APPLIED PROJECT

PSY496

ASHFORD
UNIVERSITY℠
FOUNDED 1918

Mc Graw Hill **Learning Solutions**

BOSTON BURR RIDGE, IL DUBUQUE, IA NEW YORK SAN FRANCISCO ST. LOUIS
BANGKOK BOGOTÁ CARACAS LISBON LONDON MADRID
MEXICO CITY MILAN NEW DELHI SEOUL SINGAPORE SYDNEY TAIPEI TORONTO

Applied Project
PSY496
Ashford University

This book is a McGraw-Hill Learning Solutions textbook and contains select material from the following sources:
Taking Sides: Clashing Views on Psychological Issues, Fourteenth Edition by Brent Slife. Copyright © 2006 by The McGraw-Hill Companies, Inc.
Brannigan & Merrens. "They All Look Alike to Me." The Undaunted Psychologist Copyright © 1993 by The McGraw-Hill Companies, Inc.
Essentials of Understanding Psychology, Sixth Edition by Robert S. Feldman. Copyright © 2005, 2003, 2000, 1997, 1994, 1989 by The McGraw-Hill Companies, Inc.
Wyatt. "Psychology Laboratory." 101 Success Stories Copyright © 1993 by The McGraw-Hill Companies, Inc.
Psychology: The Science of Mind and Behavior, Third Edition by Michael W. Passer and Ronald E. Smith. Copyright © 2007, 2004, 2001 by The McGraw-Hill Companies, Inc.
Research Methods in Psychology, Seventh Edition by John J. Shaughnessy, Eugene B. Zechmeister, and Jeanne S. Zechmeister. Copyright © 2006, 2003, 2000, 1997, 1994, 1990 by The McGraw-Hill Companies, Inc. Previous edition © 1985 by Alfred A. Knopf, Inc.
Chance & Harris. "A Love Affair with the Brain." and "The Life Cycle." The Best of Psychology Today Copyright © 2001 by The McGraw-Hill Companies, Inc.
All are reprinted with permission of the publisher. Many custom published texts are modified versions or adaptations of our best-selling textbooks. Some adaptations are printed in black and white to keep prices at a minimum, while others are in color.

1 2 3 4 5 6 7 8 9 0 AXE AXE 0 9 8 7

ISBN 13: 978-0-697-77530-6
ISBN-10: 0-697-77530-5

Custom Publishing Specialist: Judith Wetherington
Production Editor: Carrie Braun
Cover Design: Paul L. Illian
Printer/Binder: Axess Book Printing

Brief Contents

Chapter 1

Introduction: Unresolved Issues in Psychology

Brent Slife, Stephen C. Yanchar

Eminent psychologist Edward Bradford Titchener (1867–1927) once stated that although psychology has a short history, it has a long past. He meant that even though the science of psychology is of relatively recent origin, the subject matter of psychology extends back to ancient history. Unfortunately, this dual history—the short and the long—is rarely treated in psychology texts; most texts focus almost exclusively on the shorter history. This shorter history is thought to be guided by the scientific method, so texts are generally filled with the scientific facts of the discipline. However, we cannot fully understand psychology without also understanding its longer intellectual history, a history of age-old questions that have recently been addressed by science but rarely been completely answered. Some history texts portray this longer intellectual history, but they do not deal with its contemporary implications. *Taking Sides: Clashing Views on Controversial Psychological Issues* is dedicated to the unresolved issues that still plague psychologists from this longer history.

WHY ARE THERE UNRESOLVED ISSUES?

The subject matter of psychology is somewhat different from the subject matter of the natural sciences. In fact, psychology has been termed a "soft" science because it deals with neither the "hard" world of observable entities and physical elements—like zoology, biology, physiology, and chemistry—nor the rigorous, computational analyses of mathematics, physics, and astronomy. These hard sciences are disciplines in which the crucial questions can usually be answered through scientific observation and experimentation.

Psychologists, on the other hand, deal with the warm, "soft" world of human beings—the thoughts, attitudes, emotions, and behaviors of people interacting with other people. Psychologists are therefore concerned with many of the philosophical questions that seem so central and unique to humanity. These questions have no quick and simple answers. Indeed, these questions have occupied thinkers—scientists and philosophers alike—since at least the time of the ancient Greeks.

For example, psychologists regularly deal with the topic of mind and matter, or what is sometimes referred to as the mind-body problem. The mind-body problem essentially asks, Does the mind (which is often viewed as *not* being entirely composed of matter) control the body (which *is* entirely composed of matter), or does the brain control the mind? Yet the essence of what we mean by the mind-body problem has been a topic of debate since at least the time of the Greek philosopher Aristotle (Robinson, 1989). Aristotle (384–322 B.C.) believed that the human mind had to be distinct from the crude matter of the human body. While the human body would eventually die and decay, the human mind (or soul) was imperishable. Aristotle accounted for much of human psychology on biological grounds (i.e., in terms of matter), but he still considered the higher rational

1

activities of a human to be aspects of a mind that are independent of the body (Robinson, 1986). However, what is left out of his and other accounts is a precise explanation of how mind and body are connected. That is, if we assume that the mind is *not* composed of matter and is thus intangible, then how can it connect or interact with something material and tangible like the body? If, on the other hand, we decide that the mind *is* tangible and material, then we inherit a host of other problems associated with reductionism (see Slife & Williams, 1995, for details).

The point is that these and other such questions may not be resolved merely through scientific observation and experimentation. Scientific method is helpful for answering certain empirical questions, but its benefits are limited for many philosophical questions. And, for better or worse, psychology is infused with philosophical questions as well as empirical questions. There are basically two reasons for this infusion: the complexity of psychology's subject matter and the methods that psychologists use to study their subject matter.

Human beings—the primary subject matter of psychology—appear to operate with wills of their own within a hopelessly complex network of situations and relationships. This, it would seem, hinders the ability of scientists to attain the kind of certainty with people that they can attain with inanimate objects. Perhaps more important, it is difficult to know *why* people act in a particular manner because we cannot directly observe their intentions, thoughts, and desires. Thus, there are some aspects of human beings that elude the traditional methods of natural science.

The scientific method itself provides no irrefutable verification of an explanation. This is because data alone do not provide answers. Scientists sometimes talk as if the data from their experiments "tell" them what to believe or "give" them results, but this is somewhat misleading. Data are meaningless until they have been interpreted by the scientist (Slife & Williams, 1995). That is, scientists have a lot to do with their findings. Because there are a number of possible interpreters, there are, in principle, a number of possible interpretations. As some of the issues in this volume show, results that seem to supply indubitable proof for one interpreter might appear quite dubious to another. The reason for this is that the scientific method is set up in a manner that requires interpretation. As many who have studied this method have noted (e.g., Popper, 1959; Rychlak, 1988), the scientific method basically takes the form of a logical if-then statement: *If* my theory is correct, *then* my data will come out as I predict. However, problems can occur when we use this logic in appropriately. What if we know, for example, that we have the "then" portion of our statement, that the data did come out as I predicted? Do we then know that my theory is correct? Of course we cannot know this, because there can be an alternative theory (or many alternatives) that could explain the same data.

Unfortunately, however, this is the way in which science is conducted. We do not know the "if" portion of our logical statement—that my theory is correct; we can only know the "then" portion—that my data came out as I predicted. And our knowledge of our data cannot tell us that our theory is correct. All we can ever do is *interpret* what our data mean because our data can always mean something else.[1]

So, as a little logic has shown, data from human subjects can always be interpreted in different ways. In fact, because of these possible interpretations, there can never be a final and definitive experiment to determine what is really true about human beings (Slife & Williams, 1995). This is what scientists mean when they say that they cannot *prove* a theory but can only *support* it. Unfortunately, this simple distinction leaves many important questions unresolved, such as the mind-body problem. Still, this lack of resolution does not mean that scientists can ignore these issues. Just because certain issues are not amenable to scientific methods does not mean they go away. The issue of whether or not the mind

---

Unfortunately, falsifying the consequent—the "then" portion of our logical Statement—does not prevent us from needing to interpret either, as Slife and Williams (1995) have shown.

controls matter, for example, is vital to cancer patients who wonder whether or not positive mental attitudes will alter the course o f their disease. Such issues require exploration and debate regardless of the state of scientific knowledge. Whatever scientific information is available is important, and the lack of a complete scientific answer cannot prevent us from debating what information we do have, particularly when we may never get a complete scientific answer.

A DIALECTICAL APPROACH

This volume introduces some of the most important contemporary debates in psychology as well as some classical issues that remain unresolved. As mentioned, this volume is different from texts that focus exclusively on what is known scientifically. Most texts with an exclusive scientific focus adopt a "banking conception" of education.

The banking conception of education assumes that students are essentially "banks" in which scientific facts are "deposited." Because psychology is considered a science, there are presumably many scientific psychological facts, derived from experiments, that need to be deposited in students' minds. The banking conception makes teachers and textbooks fact distributors or information transmitters. Lectures are monologues through which the facts of experiments or the findings of method are distributed and transmitted into the mental "banks" of students. At test time, then, teachers make information "withdrawals" to discern how well students have maintained the deposits of educational currency referred to as knowledge.

Since the time of the Greek philosopher Socrates (470–399 B.C.), the banking conception of education has not been considered effective for learning about unresolved conceptual issues. One reason for this is that nestled within the banking conception lies the assumption that knowledge is above reasonable criticism and that the facts of a scholarly discipline are approximations of truth—distilled and ready for distribution to students. This is the notion of education that considers knowledge to be strictly objective. Students are thought to acquire a clear and objective picture of reality—the way things really are. As we have observed, however, it is questionable whether teachers of the "soft" sciences have access to clear and objective facts only. In many cases, the "facts" are not so clear and objective but rather puzzling and debatable. Indeed, interpretations of data are always debatable, in principle.

An alternative to the banking tradition of education is the *dialectical* tradition of education. In this tradition, there can be no meaning (and thus no knowledge) without opposition. For example, there is no way to understand what "beauty" or "upness" means without implicitly understanding what "ugliness" or "downness" is, respectively. To judge the beauty of a work of art, one must have some notion of the contrast to beauty. In other words, opposing notions only make sense when considered at the same time, one complementing the other and together forming a complete concept. In this Greek conception of the dialectic, there are no quick and easy answers to difficult questions, and there are few incontestable facts to present. Instead, there are at least two sides to every issue.

Socrates taught his students that we may begin in error or falsity, but we will eventually arrive at truth if we continue our dialectical conversation. This is because truth, for Socrates, involves uncovering what is already there. Because all conceptions—true or false—supposedly have their dialectical complements implicit within them, truth is itself already implicit and waiting to be revealed. Truth, then, according to Socrates, is uncovered by a rational analysis of the relevant (and perhaps even false) ideas and arguments already under discussion.

The discipline of psychology is often considered to be dialectical, at least in part. Any student who has studied the many different theories of human behavior (e.g., humanism, behaviorism, psychoanalysis) can attest to this. Psychology frequently consists of two or more voices on the same psychological issue. Consequently, many of the ideas of psychology develop through conversation that takes place among psychologists or among the students of psychology. Although this is understandable when we consider the complexity of psychology's subject matter, it can create problems for the banking approach to education. What can be deposited in a mental bank when two or more voices are possible and the conversation among the voices is ongoing? Some information distribution is certainly important. However, information distribution alone cannot capture this type of knowledge in the discipline, because that knowledge is dialectical in nature.

BENEFITS OF A DIALECTICAL APPROACH

The dialectical approach is the focus of this volume: Psychological issues are presented in true dialectical fashion, with two distinct sides. Students are asked to familiarize themselves with both sides of an issue, look at the supporting evidence on both sides, and engage in constructive conversation about possible resolutions. This approach to education requires students to take an active role in making sense of the issues. In so doing, students benefit in several ways.

First, students come to a richer understanding of the subject matter of psychologists. It is important to understand that there is a dialectical, or humanities, side of psychology as well as an informational, or scientific, side of psychology. As necessary as data may be, there will always be a human interpreter of the data that will never permit psychology to dispense with humanities entirely.

Second, students develop a healthy respect for both sides of a debate. There is a natural tendency to underestimate reasonable arguments on one side or the other of a debate. Often, of course, the side one favors is the "most reasonable." Without exception, the issues in this book have reasonable people and reasonable arguments *on both sides.* That is, these issues are issues in psychology precisely because they have reasonable arguments and evidence on either side. This is not to say that both sides are correct (although this too is possible). It is to say, rather, that a proper appreciation of both sides is necessary to understanding what is at issue and thus to begin to find a resolution.

A third benefit of this dialectical approach is that students better understand the nature of psychological knowledge in general. Although contemporary psychologists have taken up the scientific challenge of exploring behavior and mind, many questions are still far from being answered. Psychology's parent, like all sciences, is philosophy. Hence, philosophical (or theoretical) Issues always lurk behind the activities of psychologists. Issues such as mind versus body, free will versus determinism, nature versus nurture, and the philosophy of science are both philosophical and psychological questions. Students will necessarily have to entertain and explicate these types of issues as they learn about and advance the discipline.

Fourth, students become more aware of alternative views on controversial psychological issues. People often do not even realize that there is another point of view to an issue or evidence to the contrary. This realization, however, can help students to be more cautious in their knowledge. As the dialectician Socrates once noted, this caution is sometimes the first step toward true wisdom—knowing what it is that you don't know.

Finally, the dialectical approach promotes critical thinking skills. As authorities on critical thinking have noted (e.g., Brookfield, 1987), thinking skills require an awareness of what one *does* believe and a knowledge of alternatives regarding what one *could* believe. *Taking Sides: Clashing Views on Controversial Psychological Issues* provides both elements. Finely honed critical skills give students a better position from which to examine the psychological literature critically and to select or develop their own positions on important psychological issues.

REFERENCES

Brookfield, S. (1987). *Developing critical thinkers: Challenging adults to explore alternative ways of thinking.* San Francisco: Jossey-Bass.

Popper, K. (1959). *The logic of scientific discovery.* New York: Basic Books.

Robinson, D. (1986). *An intellectual history of psychology.* Madison, WI: University of Wisconsin Press.

Robinson, D. (1989). *Aristotle's psychology.* New York: Columbia University Press.

Rychlak, J. F. (1988). *The psychology of rigorous humanism* (2d ed.). New York: New York University Press.

Slife, B. D., & Williams, R. N. (1995). *What's behind the research: Discovering hidden assumptions in the behavioral sciences.* Thousand Oaks, CA: Sage Publications.

ON THE INTERNET . . .

Anthro.Net: Evolutionary Psychology

This site contains links and references for the study of the evolution of human behavior.

http://home1.gte.net/ericjwl/evpsych.html

Center for evolutionary Psychology

This is the Web site of the Center for Evolutionary Psychology, which is based at the University of California, Santa Barbara. Here you will find an evolutionary psychology primer, recant research in evolutionary psychology, other places to study evolutionary psychology, and more.

http://www.psych.ucsb.edu/research/cep/index.html

The Psi Cafe: A Psychology Resource Site

This site discusses different aspects of psychological research and provides helpful links to other sites that discuss research methods and popular ethical issues.

http://www.psy.pdx.edu/PsiCafe/Research/Ethics.htm

Legal, Ethical, and Professional Issues in Psychoanalysis and Psychotherapy

This site's home page offers a wealth of information about different research issues in psychology. This particular link provides access to different papers that discuss the empirically support treatment (EST) movement.

http://www.academyprojects.org/est.htm

Chapter 2

They All Look Alike to Me

Roy S. Malpass

Roy S. Malpass (Ph.D., Syracuse University) is Professor of Behavioral Science at the State University of New York, College at Plattsburgh. He has published extensively in the area of face recognition and eyewitness identification. He has been the Editor of the Journal of Cross-Cultural Psychology *(1982–1986), and is past President of the Society for Cross-Cultural Research, and President of the Division of Psychology and Law of the International Association for Cross-Cultural Psychology. Professor Malpass was born and raised in New York's Mohawk Valley, and continues to spend as much time as possible at his boathouse on a scenic lake in the Adirondacks. When out of the laboratory he may often be found pursuing his hobby of photography or his collection of antique cameras and photographs. During summer months he is more likely to be found rowing or paddling on Adirondack lakes.*

The data are always right, but they are not always the right data.

Lots of people think they are good at remembering faces. Names may be a problem, but faces are memorable. Of course, you may find yourself at a social gathering staring at someone you are just sure you've met before, but you have no recollection of when or where. But most difficult is when you stare blankly into the face of someone who has just said "Huddsfupple (your name)—I wondered when we'd meet again!"—and you have absolutely no memory for this person. But if you think these situations could be upsetting, let me tell you about an acquaintance of mine who was consulting for a well-known international agency. When she arrived in the exotic foreign location she was met by a member of the agency staff who escorted her to a hotel. She checked in, and he left her to get settled, have a nap after traveling, etc. When she went to the coffee shop she spotted him in the lobby, and waved hello. He didn't respond, and she was surprised. She took a stroll near the hotel, and again saw and greeted him. Again he did not respond. As she walked on, puzzled at his behavior, she looked up only to see him again! But this time he was dressed very differently. It was then it dawned on her that as a European in an Asian city for the first time, she was a victim of one of the oldest clichés in the book: "They all look alike to me!"

She was an experienced traveler, and was able to have a good laugh at herself for not having figured it out sooner. This is only one of the many forms of interpersonal perception and behavior in which we respond to people in terms of their group identification rather than their individuality. It is interesting, not only in its own right, but also because it represents a larger group of phenomena that are perhaps more central to intergroup identity and conflict: stereotyping and other forms of ethnocentrism. It is intriguing because it is not easily explained. A small group of researchers has been working at it for more than 20 years with some interesting findings, but no definitive explanation to show for it. This chapter is a brief description of portions of my work on this problem and how it has developed over the last two decades.

HOW DID IT ALL START?

Inquiry is driven both by theory and by the need for practical understanding. Research can take very different shapes depending on what drives it.

During the spring of 1968 a colleague and I were part of a community-action group in the Midwest. We were evaluating the examinations used to test applicants' qualifications for positions in such agencies as the fire and police departments. The town had a substantial number of black citizens, but the fire and police departments did not. We were trying to assist in the qualification of blacks on the fire and police examinations by writing training materials, and by attempting to identify any blatantly discriminatory aspects of the examinations.

We had done this for the fire department examination, and turned our attention to the police exam. The police department was cooperative, and set us up in a conference room. When we opened the examination to the second question we had a surprise. There, spread across two pages, were the photographs of eight men. Next to each photograph was a variety of facts about it. Eight minutes were given to the applicant to study this information. When we turned to the next page, there were photos of four of the eight men, and questions about the information previously given about them. All the faces displayed were white.

On the face of it (sorry) there was something discriminatory about this test when given to blacks. We thought it would be very likely that black applicants would have more difficulty recognizing white faces than black faces. We had each heard our share of racist remarks about blacks, and prominent among these was the comment that they all look alike. But that was pretty easy to understand. In the late 1960s, before school integration was widely implemented, before discrimination in housing and real-estate sales was diminished, and before black faces began to appear more widely in advertising and other media, most whites interacted with very few blacks at all, and rarely on anything like an equal basis. So there would be little personal experience as a basis for learning about them as individuals rather than as more or less equivalent examples of a category. It seemed likely that blacks' perception of whites would work the same way, and that they would have jokes about how all those whites look alike. Anyway, it seemed very likely that this particular test item would be more difficult for black than for white applicants, and therefore was an instance of racial discrimination.

As we left the police station I volunteered to go to the library to find the relevant literature documenting this problem. We agreed we would consider what to do once the nature of the evidence was known. At the library I was absolutely unable to find any literature bearing directly on this problem. I decided it must be my own incompetence in the library; so I sent my graduate assistant to find the relevant studies. He found none. Then together we convinced a couple of undergraduates to try. They reported only one marginally relevant study, but it was one more than we had gotten. We set out to design research that would give us some information on the problem. The basic question was, of course, whether there really was differential recognition for own- vs. other-race faces.

Before going on I ought to comment on the concept of "race" and how it ought to be understood in this area of research. There seems to be no good and consistent way to refer to all the various "races." To refer to a white person as "Caucasian" appears to give credence to a theory of race that has Europeans deriving from a population living at one time in the area of the Caucasus mountains. Identifying modern individuals with historical geographical populations appears to assume a kind of stability of population and within-group marriage/mating that may characterize some areas of the world well, but others not at all. Whether or not English, Poles, and Italians interbreed in Europe, people with these origins do so with great frequency in the USA, as do people of more diverse geographical origins. Similarly with "blacks." Whites in the USA tend to call anyone with discernibly "African" features "black," but in other parts of the world many more categories are used. So the old racial names just don't seem to work, especially in complex multiethnic societies. The color names also will not work, at least not consistently. While "black" and "white" are in popular usage, "yellow" will simply not do for Asians, and "black" just does not differentiate sufficiently between subgroups. "Hispanic" describes language and not even much of culture, not differ-entiating between Central American aboriginals and European Chileans. National "extraction" also provides difficulties. What do you call an American whose father was German/Italian, and whose mother was English/ Chinese, especially if his appearance is somewhat Asian? For purposes of research on facial recognition, a typology of facial appearance might be useful. Maybe the real issue is what "traditional" group a person's appearance fits into. But then a large number of people may be unclassifiable. This problem has not been solved in a satisfying way. We have to acknowledge it, and get on with the inquiry about facial recognition—even if we have to communicate by using some not so terribly appropriate terminology. But in doing so, we have to be sure that when we trans-late our research findings into inferences about the real world we do not forget the convenient fictions we accepted in order to get on with it!

NAILING IT DOWN: THE FIRST STUDY

There were important things to do. First was to obtain a suitable sample of faces to use in the research. Second was to recruit subjects, and third was to design an appropriate memory task. Fourth, although I didn't know it at the time, was a problem of the index of recognition that we would finally use. Research of this nature usually can't be done by individuals working alone. Undergraduate students often play important roles in the planning and implementation of research projects. On this project we had support for undergraduate participation in the research from the National Science Foundation, which paid the students' project expenses and provided them stipends.

We obtained photos from a variety of sources in Illinois and at Howard University, in Washington, D.C., where Jerry Kravitz, a friend from graduate-school days, was on the faculty. Kravitz had more experience with studying memory than I did, and was a good person to consult about the structure and design of the memory task for the research. My initial inclination was to stay very close to the form of the police examination that started us on this line of research. That would make it a "paired-associates" task, where faces and information about the person (face) would be associated. The test could be to produce the facts associated with each face, recognize which facts were associated with a particular face, or vice-versa.

But there would be a problem with interpretation. When the data were in, it would not be clear whether the findings had to do with recognition of facial images, with the association of verbal information with the stored representation of the images, or both. Kravitz counseled that, for sake of clarity, a simple recognition task should be used. This seemed like good advice, and so the first experiment used a simple recognition task. We first showed subjects 20 faces (10 white, 10 black) mixed semirandomly (no more than 3 black or 3 white faces could appear in sequence). Then we showed them these 20 faces mixed in with 60 more (30 white, 30 black, again mixed semirandomly). Each time a face was displayed we asked the subjects to answer "yes" or "no" to "Was it one of those shown in the first set?" (of 20).

We conducted this experiment both at Illinois and at Howard. When we were through we wrote up a basic report on the study and circulated it among a small group of researchers who we thought might be interested, and who might offer us their critical comments. We preferred to get the first round of comments from friends rather than from a journal editor's anonymous reviewers! The responses to our paper brought a very interesting surprise—one that has been influential for me in many ways. Harry Hake, an experimental psychologist of considerable reputation, returned the paper with a number of helpful comments. And at the end of the paper he penciled a note asking whether I knew about "signal detection theory." He also offered the opinion that if I published the study as it was, the human-engineering types would eat me alive.

I knew nothing about signal-detection theory, and frankly the phrase "human-engineering types" scared the hell out of me. These guys know a lot of technical stuff, and I didn't see that in my future. At the same time the prospects for continuing ignorance didn't seem so great either, so I got on the phone to Harry. He offered to come to my office and discuss it with me over a bag lunch.

Before going on, I want to emphasize the social aspects of professional life. I have learned a lot of interesting and important things from friends and colleagues over lunch and at social occasions of various kinds. Discussing ideas in a social setting is central to professional success. Do it early, and do it often.

Harry Hake did indeed come to my office, and gave me the first lesson in what has become a major interest for me—the response-decision processes that interpose between whatever it is we know personally and the actions we take on the basis of this knowledge. We often say more, less, or different from what we know, and we do so to serve our own interests. Think what the world would be like if we always said just what we have seen, thought, or remembered! In a face-recognition experiment, if we think it is important to identify as many as possible of the faces we are asked to remember (called "hits"), we will probably be willing to say "yes" to a face that looks even remotely familiar. As a result, we'll probably make some mistakes—saying yes to faces we actually didn't see before (called "false alarms"). So both hits and false alarms increase because we are more willing to say yes. If we really wanted to avoid making false alarms—as we might to avoid a mistaken identification of an innocent person in a police lineup—we would want to be much more careful about saying yes, and probably say it less often. So both hits and false alarms would decrease. But our ability to tell faces we saw before from faces we didn't see before probably would not be different. Only our willingness to say yes would be different. So if we want to know about recognition accuracy apart from people's willingness to say yes in the experiment, we need a way to adjust the accuracy score for the false-alarm rate. Signal-detection theory does that (and much more—but that's another story).

We reanalyzed our data using signal-detection-theory procedures, and what seemed like mildly confusing results were cleared up. The results and their interpretation seemed pretty obvious. First of all, there was a difference in recognizability between the white and black faces used in the experiment, for both the groups at Howard University and at Illinois. White faces were more often recognized on the average for both groups of subjects. In addition, there was a "statistical interaction" between the "race" of the faces and the "race" of the subjects, indicating that faces were better recognized by subjects of their same race.

APPEALING TO THEORY: INVESTIGATING THE OBVIOUS, AND LEARNING ABOUT WHAT ISN'T

Now what did we really have? We had a perfectly good experimental result that partially confirmed a conjecture (we can hardly call it an observation) from "real life." We had at least dragged this idea into the domain of scientific study, but two problems remained. First, we did not have a good explanation for the finding. Second, while many theories might be used to help understand this phenomenon, it was not going to be their testing ground.

The second of these—that the finding of a cross-race recognition differential would not likely be the testing ground of theories—is an important illustration of how "science" works, and deserves further comment. The primary focus of psychological research is testing propositions derived from theory, and modifying existing theory in accordance with the research findings. Development of new theory is a related activity. Theory-testing takes place in a context of well-defined techniques and methods. Theories understandably focus on problems that lend them-selves to investigation and measurement in ways that are relevant to the theory. As a result, the questions that receive the major focus of research and theory do not necessarily represent the questions "out there" awaiting explanation. At any time, many interesting phenomena and processes exist that are the focus of no theory. Therefore, they are either not investigated at all, or they are investigated as a function of their impor-tance in contemporary social events. If existing theory addresses these phenomena they may be "brought into theory." If not, their understand-ing may have to wait for the development of new theory. In the meanwhile, researchers busy with their own theory-driven research can hard-ly be blamed for not getting excited when someone says, "Yeah, but your theory can't explain my favorite phenomenon." While investigating a phenomenon that is interesting in its own right but not generated by existing theories one can feel slightly homeless.

Anyway, we began our investigations of the basis (cause) for differential recognition across race in what might be called the quarter-finals approach so well known in sports. We assembled the major contending explanations and started elimination rounds. We began with the most obvious potential explanations and set out to collect data that would allow us to choose among them.

The first study was based on the idea of "communication accuracy," which had been well worked out in the (then) newly flourishing field of language and cognition. Communication accuracy is the idea that those objects that can be more reliably described and identified from their verbal descriptions should be more reliably recognized visually. According to the theory, this is because verbal descriptions become part of the memory code for objects, and later help to trigger their memory. Observers see an object in a recognition experiment, generate a linguistic label or description of the object, and the label activates associations with other objects or concepts. Later, when the observer sees the label, the previously generated associations help to elicit the object's image. The more reliable or consistent the verbal description, the better the visual recogni-tion. We knew from a previous study that there were differences in the verbal descriptors used by blacks and whites to refer to facial features. So we reasoned that if verbal descriptions were important in facial recognition, these differences might explain the differences in facial recognition.

Henry Lavigueur, David Weldon, and I designed experiments in which subjects received different amounts of training in describing faces. More verbal-description training ought to make their descriptions more reliable, and subjects ought to get better at recognizing faces on the basis of a verbal description. So we designed a test of communication accuracy to detect whether verbal training was having this effect. Subjects also ought to get better at recognizing faces—particularly other-race faces. So they were also tested for recognition of own- and other-race faces.

The results were interesting and informative. Verbal-description training did substantially improve the communication accuracy of face descriptions, but it had no effect on visual recognition, for either own- or other-race faces. The absence of a verbal–visual relationship surprised us. We thought that perhaps face recognition might just be very difficult to improve through a relatively short training program. But in a second experiment a relatively short series of trials in which subjects were pun-ished (by electric shock) for recognition errors brought own- and other-race recognition to the same (high) levels. Improvement was pos-sible, it seemed, but verbal training didn't get it done.

It appeared that cross-race recognition has something to do with the outcomes of subjects' experience with the facial images, but that verbal processes weren't an important part of it. Therefore differences in verbal references to own- and other-race faces could not be used to explain differential recognition. These results told us something about where *not* to look for an explanation of cross-race face recognition: just what the "elimination rounds" approach does in the scientific process.

Other research programs have produced similar findings. This creates an important practical problem. If the police want to construct an image of a wanted criminal, the obvious way to do it is through the descriptions of witnesses and their verbal comments on attempted constructions. But attempts to create such images are notoriously unreliable. My conjecture is that it's because they all depend on verbal access to the subject's facial memory, *but facial memory does not use verbal categories to any great degree.* We appear to recognize faces in very short spaces of time, and we are aware of a face's identity before we are aware of its descriptive attributes.

Other studies followed, looking for other "obvious" explanations of the recognition differences in terms of well-known and important concepts. For example, we examined the relationship of racial attitudes to face recognition. If whites and blacks possess negative attitudes toward each other, racial attitudes might explain differential recognition. But we were unable to find any relationship between intergroup attitude and face recognition, in a number of studies. Other researchers have also failed to find this relationship. Our inability to find a satisfactory explanation in existing theory has been one of the things that has kept my interest in this work at a high level for many years. In many ways, it's a mystery story! Another reason is its practical implications.

TAKING IT TO COURT

We began this line of research after observing what we believed to be a racially biased test item on a police-qualification examination. From there we dug deeper into psychological theory and research until we had clearly described the differential recognition phenomenon. Later on, Bob Bothwell, Jack Brigham, and I examined a series of studies in our laboratories and elsewhere and found that differential recognition (often called the "cross-race" effect) was a stable phenomenon, applying to blacks and whites alike. We did not yet fully understand the basis of the cross-race effect, but there it was, facing us (sorry, again), as real as anything. So when I was first asked to go to court as an expert witness in a trial of a black man identified by a white man I had a sense of returning to the community from which I had derived this interesting problem that had been so good to me professionally.

Good to me professionally? I ought to explain that. How can a phenomenon like differential face recognition be good to an academic psychologist? It's simple, really. This phenomenon is inherently interesting, and it gives me a chance to work on something challenging, something that draws from a wide range of theoretical approaches and areas of psychology. But even better, it has implications for the real-world from which it was originally derived. That's a nice, diverse, but integrated package. Beyond that, however, I have been identified with the cross-race effect, since the paper I published with Kravitz in 1969 was the first (and hence "classic") study on this problem. Since the phenomenon is memorable, so is my connection with it. One should not underestimate the degree to which that opens doors, helps to begin conversations, leads to invitations to attend conferences, participate in symposia, present papers, review manuscripts and grant proposals, and many other things that enrich the life of an academic psychologist. The way it all began seems like a happy accident. But my work on this problem since that time has been very rewarding, both personally and professionally. That's how it's been good to me.

But back to court! There are some difficulties involved in testifying in court about cross-race identifications. First, it is not the role of an expert witness to make judgments about whether the identification in a particular case is or is not valid. Rather, it is the expert's role to assist the jury in their evaluation of the evidence—including the accuracy of the particular identification involved. So the expert can testify only to findings in general. Therefore, before one testifies one ought to be satisfied that there is a basis for testimony (that the own-race/other-race differential actually exists), and that the basis generalizes over populations studied, measurement techniques, and conditions of observation.

If one is satisfied on these counts, it seemed to me, one could make a real contribution. If the haunting problem of mistaken eyewitness identification is being increased by errors of cross-race identifications, it makes an already bad situation worse. Further, if it is true, as most would suspect, that white identifications of black suspects would be far more numerous than black identifications of white suspects, a note of social injustice is also added to the problem. Surely it would be a good thing to contribute our knowledge to the courts to prevent as many errors as we reasonably and practically can.

For cross-race recognition the issues are sometimes less than straightforward. We have found that a reasonable interpretation of cross-race recognition difficulty is that people are less able to distinguish other-race faces from each other. That is to say, other-race faces appear subjectively more similar to each other than they would to an own-race observer. This has two important implications.

First, when white witnesses sift through a set of black mug-shots in the process where witnesses "nominate" possible suspects, they may be more likely to identify an innocent person who looks similar to their recollection of the offender. Since these faces will appear subjectively more similar to each other, such mistakes are easily understood. At this point in the process, then, other-race nominations may be more likely to incriminate an innocent person. Also, if the identification used by the police was a "show-up," where the witness is offered a single individual for identification, there are circumstances that could easily produce an identification error. If the suspect was chosen on the basis of a good verbal description, one would understand if the suspect was similar in appearance to the offender, and also if the witness confused one for another.

Second, in some circumstances an other-race lineup might be "fairer" than an own-race lineup. The fairness of a lineup is related to the similarity of the lineup members to each other. In a chapter published in 1983, Trish Devine and I showed that, with the limitation that they must not be look-alikes, greater similarity generally means a fairer lineup. So if the lineup is otherwise appropriately constructed, the increased subjective similarity due to the lineup members being of an other race than the witness would appear to make the lineup fairer than would be true for an own-race lineup. This would be a better protection for the innocent suspect, but at the same time it might work against the identification of a guilty suspect.

Attempts to actually take our work on the cross-race effect to court met with limited success, but from my point of view it had some interesting side-effects. One day in the late 1970s I had a phone call from a public defender in a northeastern state who had read of our work. He asked if I would testify in a case that would shortly go to trial. After we dis-cussed the case, what questions he would ask me and what my responses would be, he did invite me to offer my testimony as an expert witness in the trial of a young black man accused of assault and robbery. My testimony was to center on the question of whether white witnesses would be less able to make an accurate identification of a black offender/suspect—whether an innocent black suspect would be more likely than an innocent white suspect to be wrongfully identified as the offender. My experience as an experimental psychologist active in studying this matter qualified me, at least potentially, as an expert who could assist the jury in determining the facts of the case. But first, the judge had to decide whether the jury would be allowed to hear my testimony.

To make a long story short, the judge heard my testimony in the absence of the jury (the normal procedure) and then decided that the jury would not hear it (not an unusual result). The trial judge has great discretionary latitude in such matters, but there are certain standard issues that structure the decision. One issue concerns the probative value of the testimony—whether the information an expert would contribute would actually assist the jurors in their attempt to decide what the facts of the case actually are (for example, whether or not the witness' identification was made in error). Another is whether the information the expert would contribute comes from an established and recognized field of knowledge. And still another is whether hearing testimony from an expert would tend to influence the jurors to give excessive weight to what the expert had to say. There are plenty of factors for the judge to balance, and also lots of room for the judge's personal evaluation of the issues to enter the decision.

I happened to see the judge later that day in the hallway, and I was very curious as to his reasons for disallowing my testimony. He came over to me and said he thought our research was very interesting. When I asked him why, then, he had not allowed my testimony, he began to give his legal reasoning (having to do with its probative value). I stopped him and said yes, I understood that, but I was curious about why he came to view my work as lacking in probative value. He observed that all my studies had used photographs of faces, projected as color slides on a screen, and asked what that had to do with what happens to some poor guy outside a bar at two in the morning (referring to the case in which I had testified). I had to acknowledge that this was a good point.

Whether laboratory results generalize very far beyond the laboratory was an unanswered question. Later on, as a direct result of this interaction with the judge, Trish Devine and I addressed this problem in a series of studies in eyewitness identification. We did a series of "staged crime" studies to explore differences in eyewitness identification decisions in laboratory and "apparently real" settings. We found some interesting and unexpected things. For one, it appears that if you can manipulate the beliefs witnesses have about the consequences of making an identification you can modify their willingness to make an identification in a lineup. For example, if witnesses are led to believe that the people running the lineup think the offender is actually present, they will be a lot more willing to choose someone from the lineup and say he is the offender. Of course in our system of justice the question of who is the offender is a matter for the jury to decide. It is a bit premature to make it the basis for witnesses' willingness to make an identification!

An unexpected finding concerned the witnesses' belief in the severity of punishment. We thought that most people would be particularly careful about making identifications if the consequences of mistaken identification were particularly severe. Nobody wants to cause great injury to others, at least not by mistake! But in a study where our "experimental vandal" had destroyed scientific equipment belonging to a visiting lecturer in front of an audience, members of that audience were unwilling to make identifications if the consequences for the offender would be trivial, while many were quite willing if the consequences were severe. They appeared to be quite upset by the "crime," and willing to assist the police so long as he wouldn't just get his hand slapped! Reference to these studies is in the "suggested readings," if you're interested. At the same time, research documenting a cross-race recognition differential in natural social environments has yet to be done.

Still, there were other possible explanations that seemed interesting, and we pursued a number of these in our laboratory. One promising possibility, suggested by June Chance and Alvin Goldstein, was that people may naturally look at own-race faces in a way that connects with existing information in each person's cognitive system. That information may have to do with judgments about the person's personality (e.g., their honesty, how friendly they are). In contrast, other-race faces may be seen in a more superficial, less-connected way. There was already evidence that if subjects were directed to consider aspects of a face requiring cognitive elaboration and social inferences (personality judgments, for example), recognition would be better than if subjects were directed only to superficial information (like whether the person is white or black; whether the nose is big or small).

The idea was worth checking. Trish Devine and I did a study in which we manipulated whether subjects were oriented to inferential (e.g., honest or dishonest) or superficial (e.g., black or white) attributes of own- and other-race faces. We expected an orientation to complex attributes to result in a decrease in the cross-race recognition difference. It didn't happen. Even though orienting to superficial facial information does hurt recognition, it appears people spontaneously look at all faces in an inferential way regardless of race. So, we still had to look elsewhere for an explanation. And in the meantime, with many studies being reported which searched for possible relationships between other-race face recognition and either social attitudes or personal cross-race experience, these perennial favorites still did not come through as the explanation we were looking for.

TOWARD A THEORY OF FACE RECOGNITION AND SOCIAL EXPERIENCE

Restricted social experience with other-race persons has always been the favorite explanation for the cross-race effect. And that makes good intuitive sense: how can you learn to tell "them" apart if you don't know many of "them"? For this reason it is particularly surprising that since the very first study, subjects' reports of how many other-race persons they know (and how well they know them) have been unrelated to recognition for their faces. It is possible that there are problems with the sample of subjects involved (e.g., extremely little cross-race experience, and little variation) or it could be that we simply are not asking the right questions.

Brian Mullen of Syracuse University suggests that information about small minorities (e.g., Asians, in most northeastern cities) is actually processed cognitively in different ways than information about large minorities or majorities (e.g., women or men). Mullen and his colleagues have tried to explain the cross-race effect on this basis. My own view is that we have not asked the right questions about experience. For example, people generally don't know much about the differences among U.S. nickels unless the differences are important. Similarly with people. If it is useful to differentiate among other-race individuals we will find ways to do it. For example, as I think back to my first days in school I have a couple of vivid memories of the school playground and "recess." Recess, as I remember, was not supervised to any great degree. There were mean kids there, older and bigger than I was. I can remember a couple of them very well, even now, nearly 50 years later.

If the mean kids wore black hats, like the villains in old cowboy movies, we wouldn't need to know anything more than the color of their hat to know who's what. But when there are no other markers that indicate who has good things for you, who will tease and humiliate you, who will protect you, who will hurt you, who will be friendly and cooperative, it is important to be able to identify people as individuals so you can remember whether they are one of the good guys or not. I think that's why we're pretty good at recognizing members of our own groups. Likewise, when you can identify entire categories of people that are socially irrelevant, or which can be categorically avoided with little personal or social cost, then there is little need to learn how to distinguish among them as individuals. In the absence of black hats, other social-category markers will do. This is roughly what I think is the important aspect of intergroup social experience, at least as far as inter-group face recognition is concerned. To study this idea we ought to examine the ways in which people have personal significance for each other.

This is the problem on which I will focus much of my own energy in the years ahead. I am hoping that my recent paper dealing with this issue will provide a platform for further research in cross-cultural contexts where the variations of intergroup experience may allow us to get a better look at this interesting but yet unexplained phenomenon.

If you'll pardon one final personal digression, this line of thinking about social experience relates to another of my early memories. My father collected coins, nickels in particular. He was always waiting for the one to turn up that would make us millionaires. He examined every nickel that crossed his palm. He would provide anyone who would listen with lots of details about the different types of nickels. He never found that nickel.

They all look alike to me.

SUGGESTED READINGS

Bothwell, R. K., Brigham, J. C. & Malpass, R. S. (1989). Cross-racial identification. *Personality and Social Psychology Bulletin, 15,* 19–25.

Devine, P. G., & Malpass, R. S. (1985). Orienting strategies in differential face recognition. *Personality and Social Psychology Bulletin, 11,* 33–40.

Loftus, E. F., & Ketcham, K. (1991). *Witness for the defense: The accused, the eyewitness, and the expert who puts memory on trial.* New York: St. Martin's.

Malpass, R. S. (1990). An excursion into utilitarian analysis. *Behavior Science Research, 24,* 1–15.

——— & Devine, P. G. (1981). Eyewitness identification: Lineup instructions and the absence of the offender. *Journal of Applied Psychology, 66,* 482–489.

——— & ——— (1980). Realism and eyewitness identification research. *Law and Human Behavior, 4,* 347–358.

——— & ——— (1983). Measuring the fairness of eyewitness identification lineups. In S. Lloyd-Bostock, & B. Clifford (Eds.), *Evaluating witness evidence* (pp. 81–102). London: Wiley.

——— & ——— (1984). Research on suggestion in eyewitness identification. In G. L. Wells, & E. F. Loftus (Eds.), *Eyewitness testimony: Psychological perspectives* (pp. 64–91). New York: Cambridge Univ. Press.

——— & Kravitz, J. (1969). Recognition for faces of own and other "race." *Journal of Personality and Social Psychology, 13,* 330–334.

———, Lavigueur, H., & Weldon, D. E. (1973). Verbal and visual training in face recognition. *Perception and Psychophysics, 14,* 285–292.

Mullen, B. (1991). Group composition, salience and cognitive representations: The phenomenology of being in a group. *Journal of Experimental Social Psychology, 27,* 297–323.

Wagenaar, W. A. (1988). *Identifying Ivan: A case study in legal psychology.* Cambridge, MA: Harvard Univ. Press.

Chapter 3

Research Challenges:
Exploring the Process

You probably realize by now that there are few simple formulas psychologists can follow as they carry out research. They must make choices about the type of study to conduct, the measures to take, and the most effective way to analyze the results. Even after they make these essential decisions, they must still consider several critical issues. We turn first to the most fundamental of these issues: ethics.

THE ETHICS OF RESEARCH

Put yourself in the place of one of the participants in the experiment conducted by Latané and Darley to examine the helping behavior of bystanders, in which another "bystander" simulating a seizure turned out to be a confederate of the experimenters (Latané & Darley, 1970). How would you feel when you learned that the supposed victim was in reality a paid accomplice?

Although you might at first experience relief that there had been no real emergency, you might also feel some resentment that you had been deceived by the experimenter. You might also experience concern that you had been placed in an embarrassing or compromising situation—one that might have dealt a blow to your self-esteem, depending on how you had behaved.

Most psychologists argue that deception is sometimes necessary to prevent participants from being influenced by what they think a study's true purpose is. (If you knew that Latané and Darley were actually studying your helping behavior, wouldn't you automatically have been tempted to intervene in the emergency?) To avoid such outcomes, a small proportion of research involves deception.

Nonetheless, because research has the potential to violate the rights of participants, psychologists are expected to adhere to a strict set of ethical guidelines aimed at protecting participants (American Psychological Association [APA], 2002). Those guidelines advocate the following:

- Protection of participants from physical and mental harm
- The right of participants to privacy regarding their behavior
- The assurance that participation in research is completely voluntary
- The necessity of informing participants about the nature of procedures before their participation in the experiment

All experiments that use humans as participants must be reviewed by an independent panel before being conducted, including the minority of studies that involve deception (Sales & Folkman, 2000; Fisher et al., 2002, 2003).

One of psychologists' key ethical principles is **informed consent.** Before participating in an experiment, the participants must sign a document affirming that

Informed consent: A document signed by participants affirming that they have been told the basic outlines of the study and are aware of what their participation will involve.

they have been told the basic outlines of the study and are aware of what their participation will involve, what risks the experiment may hold, and the fact that their participation is purely voluntary and they may terminate it at any time. Furthermore, after participation in a study, they must be given a *debriefing* in which they receive an explanation of the study and the procedures involved. The only time informed consent and a debriefing can be eliminated is in experiments in which the risks are minimal, as in a purely observational study in a public place (Koocher & Keith-Spiegel, 1998; Chastain & Landrum, 1999; DuBois, 2002). (To get a better understanding of ethics, try **Interactivity 4–1.**)

EXPLORING DIVERSITY

Choosing Participants Who Represent the Scope of Human Behavior

When Latané and Darley, both college professors, decided who should be chosen to participate in their experiment, they turned to the most available people: college students. In fact, college students are used so frequently in experiments that psychology has been called—somewhat contemptuously—the "science of the behavior of the college sophomore" (Rubenstein, 1982).

Using college students as participants has both advantages and drawbacks. The big benefit is that because most research occurs in university settings, college students are readily available. Typically, they cost the researcher very little: They participate for either extra course credit or a relatively small payment.

The problem is that college students may not represent the general population adequately. They tend to be younger and better educated than a significant percentage of the rest of the population of the United States. Compared with older adults, their attitudes are likely to be less well formed, and they are more apt to be influenced by authority figures and peers (Sears, 1986).

College students are also disproportionately white and middle class. However, even research that does not employ college students tends to use white, middle-class participants; the use of African Americans, Latinos, Asians, and other minorities as participants is low (Graham, 1992; Guthrie, 1998). Because psychology is a science that purports to explain human behavior in general, something is

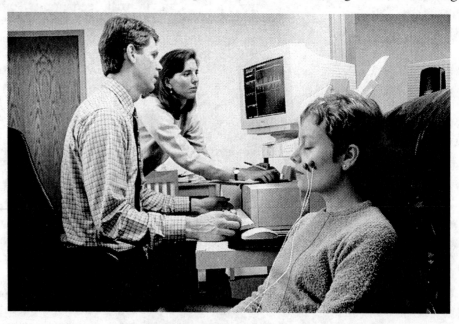

Although readily available and widely used as research subjects, college students may not represent the population at large. What are some advantages and drawbacks of using college students as subjects?

therefore amiss. Consequently, psychological researchers have become increasingly sensitive to the importance of using participants who are fully representative of the general population. Furthermore, the National Institute of Mental Health and the National Science Foundation—the primary U.S. funding sources for psychological research—now require that experiments address issues of diverse populations (Rogler, 1999; Carpenter, 2002).

SHOULD ANIMALS BE USED IN RESEARCH?

Like those who work with humans, researchers who use nonhuman animals in experiments have their own set of exacting guidelines to ensure that the animals do not suffer. Specifically, researchers must make every effort to minimize discomfort, illness, and pain, and procedures that subject animals to distress are permitted only when an alternative procedure is unavailable and when the research is justified by its prospective value. Moreover, there are federal regulations specifying how animals are to be housed, fed, and maintained. Not only must researchers strive to avoid causing physical discomfort, they are also required to promote the *psychological* well-being of some species of research animals, such as primates (Novak & Petto, 1991; APA, 1993).

Why should animals be used for research in the first place? Is it really possible to learn about human behavior from the results of research employing rats, gerbils, and pigeons? The answer is that psychological research that does employ animals has a different focus and is designed to answer different questions than is research that uses humans. For example, the shorter life span of animals (rats live an average of two years) allows researchers to learn about the effects of aging in a much smaller time frame than they could by using human participants. Moreover, some principles of behavior are similar across species, and so some basic behavioral phenomena can be studied more simply in nonhumans. Finally, some studies require large numbers of participants that share similar backgrounds or have been exposed to particular environments—conditions that could not practically be met with human beings (Gallagher & Rapp, 1997; Mukerjee, 1997).

Research using animals has provided psychologists with information that has profoundly benefited humans. For instance, it furnished the keys to detecting eye

Research involving animals is controversial but, when conducted within ethical guidelines, yields significant benefits for humans.

disorders in children early enough to prevent permanent damage, to communicating more effectively with severely retarded children, and to reducing chronic pain in people, to name just a few results (APA, 1988; Botting & Morrison, 1997).

Despite the value of research with animal participants, the use of animals in psychological research is highly controversial. For example, some critics believe that animals have rights no less significant than those of humans, and that because animals are unable to consent to participation in studies, their use is unethical. Others object to the use of animals on methodological grounds, saying it is impossible to generalize from findings on nonhuman species to humans (Plous & Herzog, 2000).

Because the issues involve complex moral and philosophical concerns, they are not easily resolved. As a consequence, review panels, which must approve all research before it is carried out, are particularly careful to ensure that research involving animals is conducted ethically (Plous, 1996a, 1996b; Barnard & Kaufman, 1997).

THREATS TO EXPERIMENT VALIDITY: EXPERIMENTER AND PARTICIPANT EXPECTATIONS

Even the best-laid experimental plans are susceptible to **experimental bias**—factors that distort the way the independent variable affects the dependent variable in an experiment. One of the most common forms of experimental bias is *experimenter expectations:* An experimenter unintentionally transmits cues to participants about the way they are expected to behave in a given experimental condition. The danger is that those expectations will bring about an "appropriate" behavior—one that otherwise might not have occurred (Rosnow & Rosenthal, 1997; Rosenthal, 2002).

A related problem is *participant expectations* about appropriate behavior. If you have ever been a participant in an experiment, you know that you quickly develop guesses about what is expected of you. In fact, it is typical for people to develop their own hypotheses about what the experimenter hopes to learn from the study. If participants form their own hypotheses, it may no longer be the experimental manipulation, but rather the participant's expectations, that produces an effect.

To guard against participant expectations biasing the results of an experiment, the experimenter may try to disguise the true purpose of the experiment. Participants who do not know that helping behavior is being studied, for example, are more apt to act in a "natural" way than they would if they knew.

Sometimes it is impossible to hide the actual purpose of research; when that is the case, other techniques are available to prevent bias. Suppose you were interested in testing the ability of a new drug to alleviate the symptoms of severe depression. If you simply gave the drug to half your participants and not to the other half, the participants who were given the drug might report feeling less depressed merely because they knew they were getting a drug. Similarly, the participants who got nothing might report feeling no better because they knew that they were in a no-treatment control group.

To solve this problem, psychologists typically use a procedure in which all the participants receive a treatment, but those in the control group receive only a **placebo,** a false treatment, such as a pill, "drug," or other substance, that has no significant chemical properties or active ingredient. Because members of both

Experimental bias: Factors that distort how the independent variable affects the dependent variable in an experiment.

Placebo: A false treatment, such as a pill, "drug," or other substance, without any significant chemical properties or active ingredient.

groups are kept in the dark about whether they are getting a real or a false treatment, any differences that are found can be attributed to the quality of the drug and not to the possible psychological effects of being administered a pill or other substance (Kirsch, 1999; Enserink, 1999, 2000a; Kim & Holloway, 2003).

However, there is one more safeguard that a careful researcher must apply in an experiment such as this. To overcome the possibility that *experimenter* expectations will affect the participant, the person who administers the drug shouldn't know whether it is actually the true drug or the placebo. By keeping both the participant and the experimenter who interacts with the participant "blind" to the nature of the drug that is being administered, researchers can more accurately assess the effects of the drug. This method is known as the *double-blind procedure*.

BECOMING AN INFORMED CONSUMER OF PSYCHOLOGY

Thinking Critically About Research

If you were about to purchase an automobile, it is unlikely that you would stop at the nearest car dealership and drive off with the first car a salesperson recommended. Instead, you would probably mull over the purchase, read about automobiles, consider the alternatives, talk to others about their experiences, and ultimately put in a fair amount of thought before you made such a major purchase.

In contrast, many of us are considerably less conscientious when we expend our intellectual, rather than financial, assets. People often jump to conclusions on the basis of incomplete and inaccurate information, and only rarely do they take the time to critically evaluate the research and data to which they are exposed.

Because the field of psychology is based on an accumulated body of research, it is crucial for psychologists to scrutinize thoroughly the methods, results, and claims of researchers. Yet it is not just psychologists who need to know how to evaluate research critically; all of us are constantly exposed to the claims of others. Knowing how to approach research and data can be helpful in areas far beyond the realm of psychology.

Several basic questions can help us sort through what is valid and what is not. Among the most important questions to ask are the following:

- *What was the purpose of the research?* Research studies should evolve from a clearly specified theory. Furthermore, we must take into account the specific hypothesis that is being tested. Unless we know what hypothesis is being examined, it is not possible to judge how successful a study has been.
- *How well was the study conducted?* Consider who the participants were, how many were involved, what methods were employed, and what problems in collecting the data the researcher encountered. There are important differences, for example, between a case study that reports the anecdotes

of a handful of respondents and a survey that collects data from several thousand people.

- *Are the results presented fairly?* It is necessary to assess statements on the basis of the actual data they reflect and their logic. For instance, when the manufacturer of car X boasts that "no other car a has a better safety record than car X," this does not mean that car X is safer than every other car. It just means that no other car has been proved safer, though many other cars could be just as safe as car X. Expressed in the latter fashion, the finding doesn't seem worth bragging about.

These three basic questions can help you assess the validity of research findings you come across—both within and outside the field of psychology. The more you know how to evaluate research in general, the better you will be able to assess what the field of psychology has to offer.

RECAP/EVALUATE/RETHINK

RECAP

What major issues confront psychologists conducting research?

- ▶ One of the key ethical principles followed by psychologists is that of informed consent. Participants must be informed, before participation, about the basic outline of the experiment and the risks and potential benefits of their participation. (p. 41)
- ▶ Although the use of college students as participants has the advantage of easy availability, there are drawbacks too. For instance, students do not necessarily represent the population as a whole. The use of animals as participants may also have costs in terms of generalizability, although the benefits of using animals in research have been profound. (p. 42)
- ▶ Experiments are subject to a number of threats, or biases. Experimenter expectations can produce bias when an experimenter unintentionally transmits cues to participants about her or his expectations regarding their behavior in a given experimental condition. Participant expectations can also bias an experiment. Among the tools experimenters use to help eliminate bias are placebos and double-blind procedures. (p. 44)

EVALUATE

1. Ethical research begins with the concept of informed consent. Before signing up to participate in an experiment, participants should be informed of

   a. The procedure of the study, stated generally
   b. The risks that may be involved
   c. Their right to withdraw at any time
   d. All of the above

2. List three benefits of using animals in psychological research.
3. Deception is one means experimenters can use to try to eliminate participants' expectations. True or false?
4. A procedure in which neither the participants nor the experimenter knows whether the participants are or are not receiving an actual treatment is known as the _____ procedure.
5. According to a report, a study has shown that men differ from women in their preference for ice cream flavors. This study was based on a sample of two men and three women. What might be wrong with this study?

RETHINK

1. A pollster studies people's attitudes toward welfare programs by circulating a questionnaire via the Internet. Is this study likely to accurately reflect the views of the general population? Why or why not?
2. A researcher strongly believes that college professors tend to show female students less attention and respect in the classroom than they show male students. She sets up an experimental study involving observation of classrooms in different conditions. In explaining the study to the professors and students who will participate, what steps should the researcher take to eliminate experimental bias based on both experimenter expectations and participant expectations?

Answers to Evaluate Questions

1. d; 2. (1) We can study some phenomena in animals more easily than we can in people, because with animal subjects we have greater control over environmental and genetic factors. (2) Large numbers of similar participants can be easily obtained. (3) We can look at generational effects much more easily in animals, because of their shorter life span, than we can with people; 3. true; 4. double-blind; 5. There are far too few participants. Without a larger sample, no valid conclusions can be drawn about ice cream preferences based on gender.

KEY TERMS

informed consent p. 41   experimental bias p. 44   placebo p. 45

Chapter 4

Psychology Laboratory

Charles R. Leith, Harlyn Hamm, and Sheila Burns, Northern Michigan University

ABSTRACT

The project created a computerized Psychology Laboratory for lower-division undergraduate psychology students. The computer lab replaced a live animal laboratory that was expensive, narrowly focused, unhealthy, and wasteful, and the new lab turned out to be cost-effective, educational, clean, and efficient.

Student evaluations show the computer lab teaches students more effectively than do traditional natural science labs. The computer lab has led to increased use of demonstration experiments in other courses and has aided both faculty and student research.

This pioneering effort required new software and unusually powerful graphics machines. The core of the project—research teams and real data—can be generalized to a variety of off-the-shelf hardware and software options available today.

IDENTIFICATION

Northern Michigan University is a regional teaching university with about 8,000 students, 350 faculty, and 28 departments. The Department of Psychology had 8 faculty members and 125 undergraduate majors when the Psychology Laboratory project was proposed.

The project was designed to improve the hands-on science laboratory experience for the 500-plus undergraduates each year who take Introductory Psychology with a laboratory to meet the schools natural science laboratory requirement. Specifically, the department sought to replace an expensive, allergy-provoking, experientially narrow, and wasteful live animal (rat) laboratory with an efficient, clean, educationally broadening, and economical computer laboratory.

DESCRIPTION

The Department of Psychology has offered an Introductory Psychology with lab course for about twenty years, and the students who use this course to fulfill a science requirement often have little additional exposure to scientific analysis.

Through 1985 the lab was based on traditional demonstrations of animal (rat) learning in a conditioning chamber. Teams of 3 students each did experiments with the rats and collaborated on a lab report. While giving the students a classic experience, the rat lab had increasingly serious drawbacks. Buying, shipping, handling, cleaning, maintaining, and systematically motivating fresh batches of rats each semester became expensive and tedious. The students spent so much time taming and maintaining their rat that the whole semester was devoted to no more than four to six simple demonstrations, all of which were closely related. At the end of each semester, 60–90 rats, who were now nearly pets, would be humanely sacrificed, leaving an uneasy sense in both students and faculty that the wisdom imparted was not quite commensurate with the waste in rat lives.

The solution proposed was to substitute a computer for each rat conditioning box and to write a program creating an artificially intelligent rat to use in experiments. This proposal had two key features: to use the computer as a lab apparatus so teams of student researchers could collect and analyze real data and to write software that would allow real experiments and not just the use of the computer as a tutorial device. The proposal called for 10 computers to serve 30 students.

To realize this plan, the psychology department sought a $28,000 National Science Foundation (NSF) grant to purchase top-of-the-line office computers. The university administration agreed to find $14,000 in matching funds. But, when the NSF grant was not funded, low-cost home computers were substituted, and the lab was developed using only the matching funds.

The key computer program was the artificially intelligent rat. Pilot work showed that the program's increased efficiency allowed all the rat experiments that had once filled a semester to be done in about three weeks. Over the winter and summer of 1987 faculty and students developed programs for additional experiments, including mapping the visual disk, reaction time, memory scanning, mental rotation, fear conditioning, and motor skill learning.

Since fall 1987, Introductory Psychology with a lab has been conducted in the computer lab every semester. At least 3 different faculty have taught the course and contributed to the computer programs or the lab manual, turning the current lab into a polished and evolved version of the original proposal.

Students prepare for each experiment by reading the Introduction and Methods section in the lab manual and passing a quiz on this material at the beginning of the lab period. Next, the students form 3-member research teams and start the program that will convert their computer station into the piece of apparatus or subject they will work with that day.

Following the method in the lab manual, the team conducts the experiment, assigning the chores of experimenter, timekeeper, data recorder, subject, etc. The students gather the data, follow the lab manual procedures for analyzing the data, and then write their conclusions as answers to questions in the manual. After completing the assignment, the team turns in a joint report. This team approach allows lab sections of 36 students to be served with only twelve computers and yields only twelve lab reports to be graded.

HUMAN RESOURCES

The initial development required one-sixth released time for 1 faculty member and the voluntary commitment of one summer by 2 faculty members. This time was used mostly for writing software but also included supervising student programers and remodeling the lab from a rat lab to a computer lab. The programers were not computer experts, but rather beginners who learned BASIC as they went along. Actual programming time took 100–300 hours per finished program. The project began with about eleven finished programs that could run some twenty experiments.

The human resources needed to continue the project are basically those required to teach any large laboratory course. Four faculty members have used the lab facility to teach Introductory Psychology courses, and only 1 was a software developer. The 3 nonprogrammers simply used the software and the computers by following instructions in the lab manual. An important human resource is the help provided by undergraduate teaching apprentices. Each apprentice earns course credit for monitoring, tutoring, grading, and keeping records for one lab section, and each section has 2 apprentices.

Many of the problems encountered in setting up the project would not apply to an implementer starting out today. Mainstream computers now have high-quality graphics ability, and professional programmers have written lab software that enables students to use computers as research apparatus. The computers are programmed to simulate sophisticated special-purpose machines such as tachistoscopes and reaction timers, which are familiar tools of the psychologist's professional education. Thus, no special knowledge of computers is necessary to run such a lab.

TECHNOLOGICAL RESOURCES

The initial implementation of the Psychology Laboratory required thirteen microcomputers: ten for the student research teams and two for backup and continued software development; the remaining one was attached to a 44-inch rear projection TV set used for demonstrations in the lab.

The computers had to be low cost and provide excellent color, animation, and sound effects to beginning BASIC programers. The Commodore C128 fit the specifications perfectly. Not only were the programming efforts rewarded by impressive displays with little effort, but also students found the machines to be user friendly.

The lab area had to be made safe for computers. Static grounding worktables were installed for each computer to prevent static spark damage, and a dust-free, dry-erase marker board was used instead of a chalkboard.

Over the five years the project has continued, the lab work space has expanded, and two computer stations have been added. The major technical support item is for repair of computer components. The Commodore C128 is a unique 8-bit machine that is not supported by the university microcomputer maintenance system, so the department found a local hobby shop that repairs Commodore machines. Maintenance costs have averaged about $10 per machine per year, representing 10 percent of the cost of maintaining the old rat lab and 20 percent of the cost of maintaining office computers in the university system.

A school wanting to replicate this computer lab would have the advantage that several prize-winning psychology computer lab programs have been written by professional programmers to run on the latest powerful hardware (the Commodore C128 is no longer produced). Most of the exercises can be duplicated with off-the-shelf software and hardware. Unlike Northern Michigan's pioneering effort, which required software development, the major hurdle today would be to write a lab manual setting up experiments designed for lab teams.

BENEFITS

Most of the benefits of using a computer in a psychology lab come from being able to program a microcomputer to simulate or emulate an astonishing range of experimental subjects and apparatus. Students can get a realistic sense of running a $3000 three-field tachistoscope without setting up ten or twelve of these fragile items for only two days a year. Because a whole new experiment can be set up in moments by running a program, it is reasonable to ask students to perform twelve different, fairly complex experiments per semester.

Faculty have found other ways to use the lab when Introductory Psychology sections are not meeting. Small-enrollment courses in Learning, Perception, and Experimental Design use the lab as a classroom and take advantage of the computers for demonstrations and experiments. In addition to classroom uses, the availability of the computers has encouraged several original experiments using the computers. Thus, the Psychology Lab has clearly enriched the curriculum and the research culture of the department.

By any measure the computer lab is cost-effective. The cost for all the apparatus to be successfully emulated elsewhere would be completely out of reach.

Tachistoscopes alone are about 400 percent over the cost of the computers. Compared to the old rat lab, the computer lab saves roughly $2000 a year in maintenance. The basic computer lab should pay for itself from accumulated savings this year or next. Using a team approach shaved two thirds off the cost of the usual one-person, one-computer lab.

The main rationale for the computer lab was that it would help to deliver superior educational experiences to students. As of winter 1991, some 1,700 students had been through the lab, and they seem to agree that it offers a superior experience. In a survey of students in natural science lab courses, conducted by the student government, students were asked, "Were the labs helpful in understanding the content of the course?" Students rated a sample of seven science labs at an average of B–; the Psychology Lab earned a B+.

The department's own evaluation asked students to recall some fact about each of twelve topics and then credit the source of this recollection. The old rat lab had been credited as the principal source of information for two topics (science and response learning) and a significant source (used by at least 10 percent of the students) for one more. The three topics credited to the rat lab were the only topics that the faculty had had time to present in that lab.

The computer lab is credited as the principal source of information for science and response learning—suggesting that the artificial rat was an adequate substitute for the real rat—and as a significant source for all nine topics taken up in the lab. There is a clear link between the computer technology and the ability to increase the breadth of training without giving up the strong science information impact that had made the old rat lab so valuable.

CRITICAL SUCCESS FACTORS

Three factors were critical to the success of the computer lab. One was using the computer as a piece of apparatus, with hardware and software allowing the emulation of a wide variety of paradigms. Second was placing students into research teams that collected and analyzed real data. Not only did the teams enjoy cooperative learning, but this was a cost-effective way to use the available computers. The third factor was the student apprentice support system that provided the constant close supervision and tutoring needed in labs.

RATIONALE

The decision to offer an Introductory Psychology lab is not to be taken lightly, since it will constitute a major logistical challenge. Given the commitment to offer labs, there is no question but that the NMU model computer lab is a most cost-effective approach. Using the latest and most powerful computers and software lets students to work on a wide variety of experimental tasks at relatively little cost in time or apparatus.

A smaller lab attached to a course for majors, such as Experimental Psychology or Experimental Design, could use this same team approach to serve, say, 20 students with seven computers. Such a small course lab would not represent a challenging logistical load and could be put together for less than $20,000.

FOR MORE INFORMATION, CONTACT:
Charles R. Leith
Department of Psychology
Northern Michigan University
Marquette, MI 49855
Phone: 906-227-2246
E-mail: FACL@NMUNUS (BITNET)

Chapter 5

The Science of Psychology

CHAPTER OUTLINE

Perhaps the most fascinating and mysterious universe of all is the one within us

Carl Sagan

A young woman appeared in the emergency room of Baltimore City Hospital three days before her 23rd birthday, pleading for help. The story she told was a strange one indeed. She and two other girls had been delivered by the same mid-wife in Georgia's Okefenokee Swamp on a Friday the 13th. The midwife, a member of a voodoo cult, had placed a curse on all three babies. She proclaimed that the first would die before her 16th birthday, the second before her 21st birthday, and the third (the patient) before her 23rd birthday.

True to the midwife's prediction, the first died in an auto accident when she was 15 years old. The second was killed during a shooting in a nightclub where she was celebrating her 21st birthday. Now the third woman waited in fear for her own death.

The emergency-room psychiatrist admitted her for observation and reassured the terrified woman that no harm would come to her in the hospital. Still, the woman believed that she was doomed. The next morning, two days before her 23rd birthday, she was found dead in her hospital bed. Doctors were unable to determine a physical cause for her death (Seligman, 1975).

Waiting in line at the theater, Ray put his arms around Kira and playfully kissed her cheek. "Remember that party where we met last year?" he asked. "You caught my eye the moment you walked into the room." "Sure," Kira laughed, "but you were so shy. Your friends practically had to drag you over to talk to me! You're lucky I'm so outgoing."

Ray knew he was shy, especially around women, yet he wasn't sure why. He had been too nervous to enjoy the few dates he had gone on in high school. During his first semester at college he met a few women he really liked but was afraid to ask them out. He didn't make many male friends either, and by winter the loneliness was getting to him. He became mildly depressed, he couldn't sleep well, and his schoolwork suffered.

After a good visit with his family during spring break, Ray turned things around. He studied hard, did well on his tests, and made friends with some guys in the dorm. His mood improved, and toward the end of the semester he met Kira. Attracted to Ray and sensing both his shyness and his interest, Kira asked Ray out. Now dating Kira for a year and doing well in school, Ray is happy and self-confident. He and Kira have even talked about getting married after they graduate.

THE NATURE OF PSYCHOLOGY

▶ **Focus 1**
What is psychology's focus? In science and daily life, what does critical thinking involve, and why is it important? (These focus questions will help you identify key concepts as you read, study, and review; they also tie in with the "Learning Objectives" in the Online Learning Center and other supplements.)

Why are some individuals shy and others outgoing? What causes people, such as Kira and Ray, to become attracted to one another and fall in love? Can we predict which relationships will last? Why is it that we remember a first date from long ago yet forget information during a test that we studied for only hours before? Where in the brain are memories stored? Why did Ray become depressed? Was it his lack of a social life, or was something else going on? And in the case of the "cursed" woman, is it possible that a psychological factor—a culturally based belief in voodoo—could have affected her biological functioning and actually brought about her death?

Welcome to psychology, the discipline that studies all of these questions and countless more. We can define **psychology** as *the scientific study of behavior and the mind.* The term *behavior* refers to actions and responses that we can directly observe, whereas the term *mind* refers to internal states and processes—such as thoughts and feelings—that cannot be seen directly and that must be inferred from observable, measurable responses. For example, we cannot see Ray's feeling of loneliness directly. Instead, we must infer how Ray feels based on his verbal statement that he is lonely.

Because behavior is so complex, its scientific study poses special challenges. As you become familiar with the kinds of evidence necessary to validate scientific conclusions, you will become a better-informed consumer of the many claims made in the name of psychology. For one thing, this course will teach you that many widely held beliefs about behavior are inaccurate. Can you distinguish the valid claims from the invalid ones in Table 5.1?

Perhaps even more important than the concepts you learn in this course will be the habits of thought that you acquire—habits that involve *critical thinking*. Critical thinking involves taking an active role in understanding the world around you, rather than merely receiving information. It's important to reflect on what that information means, how it fits in with your experiences, and its implications for your life and society. Critical thinking also means evaluating the validity of something presented to you as fact. For example, when someone tells you a new "fact," ask yourself the following questions:

What exactly are you asking me to believe?
How do you know? What is the evidence?
Are there other possible explanations?
What is the most reasonable conclusion?

We hope that after completing this course you will be more cautious about accepting psychological claims and less likely to form simplistic judgments about

TABLE 5.1   Widely Held Beliefs about Behavior: Fact or Fiction?

Directions: Decide whether each statement is true or false.

1. Most people with exceptionally high IQs are well adjusted in other areas of their life.

2. In romantic relationships, opposites usually attract.

3. Overall, married adults are happier than adults who aren't married.

4. In general, we only use about 10 percent of our brain.

5. A person who is innocent of a crime has nothing to fear from a lie detector test.

6. People who commit suicide usually have signaled to others their intention to do so.

7. If you feel that your initial answer on a multiple-choice test is wrong, leave it alone; students usually lose points by changing answers.

8. On some types of mental tasks, people perform better when they are 70 years old than when they are 20 years old.

9. Usually, it is safe to awaken someone who is sleepwalking.

10. A schizophrenic is a person who has two or more distinct personalities, hence the term *split personality.*

Answers: Items 1, 3, 6, 8, and 9 are supported by psychological research. The remaining items are false. (If you correctly answered 9 or 10 of these items, you've done significantly better than random guessing.)

why people behave and think as they do. These critical-thinking skills will serve you well in many areas of your life.

In this book we hope to share with you our enthusiasm about psychology. As you will see, psychology relates to virtually every aspect of your life. Psychological research provides us with a greater understanding of ourselves and with powerful tools to improve our lives and promote human welfare.

Psychology as a Basic and Applied Science

▶ **Focus 2**
How do basic and applied research differ? Explain how knowledge from basic research helps solve practical problems.

Science involves two types of research: **basic research,** *which reflects the quest for knowledge purely for its own sake,* and **applied research,** *which is designed to solve specific, practical problems.* For psychologists, most basic research examines how and why people behave, think, and feel the way they do. Basic research may be carried out in laboratories or real-world settings, with human participants or other species. Psychologists who study other species usually attempt to discover principles that ultimately will shed light on human behavior, but some study animal behavior for its own sake. In applied research, psychologists often use basic scientific knowledge to design, implement, and assess intervention programs. Consider the following example.

Robber's Cave and the Jigsaw Classroom

How does hostility and prejudice develop between groups, and what can be done to reduce it? In today's multicultural world, where religious and ethnic groups often clash, this question has great importance.

To provide an answer, psychologists conduct basic research on factors that increase and reduce intergroup hostility. In one experiment, researchers divided 11-year-old boys into two groups when the boys arrived at a summer camp in Robber's Cave, Oklahoma (Sherif et al., 1961). The groups, named the "Eagles" and "Rattlers," lived in separate cabins but did all other activities together. Initially, they got along well.

To test the hypothesis that competition would breed intergroup hostility, the researchers began to pit the Eagles and Rattlers against one another in athletic and other contests. As predicted, hostility soon developed between the groups. Next the researchers examined whether conflict could be reduced by having the two groups share enjoyable activities, such as watching movies together. Surprisingly, these activities only bred more taunting and fighting. The researchers then created several small emergencies to test a final hypothesis—that placing hostile groups in situations requiring cooperation to attain important, common goals would reduce intergroup conflict. In one "emergency," a heavy truck bringing food to the hungry boys supposedly stalled, forcing the Eagles and Rattlers to pool their strength and tow it with a rope to get it started. This and other cooperative experiences gradually reduced hostility between the groups, and many new friendships developed.

▶ **Focus 3**
Identify the major goals of psychology. Describe the levels-of-analysis framework.

The Robber's Cave study, which has since become a classic (that is, an older but widely known and influential study), represents basic research because its goal was to discover general principles of intergroup conflict, not to solve some preexisting problem. Prejudice between the Eagles and Rattlers did not exist from the outset; rather, the researchers created it. They showed that hostility could be bred by competition and reduced by making hostile groups dependent on one another to reach a common goal. But could this principle, derived from basic research, also be applied to real-life situations?

Years later, during a stormy desegregation of public schools in Texas, psychologist Elliot Aronson and his coworkers (1978) developed and evaluated a classroom procedure called the "jigsaw program." This program, which is now widely used to foster cooperation among children, involves creating multiethnic groups of five or six children who are assigned to prepare for an upcoming test on, for example, the life of Abraham Lincoln. Within the groups, each child is given a piece of the total knowledge to be learned. One child has information about Lincoln's childhood, another about his political career, and so on. To pass the test, group members must fit their knowledge pieces together as if working on a jigsaw puzzle. Each child must teach the others his or her piece of knowledge. Like the children at Robber's Cave, students learn that to succeed they must work together (Figure 5.1).

The jigsaw technique and other *cooperative learning programs* have been evaluated in hundreds of classrooms, with encouraging results (Johnson, 2000). Children's liking for one another generally increases, prejudice decreases, and self-esteem and school achievement improve. Cooperative learning programs show how basic research, such as the Robber's Cave experiment, provide a foundation for designing intervention programs. We will see many other examples of how basic research provides knowledge that not only satisfies our desire to understand our world but also can be applied to solve practical problems.

The Goals of Psychology

As a science, psychology has five central goals:

1. To *describe* how people and other species behave
2. To *understand* the causes of these behaviors
3. To *predict* how people and animals will behave under certain conditions
4. To *influence* behavior through the control of its causes
5. To *apply* psychological knowledge in ways that enhance human welfare

In the Robber's Cave study, the researchers carefully observed the boys' behavior under various conditions (description). They believed that competition would cause intergroup hostility and that cooperation could reduce it (tentative understanding). To test whether their understanding was correct, they predicted that competition would create hostility between the Eagles and Rattlers and that cooperation would reduce this conflict (prediction). Next they controlled the camp setting, first by pitting the Eagles and Rattlers against one another in contests and then by arranging situations that forced the groups to cooperate (influence). As predicted, competition produced hostility and cooperation reduced it, suggesting that the researchers' understanding was correct. Later, when Aronson and his coworkers sought to reduce racial hostility within newly integrated schools, they had a scientific basis for predicting what might work. They were able to apply their knowledge successfully in the form of the jigsaw program (application).

Figure 5.1 The jigsaw classroom, designed by psychologist Elliot Aronson, was inspired by basic research that showed how mutual dependence and cooperation among hostile groups can reduce intergroup hostility. Aronson's applied research had similar positive effects within racially integrated classrooms.

Psychology's Broad Scope: A Levels-of-Analysis Framework

The scope of modern psychology stretches from the borders of medicine and the biological sciences to those of the social sciences (Figure 5.2). Because we are biological creatures living in a complex social world, psychologists study an amazing array of factors to understand why people behave, think, and feel as they do. At times, this diversity of factors may seem a bit overwhelming, but we would like to provide you with a framework that will greatly simplify matters. We call it *levels of analysis:* behavior and its causes can be examined at the *biological level* (e.g., brain processes, genetic influences), the *psychological level* (e.g., our thoughts, feelings, and motives), and the *environmental level* (e.g., past and current physical and social environments to which we are exposed).

Here are two brief examples of how the levels-of-analysis framework can be applied. First, consider a behavior that you engage in every day: eating (Figure 5.3). At the biological level of analysis, various chemicals, neural circuits, and structures in your brain respond to bodily signals and help regulate whether you feel hungry or full. At the psychological level of analysis, your moods, food preferences, and motives affect eating. Do you ever eat when you're not hungry, perhaps because you feel stressed or bored? The environmental level of analysis calls attention to specific stimuli (such as the appearance or aroma of different food) that may trigger eating and to cultural customs that influence our food preferences. Does the aroma of freshly baked treats ever make your stomach growl? How about the sight of duck feet or a mound of fish gills on a plate? To most Westerners, duck feet and fish gills may not be appetizing, but during a stay in China we discovered that our hosts considered them delicious.

Now let's apply the levels-of-analysis framework to a rare and seemingly mysterious event: the case of voodoo death described earlier. How can we explain voodoo death without invoking supernatural powers?

Voodoo is practiced in several regions of the world, including parts of the United States. Decades ago, physiologist Walter Cannon (1942) suggested a possible mechanism for death by "magic curses." Cannon drew on his own research on severe stress responses in animals, as well as eyewitness reports by cultural anthropologists of deaths by magic curses. One such account described the practice of "boning," the placing of a death curse by pointing a sacred bone at the victim:

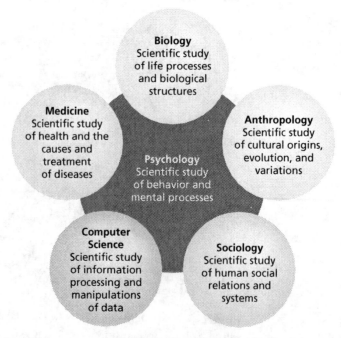

Figure 5.2 Psychology as a scientific hub. Psychology links with and overlaps many sciences.

The Biological Level

The Psychological Level

The Environmental Level

Figure 5.3 (*left*) **Biological level.** This rat weighs about triple the weight of a normal rat. As we (or rats) eat, hunger decreases as certain brain regions regulate the sensation of becoming full. Those regions in this rat's brain have been damaged, causing it to overeat and become obese. (*center*) **Psychological level.** At times we may eat out of habit, stress, or boredom. With candy bar in hand and other candies lined up, this student is ready for some autopilot munching. (*right*) **Environmental level.** Does a plateful of big, juicy insect larvae sound appetizing to you? Grubs, traditionally eaten by Australian Aboriginal peoples, are also served in some restaurants. Cultural norms influence food preferences.

> The man who discovers that he is being boned by any enemy is, indeed, a pitiable sight. . . . His cheeks blanch and his eyes become glassy. . . . His body begins to tremble and the muscles twitch involuntarily . . . soon after he writhes as if in mortal agony. Unless help is forthcoming in the shape of a countercharm administered by the . . . medicine- man, his death is only a matter of a comparatively short time. (Basedow, 1925.)

Cannon noted that in cases of death by magic curses, the victim firmly believed that he or she was doomed. For the victim, this belief represents the psychological level of analysis. At the environmental level, this belief was supported by the victim's family, friends, enemies, and culture. At the biological level of analysis, Cannon speculated that the victim's beliefs triggered a profound and persistent stress response—a flood of stress hormones (chemicals released by glands in the body)—sending the victim into physiological shock. Cannon's research had shown that one aspect of such shock is a rapid and often fatal drop in blood pressure as stress hormones allow fluid to leak out of veins and capillaries. He noted that normal autopsy procedures would not detect this mechanism of death, making it appear, as in the case of the young woman, that there was no natural cause.

Mind-Body and Nature-Nurture Interactions

Cannon's hypothesis is a plausible alternative to supernatural explanations and is consistent with research showing that negative thoughts about a stressful situation can quickly trigger the secretion of stress hormones (Borod, 2000). This work illustrates what traditionally have been called *mind-body interactions*—the relations between mental processes in the brain and the functioning of other bodily systems. Mind-body interactions focus our attention on the fascinating interplay between the psychological and biological levels of analysis. This topic has a long history within psychology, and, as you will see throughout the textbook, it remains one of psychology's most exciting frontiers.

The levels-of-analysis framework also addresses an issue that has been debated since antiquity: Is our behavior primarily shaped by nature (our biological endowment) or by nurture (our environment and learning history)? The pendulum has swung toward one end or the other at different times in history, but today growing interest in cultural influences and advances in genetics and brain research keep the nature-nurture pendulum in a more balanced position.

Perhaps most important, modern research increasingly reveals that nature and nurture interact (Jaffee et al., 2003). Just as our biological capacities affect how we behave and experience the world, our experiences influence our biological capacities. For humans and rats alike, continually depriving a newborn of physical contact, or providing a newborn with an enriched environment in which to grow, can influence its brain functioning and biological development (Rosenzweig, 1984). Thus, while it may be tempting to take sides, "nature or nurture?" usually is the wrong question. As the levels-of-analysis framework implies, nature, nurture, and psychological factors must all be taken into account to gain the fullest understanding of behavior.

Later in the chapter we'll provide a more detailed example of how looking at behavior from multiple levels enhances our understanding. For now, in concluding our discussion of psychology's scope, we'd like you to think critically about Cannon's mind-body explanation for voodoo death.

What Do You Think?

THE CASE OF VOODOO DEATH
Based on Cannon's hypothesis, why did the woman cursed by voodoo die? Do you believe that this hypothesis is reasonable? Can you think of other explanations for her death? (Think about it, then see page 27.)

IN REVIEW

- Psychology is the scientific study of behavior and the mind. The term *behavior* refers to actions and responses that can be observed and measured directly. In contrast, mental processes such as thoughts and feelings must be inferred from directly observable responses.

- Basic research reflects the quest for knowledge for its own sake. Applied research focuses on solving practical problems.

- The primary goals of psychological science are to describe, understand, predict, and influence behavior and to apply psychological knowledge to enhance human welfare.

- To understand more fully why people act, think, and feel as they do, psychologists examine behavior at the biological, the psychological, and the environmental levels of analysis.

PERSPECTIVES ON BEHAVIOR

The fact that psychologists study biological, psychological, and environmental factors that influence behavior is not new; it has been an integral part of psychology's history. But just how did psychology's scope become so broad? In part, it happened because psychology has roots in such varied disciplines as philosophy, medicine, and the biological and physical sciences. As a result, different ways of viewing people, called *perspectives*, became part of psychology's intellectual traditions. (Figure 5.4).

Figure 5.4 Youth and beauty? Or maturity and wisdom?
What we perceive depends on our perspective. If you examine this drawing, you will see either a young woman or an old one. Now try changing your perspective. The ear and necklace of the young woman are the left eye and mouth of the old woman.

If you have ever met someone who views the world differently from the way you do, you know that perspectives matter. Perspectives serve as lenses through which psychologists examine and interpret behavior. In science, new perspectives are an engine of progress. Advances occur as existing beliefs are challenged, a debate ensues, and scientists seek new evidence to resolve the debate. Sometimes, the best-supported elements of contrasting perspectives are merged into a new framework, which in turn will be challenged by still newer viewpoints.

Psychology's major perspectives guide us through its intellectual traditions and address timeless questions about human nature. To better understand how these perspectives evolved, let's briefly examine psychology's roots.

Psychology's Intellectual Roots

Humans have long sought to understand themselves, and at the center of this quest lies an issue that has tested the best minds of the ages, the so-called *mind-body* problem. Is the mind—the inner agent of consciousness and thought—a spiritual entity separate from the body, or is it a part of the body's activities?

Many early philosophers held a position of **mind-body dualism,** *the belief that the mind is a spiritual entity not subject to physical laws that govern the body.* But if the mind is not composed of physical matter, how could it become aware of bodily sensations, and how could its thoughts exert control over bodily functions? French philosopher, mathematician, and scientist René Descartes (1596–1650) proposed that the mind and body interact through the tiny pineal gland in the brain. Although Descartes placed the mind within the brain, he maintained that the mind was a spiritual, nonmaterial entity. Dualism implies that no amount of research on the physical body (including the brain) could ever hope to unravel the mysteries of the nonphysical mind.

An alternative view, **monism** (from the Greek word *monos,* meaning "one"), *holds that mind and body are one and that the mind is not a separate spiritual entity.* To monists, mental events are simply a product of physical events in the brain, a position advocated by English philosopher Thomas Hobbes (1588–1679). Monism helped set the stage for psychology because it implied that the mind could be studied by measuring physical processes within the brain. The stage was further set by John Locke (1632–1704) and other philosophers from the school of **British empiricism,** *which held that all ideas and knowledge are gained empirically—that is, through the senses.* According to the empiricists, observation is a more valid approach to knowledge than is reason, because reason is fraught with the potential for error. This idea bolstered the development of modern science, whose methods are rooted in empirical observation.

Discoveries in physiology (an area of biology that examines bodily functioning) and medicine also paved the way for psychology's emergence. By 1870 European researchers were electrically stimulating the brains of laboratory animals and mapping the surface areas that controlled various body movements. During this same period, medical reports linked damage in different areas of patients' brains with various behavioral and mental impairments. For example, damage to a specific region on the brain's left side impaired people's ability to speak fluently.

▶ **Focus 4**
Discuss psychology's philosophical and scientific roots, earliest schools of thought, and founders.

Mounting evidence of the relation between brain and behavior supported the view that empirical methods of the natural sciences could also be used to study mental processes. Indeed, by the mid-1800s, German scientists were measuring people's sensory responses to many types of physical stimuli (for example, how the perceived loudness of a sound changes as its physical intensity increases). Their experiments established a new field called *psychophysics,* the study of how psychologically experienced sensations depend on the characteristics of physical stimuli.

Around this time, Charles Darwin's (1809–1882) theory of evolution generated shock waves that are still felt today. His theory, which we will discuss later, was vigorously opposed because it seemed to contradict philosophical and religious beliefs about the exalted nature of human beings. Evolution implied that the human mind was not a spiritual entity but rather the product of a biological continuity between humans and other species. Moreover, Darwin's theory implied that scientists might gain insight about human behavior by studying other species. By the late 1800s, a convergence of intellectual forces provided the impetus for psychology's birth.

Early Schools: Structuralism and Functionalism

The infant science of psychology emerged in 1879, when Wilhelm Wundt (1832–1920) established the first experimental psychology laboratory at the University of Leipzig in Germany. Wundt, who helped train the first generation of scientific psychologists, wanted to model the study of the mind after the natural sciences (Figure 5.5). He believed that the mind could be studied by breaking it down into its basic components, as a chemist might do in studying a complex chemical compound. One of his graduate students, Englishman Edward Titchener (1867–1927), later established a psychology laboratory in the United States at Cornell University. Like Wundt, Titchener attempted to identify the basic building blocks, or structures, of the mind. Wundt and Titchener's approach came to be known as **structuralism,** *the analysis of the mind in terms of its basic elements.*

In their experiments, structuralists used the method of *introspection* ("looking within") to study sensations, which they considered the basic elements of consciousness. They exposed participants to all sorts of sensory stimuli—lights, sounds, tastes—and trained them to describe their inner experiences. Although this method of studying the mind was criticized and died out after a few decades, the structuralists left an important mark on the infant field of psychology by establishing a scientific tradition for the study of cognitive processes.

In the United States, structuralism eventually gave way to **functionalism,** *which held that psychology should study the functions of consciousness rather than its structure.* Here's a rough analogy to explain the difference between structuralism and functionalism: Consider your arms and hands. A structuralist would try to explain their movement by studying how muscles, tendons, and bones operate. In contrast, a functionalist would ask, "Why do we have arms and hands? How do they help us adapt to our environment?" The functionalists asked similar questions about mental processes and behavior. In part, they were influenced by Darwin's evolutionary theory, which stressed the importance of adaptation in

▶ **Focus 5**
Describe the psychodynamic perspective. Contrast Freud's psychoanalytic theory with modern psychodynamic theories.

Figure 5.5 At the University of Leipzig in 1879, Wilhelm Wundt (*far right*) established the first laboratory of experimental psychology to study the structure of the mind.

Figure 5.6 William James, a leader of functionalism, helped establish psychology in North America. His multi-volume book *Principles of Psychology* (1890/1950), greatly expanded the scope of psychology.

helping organisms survive and reproduce in their environment. Functionalists did much of the early research on learning and problem solving.

William James (1842–1910), a leader in the functionalist movement, was a "big-picture" person who taught courses in physiology, psychology, and philosophy at Harvard University (Figure 5.6). James's broad functionalist approach helped widen the scope of psychology to include the study of various biological processes, mental processes, and behaviors. Like Wundt, James helped train psychologists who went on to distinguished careers. Among them was Mary Whiton Calkins (1863–1930), who became the first female president of the American Psychological Association in 1905 (Figure 5.7).

Although functionalism no longer exists as a school of thought within psychology, its tradition endures in two modern-day fields: *cognitive psychology,* which studies mental processes, and *evolutionary psychology,* which emphasizes the adaptiveness of behavior.

The Psychodynamic Perspective: The Forces Within

Have you ever been mystified by why you behaved or felt a certain way? Recall the case of Ray, the student described at the beginning of the chapter who could not understand why he was so shy. The **psychodynamic perspective** *searches for the causes of behavior within the inner workings of our personality (our unique pattern of traits, emotions, and motives), emphasizing the role of unconscious processes.* Sigmund Freud (1856–1939) developed the first and most influential psychodynamic theory (Figure 5.8).

Psychoanalysis: Freud's Great Challenge

Late in the 19th century, as a young physician in Vienna, Freud was intrigued by the workings of the brain. He was confronted with patients who experienced physical symptoms such as blindness, pain, or paralysis without any apparent bodily cause. Over time he treated patients who had other problems, such as *phobias* (intense unrealistic fears). Because no disease or bodily malfunction could explain these conditions, Freud reasoned that the causes must be psychological.

Figure 5.7 Mary Whiton Calkins founded a psychology laboratory at Wellesley College, where she taught for over 30 years. She studied memory and dreams, and in 1905 became the first female president of the American Psychological Association.

Figure 5.8 Sigmund Freud founded psychoanalysis. For more than 50 years, he probed the hidden recesses of the mind.

Moreover, if his patients were not producing their symptoms consciously, Freud reasoned that the causes must be hidden from awareness—they must be unconscious. At first Freud treated his patients by using hypnosis. Later he used a technique called *free association,* in which the patient expressed any thoughts that came to mind. To Freud's surprise, his patients eventually described painful and long-"forgotten" childhood experiences, often sexual in nature. Often, after recalling and figuratively reliving these traumatic childhood experiences, the patients' symptoms improved.

Freud became convinced that an unconscious part of the mind profoundly influences behavior, and he developed a theory and a form of psychotherapy called **psychoanalysis**—*the analysis of internal and primarily unconscious psychological forces*. He also proposed that humans have powerful inborn sexual and aggressive drives and that because these desires are punished in childhood, we learn to fear them and become anxious when we are aware of their presence. This leads us to develop **defense mechanisms,** *which are psychological techniques that help us cope with anxiety and the pain of traumatic experiences. Repression,* a primary defense mechanism, protects us by keeping unacceptable impulses, feelings, and memories in the unconscious depths of the mind. All behavior, whether normal or "abnormal," reflects a largely unconscious and inevitable conflict between the defenses and internal impulses. This ongoing psychological struggle between conflicting forces is dynamic in nature, hence the term *psychodynamic*. To explain Ray's extreme shyness around women, Freud might have explored whether Ray is unconsciously afraid of his sexual impulses and therefore avoids putting himself into dating situations where he would have to confront those hidden impulses.

Freud's theory became a lightning rod for controversy. Some of his own followers strongly disagreed with aspects of the theory, especially its heavy emphasis on childhood sexuality. Other psychologists viewed the theory as difficult to test. Indeed, Freud opposed laboratory research on psychoanalytic theory, believing that his clinical observations were more valid. Nevertheless, Freud's ideas did stimulate research on topics such as dreams, memory, aggression, and mental disorders. A scholarly review of more than 3,000 scientific studies examining Freud's ideas found support for some aspects of his theory, whereas other aspects were unsupported or contradicted (Fisher & Greenberg, 1996). But even where Freud's theory was not supported, the research it inspired led to important discoveries. In addition, Freud's work forever broadened the face of psychology to include the study and treatment of psychological disorders.

Modern Psychodynamic Theory

Modern psychodynamic theories continue to explore how unconscious and conscious aspects of personality influence behavior. However, they downplay the role of hidden sexual and aggressive motives and focus more on how early family relationships, other social factors, and our sense of "self" shape our personality (Kohut, 1977). For example, psychodynamic **object relations theories** *focus on how early experiences with caregivers shape the views that people form of themselves* *and others* (Kernberg, 1984, 2000). In turn, these views unconsciously influence a person's relationships with other people throughout life. To explain Ray's shyness, a modern psychodynamic psychologist might examine Ray's conceptions of himself and his parents. Ray's shyness may stem from a fear of rejection of which he is unaware. This fear may be based on conceptions that he developed of his parents as being rejecting and disapproving, views that now unconsciously shape his expectations of how relationships with women and men will be.

The psychodynamic perspective dominated thinking about personality, mental disorders, and psychotherapy for the first half of the 20th century, and it continues to influence applied and academic psychology. Among American psychologists who provide therapy, a large group—20 to 30 percent—report their orientation as being psychodynamic. Psychoanalysis also remains a major force in European psychology (Tuckett, 2005).

Links with psychodynamic concepts can be found within several areas of psychological science. For example, biologically oriented psychologists have identified brain mechanisms that can produce emotional reactions of which we are consciously unaware (LeDoux, 2000), and cognitive scientists have shown that many aspects of information processing occur outside of awareness (Chartrand & Bargh, 2002). Thus, while most contemporary psychological scientists reject Freud's version of the unconscious mind, many support the concept that behaviors can be triggered by nonconscious processes.

The Behavioral Perspective: The Power of the Environment

The **behavioral perspective** *focuses on the role of the external environment in governing our actions.* From this perspective, our behavior is jointly determined by habits learned from previous life experiences and by stimuli in our immediate environment.

Origins of the Behavioral Perspective

▶ **Focus 6**
What are the behavioral perspective's origins and focus? Contrast radical behaviorism with cognitive behaviorism.

The behavioral perspective is rooted in the philosophical school of British empiricism, which held that all ideas and knowledge are gained through the senses. According to the early empiricist John Locke, at birth the human mind is a *tabula rasa*— a "blank tablet" or "slate"—upon which experiences are written. In this view, human nature is shaped purely by the environment.

In the early 1900s, experiments by Russian physiologist Ivan Pavlov (1849–1936) revealed one way in which the environment shapes behavior: through the association of events with one another. Pavlov found that dogs automatically learned to salivate to the sound of a new stimulus, such as a tone, if that stimulus was repeatedly paired with food. Meanwhile, in the United States, Edward Thorndike (1874–1949) examined how organisms learn through the consequences of their actions. According to Thorndike's (1911) *law of effect,* responses followed by satisfying consequences become more likely to recur, and those followed by unsatisfying consequences become less likely to recur. Thus learning is the key to understanding how experience molds behavior.

Behaviorism

Behaviorism, *a school of thought that emphasizes environmental control of behavior through learning,* began to emerge in 1913. John B. Watson (1878–1958), who led the new movement, strongly opposed the "mentalism" of the structuralists, functionalists, and psychoanalysts (Figure 5.9). He argued that the proper subject matter of psychology was observable behavior, not unobservable inner consciousness. Human beings, he said, are products of their learning experiences. So passionately did Watson hold this position that in 1924 he issued the following challenge:

> Give me a dozen healthy infants, well-formed, and my own specialized
> world to bring them up in and I'll guarantee you to take any one of them at

Figure 5.9 John B. Watson founded the school of behaviorism. He published Psychology as a Behaviorist Views It in 1913.

random and train him to become any type of specialist I might select—doctor, lawyer, artist, merchant-chief and, yes, even beggar-man and thief, regardless of his talents, penchants, tendencies, abilities, vocations, and race of his ancestors. (p. 82)

Behaviorists sought to discover the laws that govern learning, and in accord with Darwin's theory of evolution, they believed that the same basic principles of learning apply to all organisms. B. F. Skinner (1904–1990) was the leading modern figure in behaviorism (Figure 5.10). Although Skinner did not deny that thoughts and feelings occur within us, he maintained that "No account of what is happening inside the human body, no matter how complete, will explain the origins of human behavior" (1989b). Skinner believed that the real causes of behavior reside in the outer world and insisted that "A person does not act upon the world, the world acts upon him" (1971). His research, based largely on studies of rats and pigeons under controlled laboratory conditions, examined how behavior is shaped by the rewarding and punishing consequences that it produces.

In the case of our college student, Ray, a behaviorist might explain Ray's shyness around women by examining his past dating experiences. In high school, the first time Ray invited a girl to a dance he was turned down. Later, he had a crush on a girl and they went out once, after which she turned him down. Though nervous, he asked out a few girls after that but was turned down each time. Such punishing consequences decreased the likelihood that Ray would ask someone out in the future. Fortunately, Kira asked Ray out, and the positive consequences they experienced on their first date reinforced their behavior, increasing the odds that they would go out again.

Skinner believed that society could harness the power of the environment to change behavior in beneficial ways and that the chief barrier to creating a better world through "social engineering" is an outmoded conception of people as free agents. Skinner's approach, known as *radical behaviorism,* was considered ex-

Figure 5.10 B. F. Skinner, a leading behaviorist, argued that mentalistic concepts were not necessary to explain behavior and that learning principles could be used to enhance human welfare.

treme by many psychologists, but he was esteemed for his scientific contributions and for focusing attention on how environmental forces could be used to enhance human welfare. In the 1960s behaviorism inspired powerful techniques known collectively as *behavior modification.* These techniques, aimed at decreasing problem behaviors and increasing positive behaviors by manipulating environmental factors, are still used widely today (Silverman et al., 2005).

Behaviorism's insistence that psychology should focus only on observable stimuli and responses resonated with many who wanted this young science to model itself on the natural sciences. Behaviorism dominated North American research on learning into the 1960s, challenged psychodynamic views about the causes of psychological disorders, and led to highly effective treatments for some disorders. But radical behaviorism's influence waned after the 1970s as interest in studying mental processes expanded (Robins et al., 1999). Nevertheless, behaviorists continue to make important contributions to basic and applied psychology, and their discovery of basic laws of learning was one of the greatest contributions made by American psychology in the 20th century.

Cognitive Behaviorism

In the 1960s and 1970s, a growing number of psychologists showed that cognitive processes such as attention and memory could be rigorously studied by using sophisticated experiments. This led some behaviorists to challenge radical behaviorism's view that mental life was off-limits as a topic for scientific study. They developed a modified view called **cognitive behaviorism,** *which proposes that learning experiences and the environment influence our expectations and other thoughts, and in turn our thoughts influence how we behave* (Bandura, 1969, 2002). Cognitive behaviorism remains an influential viewpoint to this day (Figure 5.11).

A cognitive behaviorist might say that Ray's past dating rejections were punishing and led him to expect that further attempts at romance would be doomed. In turn, these expectations of social rejection inhibited him from asking women out and even from making male friends. While at home for spring break, family discussions helped Ray think about his situation in a new light. This helped Ray modify his behavior, become more outgoing, and improve his social relationships.

What Do You Think?

ARE THE STUDENTS LAZY?
Imagine that you are a high school teacher. Whenever you try to engage your students in a class discussion, they gaze into space and hardly say anything. You start to think that they're just a bunch of lazy kids. From a radical behavioral perspective, is your conclusion reasonable? How might you improve the situation? (Think about it, then see page 27).

Figure 5.11 Albert Bandura has played a key role in developing cognitive behaviorism, which merges the behavioral and cognitive perspectives.

The Humanistic Perspective: Self-Actualization and Positive Psychology

▶ **Focus 7**
How does humanism's conception of human nature differ from that advanced by psychodynamic theory and behaviorism?

In the mid-20th century, as the psychodynamic and behavioral perspectives vied for intellectual dominance within psychology, a new viewpoint arose to challenge them both. Known as the **humanistic perspective** (or **humanism**), *it emphasized free will, personal growth, and the attempt to find meaning in one's existence.*

Humanists rejected psychodynamic concepts of humans as being controlled by unconscious forces. They also denied behaviorism's view of humans as reactors molded by the environment. Instead, humanistic theorists such as Abraham Maslow (1908–1970) proposed that each of us has an inborn force toward *self-actualization,* the reaching of one's individual potential (Figure 5.12). When the human personality develops in a supportive environment, the positive inner nature of a person emerges. In contrast, misery and pathology occur when environments frustrate our innate tendency toward self-actualization. Humanists emphasized the importance of personal choice and responsibility, personality growth, and positive feelings of self-worth. They insisted that the meaning of our existence resides squarely in our own hands.

Thinking about Ray's shyness and loneliness, a humanist might say that no matter how many rejections Ray has had in the past, he must take personal responsibility for turning things around. A humanist also might wonder whether, in his freshman year, Ray's happiness and sense of self-worth were resting too heavily on his hope for a good romantic relationship. By focusing on building a few friendships, Ray wisely found another way to satisfy what Maslow (1954) called "belongingness," our basic human need for social acceptance and companionship.

Few early humanists were scientists and, historically, humanism has had a more limited impact on mainstream psychological science than have other perspectives. Still, it has inspired important areas of research. Humanist Carl Rogers (1902–1987) pioneered the scientific study of psychotherapy. In the 1940s and 1950s his research group was the first to audiotape counseling sessions and analyze their content. Rogers (1967) identified key processes that led to constructive changes in clients. As another example, psychologists have conducted many studies of self-concept over the past 25 years, and much of this work incorporates humanistic ideas (Verplanken & Holland, 2002).

Humanism's focus on self-actualization and growth is also seen in today's growing **positive psychology movement,** *which emphasizes the study of human*

Figure 5.12 The humanistic perspective emphasizes the human ability to surmount obstacles in the drive toward self-actualization.

strengths, fulfillment, and optimal living (Diener & Seligman, 2004). In contrast to psychology's long-standing focus on "what's wrong with our world" (e.g., mental disorders, conflict, prejudice), positive psychology examines how we can nurture what is best within ourselves and society to create a happy and fulfilling life.

The Cognitive Perspective: The Thinking Human

Derived from the Latin word *cogitare* ("to think"), the **cognitive perspective** *examines the nature of the mind and how mental processes influence behavior.* In this view, humans are information processors whose actions are governed by thought.

Origins of the Cognitive Perspective

▶ **Focus 8**
Describe the focus and the origins of the cognitive perspective and some areas of modern cognitive science.

As discussed earlier, structuralism and functionalism arose as two of psychology's earliest schools of thought. The structuralists attempted to identify the basic elements, or structure, of consciousness by using the method of introspection. In contrast, functionalists explored the purposes of consciousness. Other pioneering cognitive psychologists, such as Hermann Ebbinghaus (1850–1909) studied memory.

By the 1920s German scientists had formed a school of thought known as **Gestalt psychology,** *which examined how elements of experience are organized into wholes.* The word gestalt may be translated roughly as "whole" or "organization." Instead of trying to break consciousness down into its elements, Gestalt psychologists argued that our perceptions are organized so that "the whole is greater than the sum of its parts." Consider the painting in Figure 5.13. Many people initially perceive it as a whole—as a portrait of a strange-looking person—rather than as a mosaic of individual sea creatures. Gestalt psychology stimulated interest in cognitive topics such as perception and problem solving.

Structuralism, functionalism, and Gestalt psychology eventually disappeared as scientific schools. As behaviorism and its antimentalistic stance rose in the 1920s and 1930s to become the dominant perspective guiding North American research, the study of the mind was relegated to the back burner.

Renewed Interest in the Mind

In the 1950s several factors contributed to a renewed interest in studying cognitive processes. In part, this interest stemmed from psychologists' involvement

Figure 5.13 This painting illustrates the Gestalt principle that the whole is greater than the sum of its parts. The individual elements are sea creatures, but the whole is perceived as a portrait of a face. *The Water,* by Arcimboldo, from Kunsthistorisches Museum, Vienna.

during World War II in designing information displays, such as gauges in airplane cockpits, that enabled military personnel (e.g., pilots) to recognize and interpret that information quickly and accurately. Increasingly, psychologists began to conduct experiments that reflected an information-processing approach.

Computer technology, which was in its infancy at that time, provided new information-processing concepts and terminology that psychologists began to adapt to the study of memory and attention (Broadbent, 1958). A new metaphor was developing—the mind as a system that processes, stores, and retrieves information. The information-processing approach to studying the mind continues to be influential.

On another front in the 1950s, a heated debate arose between behaviorists and linguists about how children acquire language. The behaviorists, led by B. F. Skinner, claimed that language is acquired through basic principles of learning. The linguists, led by Noam Chomsky (b. 1928), argued that humans are biologically "preprogrammed" to acquire language and that children come to understand language as a set of "mental rules." This debate convinced many psychologists that language was too complex to be explained by behavioral principles and that it needed to be examined from a more cognitive perspective.

Interest in cognition also grew in other areas. For example, a theory developed by Swiss psychologist Jean Piaget (1896–1980), which explained how children's thinking processes become more sophisticated with age, gained widespread recognition in North America (Figure 5.14). Overall, psychologists' interest in mental processes swelled by the 1960s and 1970s—a period that sometimes is referred to as the "cognitive revolution."

The Modern Cognitive Perspective

Cognitive psychology, *which focuses on the study of mental processes,* embodies the cognitive perspective. Cognitive psychologists study the processes by which people reason and make decisions, devise solutions to problems, form perceptions and mental images, and produce and understand language. They study the nature of knowledge and expertise. Some, such as Elizabeth Loftus (b. 1944), have greatly expanded our understanding of memory and of factors that distort it (Figure 5.15). Cognitive psychologists continue to explore the nature of attention

Figure 5.14 Swiss psychologist Jean Piaget was a master of observation. Many of his conclusions about cognitive development came from carefully watching children solve problems.

Figure 5.15 Cognitive psychologist Elizabeth Loftus studies the nature of memory and how memories become distorted.

and consciousness and have increasingly become interested in how nonconscious processes influence behavior.

Cognitive neuroscience, *which uses sophisticated electrical recording and brain-imaging techniques to examine brain activity while people engage in cognitive tasks,* is a rapidly growing area that represents the intersection of cognitive psychology and the biological perspective within psychology. Cognitive neuroscientists seek to determine how the brain goes about its business of learning language, acquiring knowledge, forming memories, and performing other cognitive activities (Rajah & McIntosh, 2005).

Social constructivism, an influential cognitive viewpoint, *maintains that what we consider "reality" is largely our own mental creation,* the product of a shared way of thinking among members of social groups (Gergen, 2000). Constructivists would maintain, for example, that the long-standing conflict between Israeli Jews and Palestinian Arabs reflects immense differences in how they perceive God's plan for them and how they interpret the history of the land where they live (Rouhana & Bar-Tal, 1998).

From a cognitive perspective, we might examine Ray's shyness in terms of how he pays attention to and processes information, his perceptions, and his memory. The few times that he went on dates, Ray's nervousness may have caused him to focus on even the slightest things that weren't going well, while failing to notice other cues that suggested his date was having a good time. Ray's interpretation of his past dating failures may also be based on faulty reasoning. Ray believes he was rejected because of his personal qualities ("I'm not attractive or interesting enough") and therefore expects that future dating attempts will also be unsuccessful. If Ray correctly attributed the rejections to some temporary or situational factor ("Clarissa was already interested in someone else"), then he would not necessarily expect other women to reject him in the future. A cognitive psychologist also might ask whether Ray's memories of his past dating experiences are accurate or have become distorted over time. Ray may be remembering those events as much more unpleasant than they actually were.

The Sociocultural Perspective: The Embedded Human

Humans are social creatures. Embedded within a culture, each of us encounters ever changing social settings that shape our actions and values, our sense of identity, our very conception of reality. The **sociocultural perspective** *examines how the social environment and cultural learning influence our behavior, thoughts, and feelings.*

▶ **Focus 9**
Explain the sociocultural perspective. What are culture, norms, socialization, and individualism-collectivism?

J.M.E

Cultural Learning and Diversity

Culture *refers to the enduring values, beliefs, behaviors, and traditions that are shared by a large group of people and passed from one generation to the next.* All cultural groups develop their own social **norms,** *which are rules (often unwritten) that specify what behavior is acceptable and expected for members of that group.* Norms exist for all types of social behaviors, such as how to dress, respond to people of higher status, or act as a woman or man (Figure 5.16). For culture to endure, each new generation must internalize, or adopt, the norms and values of the group as their own. **Socialization** *is the process by which culture is transmitted to new members and internalized by them.*

In word if not in deed, psychologists have long recognized culture's impact in shaping who we are. Two influential behaviorists, Neil Miller and John Dollard, noted in 1941 that

> no psychologist would venture to predict the behavior of a rat without knowing [where in a maze] the feed or the shock is placed. It is no easier to predict the behavior of a human being without knowing the conditions of his "maze," i.e., the structure of his social environment. Culture . . . is a statement of the design of the human maze, of the type of reward involved, and of what responses are to be rewarded.

Yet despite acknowledging culture's importance, throughout much of the 20th century psychological research largely ignored non-Western groups. Such cross-cultural work usually was left to anthropologists. Even within Western societies, for decades participants in psychological research typically were white and came from middle- or upper-class backgrounds. This situation was so common that in 1976, African American psychologist Robert Guthrie published a book titled *Even the Rat Was White: A Historical View of Psychology.* There were important exceptions, however, such as research by Kenneth Clark (1914–2005) and Mamie Clark (1917–1983) and others, examining how discrimination and prejudice influenced the personality development of African American children (Clark & Clark, 1947; Figure 5.17).

Over time, psychologists increasingly began to study diverse ethnic and cultural groups. Today the growing field of *cultural psychology* (sometimes called

Figure 5.16 Social norms differ across cultures and over time within cultures. The idea of women engaging in aggressive sports or military combat is unthinkable in many cultures. Several generations ago, it was also unthinkable in the United States.

Figure 5.17 Psychologists Kenneth B. Clark and Mamie P. Clark studied the development of racial identity among African American children. Kenneth Clark also wrote books on the psychological impact of prejudice and discrimination.

RESEARCH CLOSE-UP   **Love and Marriage in Eleven Cultures**

Introduction

Would you marry someone you did not love? According to one theory, people in individualistic cultures are more likely to view romantic love as a requirement for marriage because love is a matter of personal choice (Goode, 1959). In collectivistic cultures, concern for the extended family plays a larger role in marriage decisions.

Psychologist Robert Levine and his colleagues (1995) examined college students' views about love and marriage. Whereas previous research focused on American students, these authors studied students from 11 countries. They also examined whether students from collectivistic and economically poorer countries would be less likely to view love as a prerequisite to marriage.

Method

The researchers administered language-appropriate versions of the same questionnaire to 1,163 female and male college students from 11 countries. The key question was, "If someone had all the other qualities you desired, would you marry this person if you were not in love with him/her?" The students responded "No," "Yes," or "Not Sure." The researchers determined each country's economic status and collectivistic versus individualistic orientation from data gathered by previous cross-cultural investigators.

Results

Within each country, the views of female and male students did not differ significantly. In contrast, beliefs across countries varied strongly (Table 5.2). In India, Thailand, and Pakistan, most students said they would marry or at least consider marrying someone they did not love. In the Philippines and Japan, a sizable minority—just over a third—felt the same way. In contrast, students from the other countries overwhelmingly rejected the notion of marrying somebody they did not love. Overall, students from collectivistic and economically poorer countries were less likely to view love as a prerequisite to marriage.

Discussion

Among most of our own students, the notion that you marry someone you love is a truism. They are surprised—as perhaps you are—that many students in other countries would consider marrying someone they did not love. This study reminds us that as members of a particular culture, it is easy to mistakenly assume that "our way" is the "normal way."

As in all research, we must interpret the results carefully. For example, among those students who said they would marry someone without being in

SOURCE: ROBERT LEVINE, SUGURU SATO, TSUKASA HASHIMOTO, AND JYOTI VERMA (1995). Love and Marriage in eleven cultures. *Journal of Cross-Cultural Psychology*, 26, 554–571.

(continued)

love, would it be accurate to conclude that they view love as irrelevant to marriage? Not necessarily, because other research has found that "mutual attraction/love" is viewed across most cultures as a desirable quality in a mate (Buss, 1989). Thus the results of the Levine et al. study suggest only that in some cultures love is not viewed as an *essential prerequisite* to enter into marriage.

TABLE 5.2 Love and Marriage in Eleven Cultures

If someone had all the other qualities you desired, would you marry this person if you were not in love with him/her?

Country	Percentage		
	No	**Yes**	**Not Sure**
India	24	49	27
Thailand	34	19	47
Pakistan	39	50	11
Philippines	64	11	25
Japan	64	2	34
Hong Kong	78	6	16
Australia	80	5	15
Mexico	83	10	7
England	84	7	9
Brazil	86	4	10
United States	86	4	10

SOURCE: Levine et al., 1995.

cross-cultural psychology) explores how culture is transmitted to its members and examines psychological similarities and differences among people from diverse cultures.

One important difference among cultures is the extent to which they emphasize *individualism* versus *collectivism* (Triandis & Suh, 2002). Most industrialized cultures of northern Europe and North America promote **individualism,** *an emphasis on personal goals and self-identity based primarily on one's own attributes and achievements.* In contrast, many cultures in Asia, Africa, and South America nurture **collectivism,** *in which individual goals are subordinated to those of the group and personal identity is defined largely by the ties that bind one to the extended family and other social groups.* This difference is created by social learning experiences that begin in childhood and continue in the form of social customs. In school, for example, Japanese children more often work in groups on a common assignment, whereas American children more often work alone on individual assignments.

Thinking about Ray's lonely first year in college, the sociocultural perspective leads us to ask how his cultural upbringing and other social factors contributed to his shy behavior. Throughout his teen years, cultural norms for male assertiveness may have put pressure on Ray. His shyness may have evoked teasing and other negative reactions from his high school peers, increasing his feelings of inadequacy by the time he reached college. As for Ray and Kira's relationship, we might examine how norms regarding courtship and marriage differ across cultures.

In each chapter of this book, a "Research Close-Up" provides you with a highly condensed, in-depth look at an important study, paralleling the format of re-

▶ **Focus 10**
How does the "Research Close-Up" illustrate cultural psychology's goals and importance?

▶ **Focus 11**
Describe the biological perspective and the focus of behavioral neuroscience and behavior genetics.

search articles published in psychological journals. We give you background information about the study, describe its method and key results, and discuss (evaluate) key aspects of the study. Our first "Research Close-Up" examines cross-cultural attitudes about love and marriage.

The Biological Perspective: The Brain, Genes, and Evolution

The **biological perspective** *examines how brain processes and other bodily functions regulate behavior.* Biological psychology has always been a prominent part of the field, but its influence has increased dramatically over recent decades.

Behavioral Neuroscience

Ray and Kira are in love. They study and eat together. They hold hands and kiss. Yet a year earlier, Ray was afraid to ask women out and became depressed. What brain regions, neural circuits, and brain chemicals enable us to feel love, pleasure, fear, and depression? To read, study, and feel hunger? How do hormones influence behavior? These questions are the province of **behavioral neuroscience** (also called *physiological psychology*), *which examines brain processes and other physiological functions that underlie our behavior, sensory experiences, emotions, and thoughts* (Robinson et al., 2005).

The study of brain-behavior relations was in its infancy as psychology entered the 20th century. Two pioneers of biological psychology, American Karl Lashley (1890–1958) and Canadian Donald O. Hebb (1904–1985), studied the brain's role in learning. Lashley trained rats to run mazes and then measured how surgically produced lesions (damage) to various brain areas affected the rats' learning and memory. His research inspired other psychologists to map the brain regions involved in specific psychological functions (Figure 5.18).

Hebb (1949) proposed that changes in the connections between nerve cells in the brain provide the biological basis for learning, memory, and perception. His influential theory inspired much research, continuing to this day, on how the brain's neural circuitry changes as we learn, remember, and perceive. This research led to the discovery of **neurotransmitters,** *which are chemicals released by nerve cells that allow them to communicate with one another.* The study of neurotransmitters' role in normal behavior and mental disorders represents an important area of current neuroscience research.

Because behavioral neuroscience focuses on processes that are largely invisible to the naked eye, its development has depended on technological advancements. Today, using computer-based brain-imaging techniques and devices that record brain waves, psychologists can watch activity in specific brain areas as people experience emotions, perceive stimuli, and perform tasks (Figure 5.19). These advances have led to new areas of study that forge links between various psychological perspectives. For example, cognitive neuroscience—the study of brain processes that underlie attention, reasoning, problem solving, and so

FIGURE 5.18 Karl Lashley was a pioneer of physiological psychology (behavioral neuroscience). He examined how damage to various brain regions affected rats' ability to learn and remember.

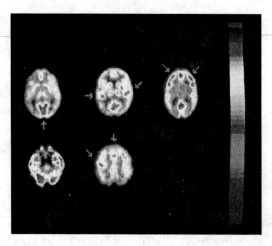

Figure 5.19 Behavioral neuroscientists use positron-emission tomography (PET) scans to measure brain activity as people perform various tasks. Viewed from above, each image pictures a horizontal slice of the brain with the front of the brain at the top. (*top left*) visual task, (*top center*) auditory task, (*top right*) cognitive task, (*bottom left*) memory task, and (*bottom right*) motor task.

forth—represents an intersection of cognitive psychology and behavioral neuroscience. As a whole, however, behavioral neuroscience is broader than cognitive neuroscience. Behavioral neuroscientists, for example, also study the biology of hunger, thirst, sex, body-temperature regulation, emotion, movement, and sensory processes such as vision, hearing, and taste.

Behavior Genetics

Psychologists have had a long-standing interest in **behavior genetics,** *the study of how behavioral tendencies are influenced by genetic factors* (DiLalla, 2004). As we all know, animals can be selectively bred for physical traits (Figure 5.20). But they can also be bred for behavioral traits such as aggression and intelligence. This is done by allowing highly aggressive or very bright males and females to mate with one another over generations. In Thailand, where gambling on fish fights is a national pastime, the selective breeding of winners has produced the highly aggressive Siamese fighting fish. The male of this species will instantly attack his own image in a mirror.

Human behavior also is influenced by genetic factors. Identical twins, who result from the splitting of a fertilized egg and therefore have the same genetic makeup, are far more similar to one another on many behavioral traits than are fraternal twins, who result from two different fertilized eggs and therefore are no more similar genetically than are nontwin siblings. This greater degree of similarity is found even when the identical twins have been reared in different homes and dissimilar environments (Plomin & Caspi, 1999).

Figure 5.20 Selective breeding can produce physical and behavioral characteristics. This tiny horse was produced by selectively breeding very small horses over a number of generations.

FIGURE 5.21 Charles Darwin, a British naturalist, formulated a theory of evolution that revolutionized scientific thinking.

Thinking about Ray, a behavior geneticist would consider the extent to which heredity contributes to differences in shyness among people. Some infants display an extremely shy, inhibited emotional style that seems to be biologically based and persists through childhood into adulthood (Kagan, 1989; Newman et al., 1997). Perhaps Ray inherited a tendency to be shy, and dating rejections in high school reinforced his natural reluctance to ask women out.

Evolutionary Psychology

Charles Darwin published his theory of evolution in 1859 (Figure 5.21). He was not the first to suggest that organisms evolve, but his theory was the best documented. His ideas were stimulated by a five-year voyage aboard a British research vessel that explored coastal regions around the globe. Darwin was struck by the numerous differences between seemingly similar species that lived in different environments. He began to view these differences as ways in which each species had adapted to its unique environment.

▶ **Focus 12**
What is natural selection? Explain the focus of evolutionary psychology.

Darwin noted that the individual members of given species differ naturally in many ways. Some possess specific traits to a greater extent than other members do. Through a process he called **natural selection,** *if an inherited trait gives certain members an advantage over others* (such as increasing their ability to attract mates, escape danger, or acquire food), *these members will be more likely to survive and pass these characteristics on to their offspring.* In this way, species evolve as the presence of adaptive traits increases within the population over generations. In contrast, traits that put certain members at a disadvantage tend to become less common within a species over time because members having these traits will be less likely to survive and reproduce.

As the environment changes, the adaptiveness of a trait may increase or decrease. Thus through natural selection, a species' biology evolves in response to environmental conditions (Figure 5.22). Darwin assumed that the principle of natural selection could be applied to all living organisms, including humans.

Evolutionary psychology *is a growing discipline that seeks to explain how evolution shaped modern human behavior* (Buss, 2005). Evolutionary psychologists stress that through natural selection, human mental abilities and behavioral tendencies evolved along with a changing body (Tooby & Cosmides, 1992). Consider how the brain evolved over millions of years, with the greatest growth occurring in brain regions involving higher mental processes.

According to one theory, as our humanlike ancestors developed new physical abilities (such as the ability to walk upright, thus freeing the use of the arms and hands), they began to use tools and weapons and to hunt and live in social groups (Pilbeam, 1984). Certain psychological abilities—memory, thought, language, and the capacity to learn and solve problems—became more important to survival as our ancestors had to adapt to new ways of living.

Within any generation, genetically based variations in brain structure and functioning occur among individuals. Ancestors whose brain characteristics better supported adaptive mental abilities were more likely to survive and reproduce.

Figure 5.22 Natural selection pressures result in physical changes. The peppered moth's natural color is that of the lighter insect. However, over many generations, peppered moths who live in polluted urban areas have become darker, not from the pollution but because moths who inherited slightly darker coloration blended better into their grimy environment. Thus they were more likely to survive predators and pass their "darker" genes on to their offspring. However, a trip into the countryside to visit their light-colored relatives could easily prove fatal for these darker urban insects.

Thus through natural selection, adaptations to new environmental demands contributed to the development of the brain, just as brain growth contributed to the further development of human behavior.

Evolutionary psychologists also attempt to explain the evolution of human social behaviors. For example, recall that Ray and Kira are contemplating marriage. As a species, why have we evolved to seek out a long-term bond with a mate? And why is it that across the world, on average, men desire a younger mate and attach greater importance than women to a potential mate's physical attractiveness, whereas women tend to seek an older mate and attach more importance than men to a potential mate's ambition? As we'll discuss more fully in Chapter 10, whereas sociocultural psychologists argue that socialization and gender inequality in job opportunities cause most sex differences in mate preferences, some evolutionary psychologists propose that through natural selection men and women have become biologically predisposed to seek somewhat different qualities in a mate (Buss, 1989, 2005).

IN REVIEW

- Psychology's intellectual roots lie in philosophy, biology, and medicine. Several major perspectives have shaped psychology's scientific growth. In the late 1800s Wundt and James helped found psychology. Structuralism, which examined the basic components of consciousness, and functionalism, which focused on the purposes of consciousness, were psychology's two earliest schools of thought.

- The psychodynamic perspective calls attention to unconscious motives, conflicts, and defense mechanisms that influence our personality and behavior. Freud emphasized how unconscious sexual and aggressive impulses and childhood experiences shape personality. Modern psychodynamic theories focus more on how early family relationships and our sense of self unconsciously influence our current behavior.

- The behavioral perspective emphasizes how the external environment and learning shape behavior. Behaviorists such as Watson and Skinner believed that psychology should only study observable stimuli and responses, not unobservable mental processes. Behaviorists discovered basic laws of learning through controlled research with laboratory animals and applied these principles to enhance human welfare. Cognitive behaviorists believe that learning experiences influence our thoughts, which in turn influence our behaviors.

- The humanistic perspective emphasizes personal freedom and choice, psychological growth, and self-actualization. Humanism has contributed to research on the self, the process of psychotherapy, and today's positive psychology movement.

- The cognitive perspective, embodied by the field of cognitive psychology, views humans as information processors who think, judge, and solve problems. Its roots lie in the early schools of structuralism, functionalism, and Gestalt psychology. Cognitive neuroscience examines the brain processes that occur as people perform mental tasks. Social constructivism maintains that much of what we call reality is a creation of our own mental processes.

- The sociocultural perspective examines how the social environment and cultural learning influence our behavior and thoughts. Cultural psychologists study how culture is transmitted to its members and examine similarities and differences among people from various cultures. An orientation toward individualism versus collectivism represents one of many ways in which cultures vary.

- With roots in physiology, medicine, and Darwin's theory of evolution, the biological perspective examines how bodily functions regulate behavior. Behavioral neuroscientists study brain and hormonal processes that underlie our behavior, sensations, emotions, and thoughts. Behavior geneticists study how behavior is influenced by our genetic inheritance. Evolutionary psychologists examine the adaptive functions of behaviors and seek to explain how evolution has biologically predisposed modern humans toward certain ways of behaving.

TABLE 5.3 Comparison of Six Major Perspectives on Human Behavior						
	Psychodynamic	**Behavioral**	**Humanistic**	**Cognitive**	**Sociocultural**	**Biological**
Conception of human nature	The human as controlled by inner forces and conflicts	The human as reactor to the environment	The human as free agent, seeking self-actualization	The human as thinker	The human as social being embedded in a culture	The human animal
Major causal factors in behavior	Unconscious motives, conflicts, and defenses; early childhood experiences and unresolved conflicts	Past learning experiences and the stimuli and behavioral consequences that exist in the current environment	Free will, choice, and innate drive toward self-actualization; search for personal meaning of existence	Thoughts, anticipations, planning, perceptions, attention, and memory processes	Social forces, including norms, social interactions, and group processes in one's culture and social environment	Genetic and evolutionary factors; brain and biochemical processes
Predominant focus and methods of discovery	Intensive observations of personality processes in clinical settings; some laboratory research	Study of learning processes in laboratory and real-world settings, with an emphasis on precise observation of stimuli and responses	Study of meaning, values, and purpose in life; study of self-concept and its role in thought, emotion, and behavior	Study of cognitive processes, usually under highly controlled laboratory conditions	Study of behavior and mental processes of people in different cultures; experiments examining people's responses to social stimuli	Study of brain-behavior relations; role of hormones and biochemical factors in behavior; behavior genetics research

USING LEVELS OF ANALYSIS TO INTEGRATE THE PERSPECTIVES

As summarized in Table 5.3, psychology's major perspectives (presented in the order we have discussed them) provide us with differing conceptions of human nature. Fortunately, we can distill the essence of these perspectives into the simple three-part framework that we briefly introduced earlier in the chapter: Behavior can be understood at biological, psychological, and environmental levels of analysis.

First, we can analyze behavior and its causes in terms of brain functioning and hormones, as well as genetic factors shaped over the course of evolution. This is *the biological level of analysis*. The biological level can tell us much, but not everything. For example, we may know that certain thoughts and emotions are associated with activity in particular brain regions, but this does not tell us what those thoughts are. Thus we must also examine the *psychological level of analysis*. Here we might look to the cognitive perspective and analyze how thought, memory, and planning influence behavior. Borrowing from the psychodynamic and humanistic perspectives, we also can examine how certain motives and personality traits influence behavior. Finally, we must also consider the *environmental level of analysis*. Here we can use the behavioral and sociocultural perspectives to examine how stimuli in the physical and social environment shape our behavior, thoughts, and feelings.

▶ **Focus 13**
Use the three-level framework to integrate psychology's perspectives and discuss causes of depression.

Realize that a full understanding of behavior often moves us back and forth between these three levels. Consider Ray and Kira. When we describe aspects of the culture in which they were raised, such as its religious values and social customs, we are operating at the environmental level of analysis. However, once Ray and Kira adopted those cultural values as their own, those values became an essential part of their identities, which represent the psychological level of analysis. Similarly, we might describe a family environment as highly abusive, but an abused child's tendency to worry and feel anxious—and the chemical changes in the brain that underlie this anxiety—move us to the psychological and biological levels of analysis.

An Example: Understanding Depression

To appreciate how the levels-of-analysis framework can help us understand behavior, let's examine a common but complex psychological problem in our culture: depression. Most people experience sadness, grief, or the blues at some time in their lives. Recall that Ray was lonely during his first year at college and became mildly depressed for a short time. These feelings often are normal responses to significant negative events or losses that we have experienced. However, when these emotions are intense, persist over a long period, and are accompanied by thoughts of hopelessness and an inability to experience pleasure, we have crossed the boundary between a normal reaction and clinical depression.

To better understand depression, let's begin at the biological level of analysis. First, genetic factors appear to predispose some people toward developing depression (Neumeister et al., 2004). In one study, relatives of people who had developed major depression before age 20 were 8 times more likely to become depressed at some point than were relatives of nondepressed people (Weissman et al., 1984).

Biochemical factors also play a role. Recall that neurotransmitters are chemicals that transmit signals between nerve cells within the brain. For many depressed people, certain neurotransmitter systems do not operate normally, and the most effective antidepressant drugs restore neurotransmitter activity to more normal levels.

From an evolutionary perspective, ancestors who developed effective ways to cope with environmental threats increased their chances of surviving and passing on their genes. At times, the psychological and physical ability to withdraw and conserve one's resources was undoubtedly the most adaptive defense against an environmental stressor, such as an unavoidable defeat or personal loss. Some evolutionary theorists view depression (and its accompanying disengagement and sense of hopelessness) as an exaggerated form of this normally adaptive, genetically based withdrawal process (Gilbert, 2001).

Moving to a psychological level of analysis, we find that depression is associated with a thinking style in which the person interprets events pessimistically (Seligman & Isaacowitz, 2000). Depressed people can find the black cloud that surrounds every silver lining. They tend to blame themselves for negative things that occur and take little credit for the good things that happen in their lives; they generally view the future as bleak and may have perfectionistic expectations that make them overly sensitive to how other people evaluate them (Bieling et al., 2004).

Are some personality patterns more prone to depression than others? Many psychodynamic theorists believe that severe losses, rejections, or traumas in childhood help create a personality style that causes people to overreact to setbacks, setting the stage for future depression. In support of this notion, studies show that depressed people are more likely than nondepressed people to have experienced parental rejection, sexual abuse, or the loss of a parent through death or separation during childhood (Bowlby, 2000a).

Finally, at the environmental level of analysis, behaviorists propose that depression is a reaction to a nonrewarding environment. A vicious cycle begins when the environment provides fewer rewards for the person. As depression intensifies, some people feel so badly that they stop doing things that ordinarily give them pleasure, which decreases environmental rewards still further. To make things worse, depressed people may complain a lot and seek excessive support from others. These behaviors eventually begin to alienate other people, causing them to shy away from the depressed person. The net result is a worsening environment with fewer rewards, reduced support from others, and hopeless pessimism (Lewinsohn et al., 1985; Nezlek et al., 2000).

Sociocultural factors also affect depression. As noted above, abusive family environments and other traumatic social experiences increase children's risk for depression later in life. Moreover, although depression is found in virtually all cultures, its symptoms, causes, and prevalence may reflect cultural differences (Kleinman, 2004). For reasons still unknown, in the United States, Canada, and other Western nations, women are about twice as likely as men to report feeling depressed; no such sex difference is found in developing countries (Culbertson, 1997).

Figure 5.23 organizes causal factors in depression into three classes: biological, psychological, and environmental. Keep in mind, however, that the specific

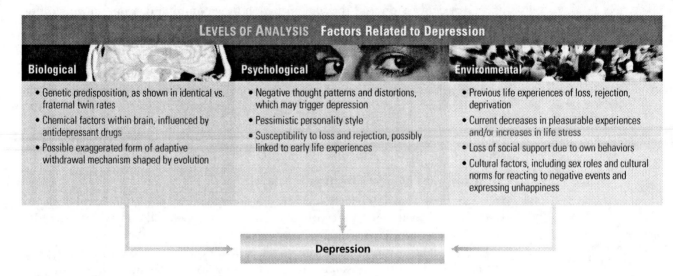

LEVELS OF ANALYSIS Factors Related to Depression

Biological

- Genetic predisposition, as shown in identical vs. fraternal twin rates
- Chemical factors within brain, influenced by antidepressant drugs
- Possible exaggerated form of adaptive withdrawal mechanism shaped by evolution

Psychological

- Negative thought patterns and distortions, which may trigger depression
- Pessimistic personality style
- Susceptibility to loss and rejection, possibly linked to early life experiences

Environmental

- Previous life experiences of loss, rejection, deprivation
- Current decreases in pleasurable experiences and/or increases in life stress
- Loss of social support due to own behaviors
- Cultural factors, including sex roles and cultural norms for reacting to negative events and expressing unhappiness

Depression

Figure 5.23 Levels of Analysis: Factors related to depression

Beneath the Surface

WHAT DID YOU EXPECT?

We'd like you to reflect for a moment on a simple question: What have you learned thus far about psychology that differs from your initial expectations? We ask you this question because, up to now, we've focused on what psychology is. We would now like to point out what psychology isn't.

Perhaps like many of our own students you may have equated psychology with counseling or therapy. If so, then you have already seen that psychology is much more. Many students do not expect psychologists to study brain processes and genetics; others are surprised at the overlap between psychology and disciplines such as sociology and anthropology.

Perhaps you did not expect the rich diversity of theoretical perspectives within psychology. You may have heard of Sigmund Freud and psychoanalysis, or possibly of B. F. Skinner and behaviorism. Indeed, in popular cartoons, psychologists are often stereotyped as therapists who analyze patients lying on couches, or as researchers in white lab coats studying rats in a maze. Now you know that other major perspectives are important parts of psychology's past and present.

Given psychology's theoretical diversity, perhaps you did not expect how environmental, psychological, and biological factors intertwine to influence behavior. And, with regard to influencing behavior, we hasten to dispel the notion that psychology is about mind control. Psychology's goal is not to control people's minds in the sense that control means inducing people to think or do things against their will. Rather, psychologists conduct basic research to learn how people behave, think, and feel; many also apply that knowledge to promote positive changes for individuals, groups, and society as a whole.

We've observed that some students mistakenly expect psychology to be just plain common sense. After all, each of us has spent much of our lives interacting with other people, and we all form notions about human behavior and why people act as they do. For many reasons (which we'll explore in later chapters), our common sense often misleads us. For example, we usually don't subject our commonsense notions to a careful test. Perhaps when you took the true-false test in Table 5.1 you found that some of your commonsense answers were not consistent with the scientific findings.

Finally, we have found that many students underestimate the amount of work required to succeed in this course and therefore mistakenly expect introductory psychology to be easy. However, because of the breadth of topics and the nature of the concepts and information covered in this course, you may find that it takes a lot more effort than you anticipated to gain a true understanding of the material.

In the coming chapters, you will read about many research findings that are likely to contradict your expectations and many popular misconceptions about behavior. We look forward to helping you explore our exciting and important branch of science.

causes of depression and the way in which they combine or interact may differ from case to case. **Interaction** *means that the way in which one factor influences behavior depends on the presence of another factor.* For example, someone who experiences a minor setback in life may become depressed if she or he has a strong biological predisposition for depression. The same setback might barely faze a person with a weak biological predisposition for depression; only a catastrophic loss might cause this other person to become depressed. Thus the intensity of life stress and strength of biological predisposition would interact to influence behavior. Just as boiling water softens celery and hardens an egg, the same environment can affect two people differently.

Summary of Major Themes

Our excursion through psychology's major perspectives and levels of analysis reveals several principles that you will encounter repeatedly as we explore the realm of behavior:

- As a science, psychology is empirical. It favors direct observation over pure intuition or reasoning as a means of attaining knowledge about behavior.
- Although committed to studying behavior objectively, psychologists recognize that our personal experience of the world is subjective.
- Behavior is determined by multiple causal factors, including our biological endowment ("nature"), the environment and our past learning experiences ("nurture"), and psychological factors that include our thoughts and motives.
- Behavior is a means of adapting to environmental demands; capacities have evolved during each species' history because they facilitated adaptation and survival.
- Behavior and cognitive processes are affected by the social and cultural environments in which we develop and live.

▶ **Focus 14**
Discuss five major themes identified in this chapter.

IN REVIEW

▦ Factors that influence behavior can be organized into three broad levels of analysis. The biological level examines how brain processes, hormonal and genetic influences, and evolutionary adaptations underlie behavior. The psychological level focuses on mental processes and psychological motives and how they influence behavior. The environmental level examines physical and social stimuli, including cultural factors, that shape our behavior and thoughts.

▦ To understand behavior, we often move back and forth between these levels of analysis. For example, when as children we are first exposed to cultural norms, those norms reflect a characteristic of our environment. However, once we adopt norms as our own, they become a part of our worldview and now represent the psychological level of analysis.

▦ Biological, psychological, and environmental factors contribute to depression. These factors can also interact. A mild setback may trigger depression in a person who has a strong biological predisposition toward depression, whereas a person who has a weak biological predisposition may become depressed only after suffering a severe setback.

PSYCHOLOGY TODAY

To many people, when you say the word *psychologist,* the first image that comes to mind is that of a therapist. This is understandable, as a large number of psychologists are indeed *clinical psychologists,* who diagnose and treat people with psychological problems in clinics, hospitals, and private practice. Yet many clinical psychologists also are scientists who conduct research on the causes of mental disorders and the effectiveness of various kinds of treatment. Moreover, there are many other types of psychologists who have no connection with therapy and instead work as basic or applied researchers.

▶ **Focus 15**
Describe some of psychology's major subfields and professional organizations.

A Global Science and Profession

As a science and profession, psychology today is more diversified and robust than ever before. Because of psychology's enormous breadth, no psychologist can be an expert on all aspects of behavior. As in other sciences, many areas of specialization have emerged. Table 5.4 describes some of psychology's major subfields, but realize that psychological research often cuts across subfields. For example, developmental, social, clinical, and physiological psychologists might all study the causes of antisocial behavior among children.

Modern psychology also is geographically, ethnically, and gender diversified. A century ago, psychological research was conducted almost entirely in Europe, North America, and Russia by White males. Today these regions remain scientific powerhouses, but you will find women and men from diverse backgrounds conducting psychological research and providing psychological services around the globe. Founded in 1951 to support psychology worldwide, the International Union of Psychological Science consists of major psychological organizations from 70 countries (IUPsyS, 2005). Moreover, across the world, college students are eagerly studying psychology. In the United States, psychology ranks among the top five disciplines in the number of undergraduate degrees and doctoral degrees awarded annually (National Center for Education Statistics, 2001).

The American Psychological Association (APA), founded in 1892, is the largest individual psychological association in the world. Its 150,000 members and 53 - divisions represent not only the subfields shown in Table 5.4 but also areas that focus on psychology's relation to the arts, religion, the military, the environment, sports, social policy issues, the law, and the media (APA, 2005). The American Psychological Society (APS), a newer organization consisting primarily of researchers, has grown to 12,000 members in just two decades (APS, 2005). Both APA and APS have international members in dozens of countries.

A career in most of the subfields described in Table 5.4 requires a doctoral degree based on four to six years of training beyond the bachelor's degree. Graduate training includes broad exposure to knowledge in psychology, concentrated study in one or more subfields, and extensive training in research methods. In some areas, such as clinical, counseling, school, and industrial/organizational psychology,

TABLE 5.4 Major Specialty Areas within Psychology

Specialty	Major Focus
Animal behavior (comparative)	Study of nonhuman species in natural or laboratory environments; includes genetics, brain processes, social behavior, evolutionary processes
Behavioral neuroscience	Examination of brain and hormonal processes that underlie behavior; behavior genetics and evolutionary psychology are sometimes grouped under behavioral neuroscience
Clinical	Diagnosis and treatment of psychological disorders; research on causes of disorders and treatment effectiveness
Cognitive	Study of mental processes such as memory, problem solving, planning, consciousness, and language (psycholinguistics)
Counseling	Consultation with clients on issues of personal adjustment; vocational and career planning; interest and aptitude testing
Cultural/cross-cultural	Study of cultural transmission, psychological similarities and differences among people from different cultures
Developmental	Study of physical, mental, emotional, and social development across the entire life span
Educational	Study of psychological aspects of the educational process; curriculum and instructional research; teacher training
Experimental	Research (typically laboratory experiments, often with nonhumans) on basic processes such as learning, perception, and motivation
Industrial/organizational	Examination of behavior in work settings; study of factors related to employee morale and performance; development of tests to select job applicants; development of machines and tasks to fit human capabilities
Personality	Study of individual differences in personality and their effects on behavior; development of personality tests
Social	Examination of how the social environment—the presence of other people—influences an individual's behavior, thoughts, and feelings
Quantitative	Measurement issues and data analysis; development of mathematical models of behavior

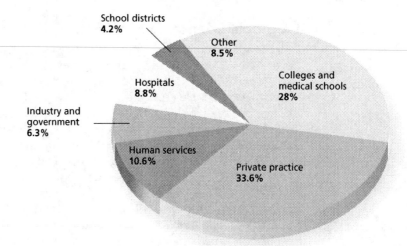

Figure 5.24 Work settings of psychologists. SOURCE: Adapted from data in Table 4. American Psychological Association Research Office, 2001.

additional supervised practical experience in a hospital, clinic, school, or workplace setting is generally required. Please note, however, that psychologists who perform mental health services are not the same as psychiatrists. *Psychiatrists* are medical doctors who, after completing their general training in medicine, receive additional training in diagnosing and treating mental disorders.

Besides its fascinating subject matter, psychology attracts many people with its rich variety of career options. Figure 5.24 shows the major settings in which psychologists work. Many psychologists teach, engage in research, or apply psychological principles and techniques to help solve personal or social problems. For more information on careers in psychology, visit the Online Learning Center (OLC) that accompanies this book.

Psychology and Public Policy

Modern society faces a host of complex social problems. Psychology, as a science and profession, is poised to help solve them. Through basic research, psychologists provide fundamental knowledge about behavior. In applied research, they use this knowledge to design, implement, and assess intervention programs. Together, basic research and applied research are pillars for *evidence-based public policies* that affect the lives of millions of people.

Increasingly, psychologists are being called on to tackle social issues and shape public policy. Consider three of many examples:

• *Education:* From grade school through college, how can we best teach students? In 2002 psychologist Grover Whitehurst became the first director of the U.S. Institute for Education Sciences, a new research unit within the U.S. Department of Education. The Institute's goal is to transform education "into an evidence-based field in which decision makers routinely seek out the best available research and data before adopting programs or practices" (Institute of Education Sciences, 2005).

• *Violence prevention:* Based on decades of aggression research, the APA and other organizations are conducting a program to provide children with nonviolent role models and to improve the violence-prevention skills of teachers, parents, and other caregivers. Training sessions are held in local communities, and almost 170,000 antiviolence public-service announcements aired on television and radio nationwide within the program's first two years (Farberman, 2002).

• *Mental health:* When research indicated that college students needed greater access to on-campus mental health care, the APA crafted the Campus Care and Counseling Act to help meet this need. Some provisions of this act were incorporated into legislation that was passed by the U.S. Congress in 2004.

▶ **Focus 16**
How does psychology help shape public policy?

▶ **Focus 17**
Describe scientifically-based strategies that can enhance students' learning and academic performance.

Psychologists also influence national policy by helping politicians craft legislation dealing with a host of other social issues, from preventing AIDS and obesity to enhancing child care and homeland security. Moreover, their influence is not limited to the United States. School bullying, for example, is a serious problem in several countries. Norwegian psychologist Dan Olweus, a leading researcher on bullying, developed a prevention program that the Norwegian government makes available to all of its public schools (Olweus, 2004). Some American schools also have adopted it.

Psychology and Your Life

We're biased, of course, but to us psychology is the most fascinating subject around, and we hope that some of this enthusiasm rubs off on you. We also hope that as you learn new concepts in your psychology course, you will reflect on how they relate to your own experiences. Psychological principles can not only help solve societal problems but also enhance your own life. For example, research by behavioral, cognitive, and educational psychologists on learning and memory provides guidelines that can improve your academic performance. To conclude this chapter, our first "Applying Psychological Science" feature describes some of these guidelines.

Applying Psychological Science

HOW TO ENHANCE YOUR ACADEMIC PERFORMANCE

College life presents many challenges, and working smart can be as important for meeting those challenges as working hard. The following strategies can help you increase your learning and academic performance (Figure 5.25).

Effective Time Management

If you efficiently allocate the time needed for study, you will have a clear conscience when it's time for recreational activities and relaxation. First, *develop a written schedule.* This forces you to decide how to allocate your time and increases your commitment to the plan. Begin by writing down your class meetings and other responsibilities. Then block in periods of study, avoiding times when you are likely to be tired. Distribute study times throughout the week, and schedule some study times immediately before enjoyable activities, which you can use as rewards for studying.

Second, *prioritize your tasks* (Lakein, 1973). Most of us tend to procrastinate by working on simple tasks while putting off the toughest tasks until later. This can result in never getting to the major tasks (such as writing a term paper or studying for an exam) until too little time remains. Ask yourself, each day, "What is the most important thing to get done?" Do that task first, then move to the next most important task, and so on.

Third, *break large tasks into smaller parts* that can be completed at specific times (Catrambrone, 1998). Important tasks often are too big to complete all at once, so break them down and define each part in terms of a specific but realistic goal (e.g., number of pages to be read or amount of material to be studied). Successfully completing each goal is rewarding, strengthens your study skills, and increases your feelings of mastery.

Studying More Effectively

After planning your study time, use that time effectively. *Choose a study place where there are no distractions and where you do nothing but study,* say, a quiet library rather than a busy cafeteria. In time, you will learn to associate that location with studying, and studying there will become even easier (Watson & Tharp, 1997).

How you study is vital to your academic success. Don't read material passively and hope that it will just soak in. Instead, *use an active approach to learning* (Glaser & Bassok, 1989). For example, when reading a textbook chapter, first look over the chapter outline, which will give you a good idea of the information you are going to be processing. As you read the material, think about how it applies to your life or how it relates to other information that you already know.

(continued)

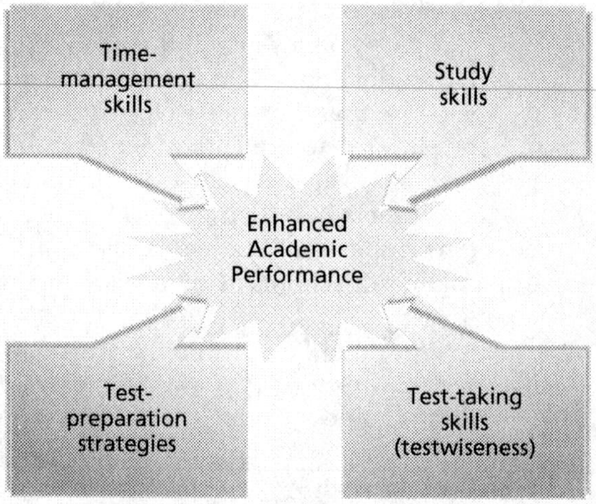

Figure 5.25 Improving Academic Performance. Academic performance-enhancement methods include strategies for managing time, studying more effectively, preparing for tests, and taking tests.

Use Focus Questions to Enhance Active Learning

You can also increase active learning by using the focus questions that appear in the margins of this book. These questions call attention to major concepts and facts. Use them to help you anticipate key points before you read a section, and use them again after you have read each section to test your understanding of the material. This will require you to stop and think about the content. Research shows that responding to these types of questions promotes better recall (Moreland et al., 1997).

Realize that these questions focus on only a portion of the important material. We could have written more questions, but just because some sections don't have focus questions doesn't mean that you can skip the material. In fact, you will learn even more if you supplement our questions with ones of your own—especially for sections that do not already have focus questions. Answering the focus questions and writing questions of your own will require more effort than passive reading does, but it will result in better learning (Estes & Vaughn, 1985; Hamilton, 1985).

Preparing for Tests

Contrary to what many students believe, introductory psychology is not an easy course. It covers a lot of diverse material, and many new concepts must be mastered. Many students who are new to college don't realize that the academic demands far exceed those of high school. Moreover, many students don't realize how hard high achievers actually work. In one study, researchers found that failing students spent only one third as many hours studying as did A-students (who studied about two hours for every hour spent in class). Yet the failing students *thought* they were studying as much as anyone else, and many wondered why they were not doing well (Watson & Tharp, 1997).

As we noted earlier, a written study schedule helps spread your test preparation over time and helps avoid last-minute cramming. Cramming is less effective because it is fatiguing, taxes your memory, and may increase test anxiety, which interferes with learning and test performance (Sarason & Sarason, 1990). Ideally, as the exam day nears, you should already understand the material. Then use the time before the test to refine your knowledge. Using the focus questions can pay big dividends in the final days before an exam.

Test-Taking Strategies

Some students are more effective test takers than others. They know how to approach different types of tests (e.g., multiple choice or essay) to maximize their performance.

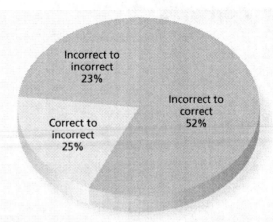

Figure 5.26 Changing answers on multiple-choice tests. Researchers analyzed the eraser marks on 6,412 exams taken by introductory psychology students. Contrary to popular wisdom, changing one's answer was twice as likely to result in gaining points rather than losing points. SOURCE: Based on Kruger et al., 2005.

Such skills are called *testwiseness* (Fagley, 1987). Here are some strategies that testwise students use:

- Use time wisely. Check your progress occasionally during the test. Answer the questions you know first (and, on essay exams, the ones worth the most points). Do not get bogged down on a question you find difficult. Mark it and come back to it later.
- On essay exams, outline the points you want to make before you begin writing, then cover the key points in enough detail to communicate what you know.
- On multiple-choice tests, read each question and try to answer it before reading the answer options. If you find your answer among the alternatives, that alternative is probably the correct one. Still, read all the other alternatives to make sure that you choose the best one.
- Many students believe that they should not change answers on multiple-choice tests because the first guess is most likely to be correct. Eighty years of research shows that this belief is false (Kruger et al., 2005). As Figure 5.26 shows, changing an answer is far more likely to result in a wrong answer becoming a correct one than vice versa. Don't be reluctant to change an answer if you are fairly sure that the alternative is better.
- Some multiple-choice questions have "all of the above" as an alternative. If one of the other answers is clearly incorrect, eliminate the "all of the above" option; if you are sure that at least two of the other answers are correct but are not sure about the third, choose "all of the above."

Time management, study skills, test-preparation strategies, and testwiseness are not acquired overnight; they require effort and practice.

IN REVIEW

- Psychologists today conduct research and provide services around the globe.
- Psychologists specialize in various subfields and work in many settings. They teach, conduct research, perform therapy and counseling, and apply psychological principles to solve personal and social problems.
- You can use principles derived from psychological science to enhance your learning and increase your likelihood of performing well on tests. These include time-management principles, strategies for studying more effectively, test-preparation strategies, and techniques for taking tests.

KEY TERMS AND CONCEPTS

Each term has been boldfaced and defined in the chapter

applied research
basic research
behavioral neuroscience
behavioral perspective
behavior genetics
behaviorism
biological perspective
British empiricism
cognitive behaviorism
cognitive neuroscience
cognitive perspective
cognitive psychology
collectivism
cultural psychology
culture
defense mechanisms
evolutionary psychology
functionalism
Gestalt psychology

humanistic perspective
  (humanism)
individualism
interaction
mind-body dualism
monism
natural selection
neurotransmitters
norms
object relations theory
positive psychology movement
psychoanalysis
psychodynamic perspective
psychology
social constructivism
socialization
sociocultural perspective
structuralism

What Do you Think

THE CASE OF VOODOO DEATH

According to Cannon's hypothesis, the woman's belief in voodoo and knowledge that she had been "cursed" caused her to experience persistent, excessive stress. She became increasingly terrified as her 23rd birthday neared, and her stress response eventually triggered a fatal drop in blood pressure, producing shock and causing death.

Does this explanation seem reasonable to you? In forming your answer, one issue to consider is whether any good evidence supports Cannon's explanation. Cannon's research with animals suggested that a persistent, intense stress response could cause death in a way that would not be easily detectable upon autopsy, and more recent psychological and medical research points to negative effects that stress (caused by fear, worry, or other factors) can have on bodily functioning. However, we also need to consider other possible explanations for the woman's death.

First, in many cases, even ones that Cannon described, voodoo victims refuse all food and drink after they have been cursed, and prolonged severe dehydration may be the cause of death (Barber, 1961). However, in other documented cases, food and drink restriction can be ruled out. Had the woman in our example been severely dehydrated, it seems unlikely that the hospital medical staff would have failed to notice this.

Second, voodoo victims often seem to surrender psychologically; they feel helpless and hopeless, believing that there is no place to hide from impending death (Cohen, 1985). Some scientists argue that this hopelessness increases victims' susceptibility to disease, which then leads to death (Lester, 1972). Others propose that this hopelessness has a more direct effect, triggering bodily responses that eventually decrease one's heart rate and cause death (Richter, 1957). Realize that all of these explanations, although different from Cannon's, still illustrate mind-body interactions, and they support the general point that psychological beliefs can trigger responses that—one way or another—impair health.

Finally, even without the voodoo curse, perhaps the woman would have died that night anyway. Sudden death at such a young age is rare, and the timing would have been an amazing coincidence, but we can't completely rule out the possibility that the woman suffered from a life-threatening medical condition that the physicians did not detect.

In our opinion, Cannon's explanation seems plausible, but as a critical thinker, you should keep the bottom line in mind: We can't say for sure why the woman died. For obvious ethical reasons, researchers don't expose people to voodoo curses in controlled experiments to carefully examine whether and how they die! Instead, scientists obtain clues from natural cases of voodoo death and from research on stress and mind-body interactions and then try to formulate the most plausible explanation.

Are the Students Lazy?

It may be tempting to blame the students' unresponsiveness on laziness, but a radical behaviorist would not focus on internal mental states to explain their inaction. First, to say that students are unresponsive because they're lazy doesn't explain anything. Consider this reasoning: How do we know that the students are lazy? Answer: because they are unresponsive. Therefore, if we say that students are lazy because they're unresponsive and then turn around and conclude that students are unresponsive because they are lazy, all we are really saying is that "students are unresponsive because they are unresponsive." This is not an explanation at all but rather an example of circular reasoning.

From a behavioral perspective, people's actions are shaped by the environment and learning experiences. Put yourself in the hypothetical role of the high school teacher: You may not realize it, but when students sit quietly, you smile and seem more relaxed. When students participate in class discussions, you are quick to criticize their ideas. In these ways you may have taught your students to behave passively.

To change their behavior, you can modify their educational environment so that they will learn new responses. Reward behaviors that you want to see (raising hands, correctly answering questions, and so on). For example, praise students not only for giving correct answers but also for participating. If an answer is incorrect, point this out in a nonpunitive way while still reinforcing the student's participation.

Modifying the environment to change behavior is often not as easy as it sounds, but this example illustrates one way a behaviorist might try to rearrange the environmental consequences rather than jump to the conclusion that the situation is hopeless.

Chapter 6

Unobtrusive Measures
of Behavior

OVERVIEW

We have described observational methods in which the researcher directly observes and records behavior in a natural setting. We have also described how researchers can use survey-research methods to learn about people's thoughts and feelings by asking people directly about their opinions and attitudes. In this chapter we consider methods that do not require direct observation or direct questioning of people. Researchers can gain important insights into people's behavior by examining physical traces of behavior (e.g., graffiti) and archival records (e.g., high school yearbooks). These indirect methods for investigating behavior are called **unobtrusive (nonreactive) measures**. When unobtrusive observation is used, the individuals being observed are not aware of the presence of the observer. When the researcher obtains data from physical traces or archival records, the method of gathering information is even more unobtrusive because the individuals being studied often are no longer present when the researcher is collecting the data. Although unobtrusive measures often yield important information in themselves, they also frequently provide a means of confirming or challenging the validity of conclusions reached using direct observation or surveys. Thus, unobtrusive measures can make important contributions to the multimethod approach to research.

The examination of *physical traces* produced by individuals' behavior represents one type of unobtrusive measure. Consider, for example, the possibility that Latin Americans differ from North Americans in their concern for punctuality. Possible cultural differences in a concern for "being on time" could be investigated using surveys that directly ask people about how often they are late for events, how they feel about concerts and sports events that start later than scheduled, and so on. One unobtrusive measure of people's concern for time, however, might be how accurately clocks are set. In fact researchers found that public clocks (those located in banks) in a Brazilian city were less accurate than those in a similar-sized city in the United States (Levine, West, & Reis, 1980). Although there may be alternative explanations for this finding, differences in this physical-trace measure support the notion that cultural differences in concern for being on time do exist. Levine (1990) (whose research on pace of life.) also examined the accuracy of public clocks in cities and countries around the world. Levine found that measures of walking speed of a country's citizens (direct observation) correlated positively with the accuracy of the country's public clocks (unobtrusive measures).

Archival records are the public and private documents describing the activities of individuals, institutions, governments, and other groups. *Archival data* may be obtained by inspecting these archival records. For example, researchers have claimed that analyses of mortality data reveal a lower than expected frequency of deaths before important events, such as birthdays and religious holidays, and a higher than expected frequency of deaths after these important events (the death "dip/peak" hypothesis). The general procedure for investigating the relationship between death and important occasions is to examine archival data revealing the death dates of individuals in relation to certain important events (see, for example, Phillips, Van Voorhees, & Ruth, 1992; Schulz & Bazerman, 1980). Three major positive events have been examined by researchers: birthdays, national elections, and religious holidays. For instance, one of the early studies to offer data supporting a death-dip/peak hypothesis used birth dates and death dates of persons listed in the book *Four Hundred Notable Americans* (Schulz & Bazerman, 1980). Based on chance alone, one would expect that an individual's death is equally likely in any of the 12 months. However, the number of deaths during the month prior to the month of an individual's birth was found to be lower than the death rate for other months, thus supporting the death-dip/peak hypothesis. According to Schulz and Bazerman, a general explanation for this type of finding is that people somehow prolong their lives or delay death until a special event, such as a birthday, has been experienced.

Phillips and his colleagues demonstrated that a death dip/peak hypothesis is supported more for women than men (Phillips et al., 1992). Female mortality dips below normal the week before the birthday and peaks the week after, whereas male mortality peaks shortly before the birthday. The researchers suggested that for women birthdays act as a "lifeline," and for men birthdays act as a "deadline." Phillips has also shown support for the death dip/peak hypothesis as it relates to religious holidays. Mortality within a Jewish group showed the dip/peak pattern around the Jewish holiday of Passover (Phillips & King, 1988), and mortality within a Chinese group showed this pattern around the Harvest Moon Festival (Phillips & Smith, 1990).

Exactly how people might prolong their life is not particularly clear. One suggestion is that looking forward to a positive event creates a state of positive anticipation that precipitates beneficial neurochemical changes. Another possible explanation is that elderly persons are more likely to follow their health and medical regimens closely as an important date nears, so as to reduce the chances of dying before the event arrives.

In this chapter we present the rationale for using physical traces and archival data. Particular kinds of physical traces are identified and examples of their use in psychological studies are offered. Types of archives and the kinds of data that can be drawn from archival records are also reviewed. Several important advantages of the use of physical traces or archival data are highlighted. There are some limitations and problems with these unobtrusive measures, and they, too, are discussed.

PHYSICAL TRACES

Rationale

* The problem of reactivity (people changing their behavior because they know they are being observed) does not arise when unobtrusive measures of behavior such as physical traces are used.

* The investigation of physical traces represents a valuable component of the multimethod approach to hypothesis testing.

As everyone who has read a few detective stories knows, examining physical evidence of past behavior can provide important clues to the characteristics of individuals and events. For example, the size of footprints in the ground says something about the size and age of the person who stepped there. The distance between footprints can indicate whether the person was walking or running.

Physical traces are especially valuable to researchers because they provide nonreactive measures of behavior (Webb et al., 1981). *A behavioral measure is reactive when participants' awareness of an observer affects the measurement process*. This is often the case when direct observations are made, and it is nearly always the case when surveys are conducted. Aware that their responses are being recorded, participants may behave in a way that does not correspond to their normal behavior. Survey data are particularly susceptible to reactive effects because respondents may give answers they feel the researcher wants to hear or may answer in a way that makes them (the respondents) look good. For instance, social scientists are well aware that responses to surveys asking about degree of political activity, such as past voting behavior, typically overestimate this activity (e.g., Endersby & Towle, 1996).

Physical-trace measures are nonreactive because they are obtained indirectly—the participant is often not present when the data are collected. Thus, unobtrusive measures are valuable alternatives to the reactive measures obtained via direct observation or surveys. In some studies it might be possible for a physical-trace measure to be the only measure of behavior. More commonly, physical traces are used in combination with other measures. As we emphasized researchers investigating a particular research question gain a great deal by including several different measures of behavior. A *multimethod approach* to examining a research question is recommended because it reduces the likelihood that research findings are due to some artifact of a single measurement process (Webb et al., 1981). There are few (if any) perfect measures in the social sciences. Therefore, the results of a study must be carefully scrutinized to determine whether some characteristic of the measurement instrument (such as its reactivity) has contributed to the results. Even then, it is possible that some artifact has been overlooked. The most persuasive argument supporting the validity of a particular research hypothesis is one based on evidence obtained by applying a combination of different measures.

Researchers investigating cultural differences in time perception used such a multimethod approach. They surveyed individuals living in Latin America and in the United States to find out how frequently their subjects were late for appointments and to discover their attitudes toward being late (Levine et al., 1980). Citizens of Brazil reported themselves more often late for appointments and expressed less regret at being late than did citizens of the United States. However, a bias in these responses could be present if people described themselves in a way that fit their cultural "image," rather than as they actually behaved. As we mentioned earlier, however, the researchers also found that public clocks were less accurate in Brazil than in the United States. Further, the researchers observed that watches worn by people in the United States deviated less from the correct time than watches worn by people in Brazil. The data obtained by examining public clocks and the watches worn by citizens of each country tended to confirm the validity of the survey responses and, in combination with the survey results, provided strong evidence for the research hypothesis.

Types of Physical Traces

- Two categories of physical traces are "use traces" and "products."
- Use traces reflect the physical evidence of use (or nonuse) of items, and can be measured in terms of natural or controlled use.
- By examining the products people own or the products produced by a culture, researchers test hypotheses about attitudes and preferences.

Physical traces are the remnants, fragments, and products of past behavior. Two broad categories of physical traces are "use traces" and "products." *Use traces* are what the label implies—the physical evidence that results from use (or nonuse) of an item. Clock settings are an example of a physical-use trace. So are the remains of cigarettes in ashtrays and the marks made in textbooks. *Products* are the creations, constructions, or other artifacts of earlier behavior. Anthropologists are often interested in the surviving products of ancient cultures. By examining the types of vessels, paintings, and other artifacts that remain, the anthropologist can often describe precisely the pattern of behavior exhibited in a setting that is thousands of years old. Psychologists may also examine physical products in order to describe behavior or to test hypotheses. Psychologists who study animal behavior, for instance, may learn about the behavior of different species by examining the types of nests that are constructed. Newhagen and Ancell (1995) examined bumper stickers used by Black and White residents of a Washington, DC, suburb to investigate racial differences in degree of emotional expressiveness.

Use Traces Physical-use traces are classified as either natural or controlled (planned). *Natural-use traces* are produced without any intervention by the - investigator. Their appearance is the result of naturally occurring events. *Controlled-use (or planned-use) traces* result when there is some degree of intervention or manipulation by an investigator. A study by Friedman and Wilson (1975) illustrates the distinction between these two types of measures.

The investigators employed both controlled and natural accretion measures to investigate college students' use of textbooks. They affixed tiny glue seals between adjacent pages of textbooks before the students purchased the books for a course. At the end of the semester the investigators obtained the books from the students and recorded how many seals in the textbooks had been broken and where the broken seals were located. Because the researchers controlled the presence of glue seals in the books, this constituted a conrrolled-use trace. The investigators also analyzed the frequency and nature of underlining by students in the textbooks. Because underlining is typically associated with textbook use, the amount of underlining represents a natural-use measure. Analysis of these physical-use measures indicated that students more often read the chapters that appeared early in the book than those that appeared later in the book.

Table 6.1 includes examples of how physical-use traces can be used as unobtrusive measures of interesting variables. These measures either were used as part of an actual scientific study or represent suggestions by researchers of possible novel and nonreactive measures of behavior (see Webb et al., 1981). The examples given in Table 6.1 are organized according to whether the use traces are natural or controlled. As you examine the contents of Table 6.1, try to think of other possible physical traces that could serve as measures of the variables listed.

Products Physical products have been examined less frequently in psychological studies than have physical-use traces. Nevertheless, this category of physical traces has been used in interesting and meaningful ways to test hypotheses about

TABLE 6.1   EXAMPLES OF PHYSICAL-USE TRACES AND VARIABLES BEING MEASURED*

Trace	Variable
Natural-Use Traces	
Inscriptions (graffiti) on walls of public rest rooms	Sexual preoccupation
Fingerprints or smudges on pages of books	Book usage
Liquor bottles in trash cans	Alcohol consumption of households
Litter	Effectiveness of antilitter posters
Garbage	Food use and lifestyle
Locked/unlocked cars	Concern for property
Lengths of cigarette butts	Cultural differences in death rate due to cancer
Wear on floor or steps	Amount of foot traffic
Wear on library books	Frequency of use
Food consumed	Eating behavior
Spots (produced by rubbing) on statues or religious objects	Level of religious belief
Controlled-Use Traces	
Glue seals broken (seals inserted prior to distribution)	Index of specific pages read
Nose prints on windows of museum exhibit (windows wiped clean each night)	Popularity (frequency) and age (height of points) of viewers
Wear on children's shoes (measured at two points in time)	Activity level of children
Removal of "tear-away" tags on ads or notices	Interest in notice
Wear on mats or other floor coverings placed in specific areas	Amount of foot traffic
Change in statues or objects coated with substances sensitive to touching	Superstitious behavior

*From Webb et. al. (1981).

behavior. For example, researchers recently examined food-related products of both the United States and France to investigate what has been called the "French paradox" (Rozin, Kabnick, Pete, Fischler, & Shields, 2003). The term "French paradox" refers to the fact that the mortality rate from heart disease is much lower in France than the United States despite the fact that the French eat more fatty foods and less reduced-fat foods than Americans. Moreover, Americans are much more likely to be overweight or even obese than are the French. What accounts for these differences? The fact that the French drink much more red wine has been suggested as an explanation. Other explanations are genetic differences in metabolism and lower stress levels in France than the United States (see Rozin et al., 2003). Yet another possible explanation is that the French eat less, and Rozin et al. studied products of France and the United States, looking for evidence to support this hypothesis. They made on-site observations of portion sizes in comparable restaurants in France and the United States. In addition, they examined product sizes in French and American supermarkets. The researchers found that American portions were on average 25% greater than those in French restaurants, and food products on American supermarket shelves were generally larger. These findings provide evidence for yet another explanation of the French paradox—namely, that the French eat less and this contributes to their lower weight and lower mortality from heart disease.

Brandt (1972) points out that the products that people own provide important clues to their lifestyle and behavior patterns. What personality differences, for instance, are reflected in the purchase of different models of cars or in the extras and options that are ordered with a car? Besides serving as a measure of social status or personality, the products a person owns can be used to assess the validity of certain kinds of verbal reports. Are individuals' statements about their

FIGURE 6.1   Bumper stickers are an unobtrusive measure of people's attitudes.

attitude toward energy conservation, for instance, related to the kinds of products they own and use?

Consider the American driving public's interest in bumper stickers. You probably have seen stickers that state, "Guns Don't Kill, People Do," or "Abortion Stops a Beating Heart." As Newhagen and Ancell (1995) point out, bumper stickers are unique in that they "allow for the expression of highly personal opinions about strongly held views to a large audience without any real commitment to interact with them." And, unlike graffiti, which is often illegal and socially undesirable, bumper stickers permit an acceptable outlet for the expression of public emotion. When Newhagen and Ancell analyzed bumper sticker messages of suburban Blacks and Whites in the Washington, DC, area, they found overall frequency of bumper sticker usage was highest in low-income areas regardless of race. High-income White neighborhoods showed most evidence of positive and intense stickers, whereas bumper stickers were least frequently observed and, when they were, the messages were the most subdued, in high-income Black neighborhoods. The researchers suggested that the results illustrate examples of discretely different forms of public expression of emotion as a function of race and income. This conclusion seems to fit with Endersby and Towle's (1996) characterization of bumper stickers as reflecting "a form of identification and solidarity with a group sharing common beliefs."

Problems and Limitations

- Before concluding that a measure of physical traces is a valid indicator of behavior or attitudes, a researcher should make sure no sources of bias exist.
- Validity of physical-trace measures can be ascertained by examining converging evidence.

Physical measures offer a researcher valuable and sometimes novel means to study behavior, and the measures available are limited only by the ingenuity of the investigator. However, the validity of physical traces must be carefully

FIGURE 6.2 The classic "lost-letter technique" illustrates some of the problems with the analysis of physical traces (see text).

examined and verified through independent sources of evidence. Bias can be introduced in the way physical-use traces are laid down and in the manner in which traces survive over time. Does a well-worn path to the right indicate people's interest in objects in that direction or simply a natural human tendency to turn right? Is the setting of clocks a good measure of people's regard for punctuality, or do inaccurate clock settings indicate poor artisan-ship, inadequate maintenance, or irregular electrical service? To what extent is frequency of bumper sticker usage affected by the recent success of local sports teams?

Problems associated with the analysis of physical traces are illustrated in a classic study of honesty carried out using the "lost-letter technique" (see Merritt & Fowler, 1948). The investigators "accidentally" dropped postcards and envelopes at various locations in cities of the East and Midwest. Two types of envelopes were "lost." One contained a written message, and the other contained a lead slug the size of a 50-cent piece. All the letters were addressed and bore proper postage, but no return address was shown. Although 85% of the empty envelopes were returned, only 54% of the envelopes with a slug found their way to a mailbox. Further, more than 10% of the envelopes with a slug were returned after having been opened.

Before the researchers could conclude that the return rates represented a valid measure of the public's honesty (or dishonesty), several possible biases associated with this physical trace had to be considered. Postcards, for instance, were less likely than sealed envelopes to be returned. This difference may have been due, however, to the fact that postcards are more easily affected by the wind and other natural conditions than are larger envelopes. On the other hand, envelopes with a slug are heavier and less likely to be blown away—and these were still less likely to be returned. Letters that were dropped in certain locations (e.g., where many children are present) or at certain times of the day (e.g., just before nightfall) are also likely not to be returned for reasons other than the public's dishonesty or apathy.

BOX 6.1

LOST "LETTERS" ON THE INTERNET

Stern and Faber (1997) used the Internet to produce a "lost e-mail" version of the lost-letter technique. In one study the researchers investigated people's attitudes toward the 1996 presidential candidate, Ross Perot. The researchers sent messages that were supposed to look like misdirected e-mail messages to randomly selected e-mail addresses across the country. The messages went to "Steve" and asked for help with fund raising. The researchers were most interested in the e-mail replies when the original message mentioned that the fund raising was for Ross Perot. The returned messages indicated little support for Ross Perot.

For instance, a number of people returning the Ross Perot message went out of their way to say they were voting for someone else, while none said they planned to vote for him.

The e-mail version of the lost-letter techniques raises ethical concerns that do not apply to the original version. For example, dropping letters on the street can be considered part of the public domain and the person's response is anonymous. A returned e-mail, on the other hand, typically includes the sender's e-mail address making an anonymous response impossible. How would you address these ethical concerns?

The researchers avoided some possible biases associated with the lost-letter technique by the methods they used to "drop" the letters. They checked for other possible biases by directly observing a letter's fate. Their observations of a sample of dropped letters revealed that a letter was picked up 90% of the time by the first person who saw it, suggesting that dropped letters were soon in the hands of unknowing participants.

The consideration of possible biases in the lost-letter technique illustrates a more general principle. Whenever possible, supplementary evidence for the validity of physical traces should be obtained (see Webb et al, 1981). Alternative hypotheses for changes in physical traces must be considered, and data must be collected that allow alternative interpretations to be dismissed. Care must also be taken when comparing results across studies to make sure that measures are defined similarly. For example, when Newhagen and Ancell (1995) tallied bumper stickers, they included only those literally found on car bumpers; Endersby and Towle (1996) operationally defined bumper stickers as any message visible from the rear of the vehicle, which included rear window decals. Different operational definitions of a concept can easily lead to different results.

ARCHIVAL DATA

Rationale

- Archival data comprise the records or documents of the activities of individuals, groups, institutions, and governments.
- Archival data are used to test hypotheses as part of the multimethod approach, to establish the external validity of laboratory findings, and to assess the effects of natural treatments,
- Archival data represent a rich, plentiful source of observations for psychological studies.

When we were born, a record was made of our birth. Information on the birth record probably included the city and state in which we were born, the date and time of our birth, our parents' names, and our name. When we die, another record will be made. It will include such details as probable cause of death, date and time of death, and our age. In between these two events, innumerable records are made of our behavior. Physicians record visits. Hospitals keep a record of when we enter

STRETCHING EXERCISE

A researcher wishes to test the hypothesis that youth attending private high schools are not as "dirty-minded" as students attending public high schools. He chooses two schools (one a church-affiliated school and one public) that are located in the same neighborhood, approximately one mile apart. Both schools include grades 9 through 12. To test the hypothesis, the investigator decides to use both natural and controlled physical-use traces. Specifically, the researcher operationally defines "dirty-mindedness" as the number of obscene words (from a predetermined list) that are found in the restrooms of each school. The natural-use measure is simply the number of new target words appearing on the walls of the restrooms at the end of each week. As a measure of controlled use, the investigator obtains permission from the school authorities to place pads of paper and pencils in the toilet stalls of the restrooms at each school. On each pad of paper is written: "Leave me a note," At the end of each week the investigator replaces the pad with a fresh one and examines the pages that have been written on for the appearance of obscene words.

1. Comment on possible biases that could affect the validity of the physical-trace measures proposed in this study.
2. Frame questions that might be asked concerning the external validity of this study.
3. Suggest ways in which the investigator might use a multimethod approach to this problem.

and when we leave. Schools record our grades and extracurricular activities. Our employer may record the number of times we are late or how often we fail to show up for work. Newspapers describe notable successes and failures. Local governments record when we get married and to whom, as well as when we buy a house and how much it costs. The federal government records, among other things, what we pay in income taxes.

Records are kept not only of individuals but also of countries, institutions, cities, and businesses. The gross national product of a country, its major exports and imports, the size of its defense budget, the distribution of its population, and the number of television sets owned by its populace are just a few of the facts that are frequently recorded. How much profit a company makes is part of its report to stockholders. Voting behaviors of state and federal legislators are recorded, as is the amount of money a city spends on social services. Analysis and interpretation of local and world events flood the media. The contents of the media and of documents and books (published and unpublished) are a source of information about current fads and prejudices, changing patterns of belief, and the ideas of important (and not so important) members of society. The Internet has increased both the number of records that are kept and the ease with which these records can be accessed by individuals.

Archival data are obtained from records or documents recounting the activities of individuals or of institutions, governments, and other groups. As measures of behavior, archival data share some of the same advantages as physical traces. Archival data represent unobtrusive measures that provide a valuable alternative to direct observation and survey research. Like physical-trace measures, archival data can be used to check the validity of other measures as part of a multimethod approach to hypothesis testing. Research done by Frank and Gilovich (1988) provides an excellent illustration of the use of archival data in the context of a multimethod approach to hypothesis testing.

Frank and Gilovich (1988) investigated the strong cultural association that exists between the color black and "badness," or evil. They point out that you could always tell the good guys from the bad guys in vintage American Western movies. The good guys, of course, wore white hats and the bad guys wore black hats. The strong cultural association between black and badness is reflected in other ways. We speak of people being "blackballed," "blacklisted," "blackmailed" and a person's reputation's being "blackened." When terrible things happen it is a "black day." Black is seen in many cultures as the color of death. The good and bad sides of human nature are also contrasted using black-and-white images, as was illustrated by the characters of the famous Star Wars movies. Viewers of these classic films likely will remember the confrontation between the villain, Darth Vader (dressed completely in black), and the young hero, Luke Skywalker (dressed in white or light colors). Vader, unfortunately, had "gone over" to the dark side. (See also Meier et al., 2004.)

Frank and Gilovich wanted to find out if this strong cultural association between black and evil would affect the way people behave. Specifically, they asked whether professional sports teams that wear black uniforms are more aggressive than those that wear nonblack uniforms. Using archival data obtained from the central offices of the National Football League (NFL) and the National Hockey League (NHL), Frank and Gilovich analyzed penalty records of each major professional team in these sports between 1970 and 1986. As measures of aggressiveness they used yards penalized in the NFL and minutes that a player was assigned to the penalty box in the NHL. They chose these particular measures rather than simply counting the number of infractions because penalties for over-aggressiveness are generally more severe (in yards or minutes) than are those for simple rule violations. The operational definition of a "black uniform" was that the colored version of the team's uniform (the one used typically for away games in the NHL and for home games in the NFL) was more than 50% black. (The dark blue uniforms of the Chicago Bears in the NFL were included among the black-uniform teams because many people mistakenly remember their uniforms as black.) The authors predicted that teams wearing black should be penalized more than would be expected simply by chance. And that's just what they found! Teams with black uniforms, such as Oakland, Chicago, and Cincinnati in the NFL, and Philadelphia, Pittsburgh, and Vancouver in the NHL, were reliably penalized more than many other teams that did not wear black uniforms. Thus, a clear connection between aggressiveness and wearing black uniforms was established.

What psychological processes might account for these effects? Frank and Gilovich suggest that both social-perception and self-perception processes are at work. They argue that social perception plays a role because others (specifically, referees) "see" players in black as more aggressive than players not wearing black and therefore award more penalties to players in black. Self-perception leads the players themselves to behave more aggressively when they put on black uniforms. Frank and Gilovich used a multimethod approach to provide support for their explanations based on the archival data by conducting two laboratory experiments. In one experiment, both college students and referees watched staged football games between teams wearing black or white uniforms and rated the players' aggressiveness. In a second experiment, students donned either black or white uniforms in anticipation of an athletic competition before choosing a game from a list of aggressive and nonaggressive games. In the first experiment, both referees and college students were more likely to rate a team wearing black as aggressive. The second experiment showed that students who donned black uniforms chose more aggressive games. By combining data obtained from archival analyses and laboratory experiments, Frank and Gilovich provide a strong case for their explanations of this interesting cultural phenomenon.

Archival data can also be used to test the external validity of laboratory findings. Researchers have used laboratory-based experiments to investigate *causal attributions:* the reasons people give for a certain outcome. A major finding from laboratory studies of causal attributions is that people make different attributions for their successes and failures. People tend to make internal attributions for their successes; they assume that the outcome is due to some characteristic within themselves. For failures, however, people tend to make external attribu-

FIGURE 6.3 Archival records permit psychologists to study the "home advantage" in sports competitions.

tions; they assume that the outcome is due to something beyond their control. Lau and Russell (1980) analyzed the contents of the sports pages in eight daily newspapers in order to test whether results obtained from laboratory experiments were relevant to "real-world" settings. Lau and Russell's analysis of explanations given by sportswriters or team members for the outcome of baseball and football games supported the conclusion based on the lab findings. Specifically, they identified 594 explanations for success and failure involving 33 major sporting events. From the perspective of the winning team, 75% of the attributions were internal, whereas only 55% of the attributions of the losing team were internal.

Researchers can use archival data for two additional purposes—to test hypotheses about past behavior and to assess the effect of a natural treatment. For example, archival data play a central role in studies of the "home advantage" in sports competitions (see, for example, Courneya & Carron, 1992). Sports teams typically play "at home" and "away" over the course of a season and so researchers can ask how this difference affects a team's performance. The *home advantage* refers to the fact that in many sports competitions a team wins consistently more games played at home than it does games played away. Baumeister (1995) has investigated an interesting and somewhat counterintuitive finding that runs counter to the home advantage. Even though teams playing at home tend to win more consistently, they do not necessarily perform well in key games played at home, such as those that decide a championship. The "home choke" phenomenon, nevertheless, has not always found support through archival analyses (Schlenker, Phillips, Boniecki, & Schlenker, 1995a, 1995b).

Natural treatments are naturally occurring events that have significant impact on society at large or on particular members of society. Because it is not always possible to anticipate these events, researchers who want to assess their impact must use a variety of behavioral measures, including archival data. Acts of terrorism, drastic changes in the stock market, and the passage of new laws are examples of the kinds of events that may have important effects on behavior and that might be investigated using archival data. So, too, are the naturally occurring events of a natural life history, such as death or divorce of parents, a chronic illness, or marital difficulties.

In 1921, Lewis Terman began a longitudinal study of intelligence by recruiting more than 1,500 above average children in the San Francisco and Los Angeles schools (see Terman & Oden, 1947). The children, 856 boys and 672 girls, were preadolescents at the time and have been followed at 5- to 10-year intervals since that time. Friedman et al. (1995) have taken advantage of the archival data associated with Terman's study of gifted children to investigate "psychosocial and behavioral predictors of longevity" Friedman and his colleagues also interviewed surviving members of the original group of children for their study.

Friedman et al. (1995) used the archival data from Terman's study to examine the effect of parental divorce on longevity. There is considerable evidence in the psychology literature indicating that children who experience parental divorce or conflict have more conduct and behavioral problems, greater academic difficulties, and poorer health than children whose parents did not divorce (see Tucker et al., 1997). The question in the Friedman et al. (1995) study was whether divorce would also affect mortality rates. The sample of gifted children was relatively homogeneous in that the children were very bright (IQs greater than 135), nearly all White, and mostly middle-class. Nonetheless, the results for this group are clear; parental divorce is associated with premature death. Friedman et al. (1995) found that men from divorced homes were predicted to die at age 76, whereas those from intact homes were predicted to die at age 80; for women the corresponding predicted ages of death were 82 and 86. The reasons for this clear relationship between parental divorce and children's longevity are complex and not completely understood. For example, children from divorced homes were also more likely to be divorced themselves, men were more likely to die from physical injuries, and women from divorced homes smoke more (Tucker et al., 1997). Results of these archival analyses indicate, nevertheless, that "parental divorce sets off a negative chain of events, which contribute to a higher mortality risk among individuals from divorced homes" (Tucker et al, 1997).

One final important reason for considering the use of archival data in research is simply because archival data are so plentiful. We noted earlier the extensive records that society keeps on individuals, groups, and institutions. We also described how researchers can now gain access to archival data more easily by using the Internet. Through careful analysis of archival information, researchers can gain evidence to test numerous hypotheses. There are practical advantages as well. Researchers can avoid the often lengthy data collection phase of research because archival data have already been collected. Archival records can even contain initial summary descriptions. Ethical concerns are also less worrisome because archival information is frequently part of the public record and is usually reported in a manner that does not identify individuals. One goal of this chapter is to alert you to the rich resource that is available if you choose to analyze archival data when you are investigating psychological questions.

Types of Archival Data

- Types of archival data include running records, news media, and other types of records; archival data can consist of public or private documents.

The sheer diversity and extent of archival sources make their classification rather arbitrary. Records that are continuously kept and updated are frequently referred to as *running records*. Tax records and records of various government agencies are good examples, as are the myriad records of sports teams. Because of their continuous nature, running records are particularly useful in longitudinal studies or in the documentation of trends. Other records, such as personal documents, are more likely to be discontinuous or episodic (see Webb et al., 1981). Archival records can also be distinguished by the degree to which they are available for public inspection. Many records kept by government agencies are easily obtainable. Most records of private institutions and businesses, however, are not open to public scrutiny or can be obtained only after many requests and considerable patience on the part of the researcher.

The news media are yet another important source of archival data. Various records, ranging from stock market reports to crime statistics, are published in newspapers and reported on television and on the Internet. The content of media reports is also a form of archival record and is subject to analysis. Earlier we described how the contents of sports pages were used to test a theory of causal attribution. The placement of "Found" advertisements in the Lost and Found section of a newspaper can be used to measure public altruism (see Goldstein, Minkin, Minkin, & Baer, 1978). Researchers investigating the "French paradox" examined restaurant guides in Philadelphia and Paris, recording the number of references to "all-you-can-eat" buffets. There was no mention of all-you-can-eat options in Paris; there were 18 such cases in Philadelphia (Rozin et al., 2003).

Phillips (1977) used running records of motor vehicle fatalities kept by the California Highway Patrol and a measure of suicide publicity derived from California newspapers to determine whether there is a significant suicidal component to motor vehicle fatalities. He hypothesized that a substantial number of deaths arising from motor vehicle accidents are actually the result of individuals using their cars to commit suicide. To test this hypothesis, Phillips investigated whether motor vehicle fatalities would, like suicides in general, increase after a well-publicized suicide story. Components of the publicity measure included the daily circulation of each newspaper and the number of days the newspaper carried the suicide story. This publicity measure correlated significantly with changes in motor vehicle fatalities after each story. The number of motor vehicle fatalities increased significantly during the few days after a well-publicized suicide story, reaching a peak on day 3. This result is shown in Figure 6.4. Phillips did additional analyses to confirm that the pattern shown in Figure 6.4 was indeed associated with the publication of a suicide story. He compared changes in the frequency of motor vehicle fatalities during experimental periods (the week right after the story) with control periods that were free from suicide stories. The control periods were matched with the experimental periods in terms of day of the week, presence or absence of holidays, and time of the year. Phillips concluded

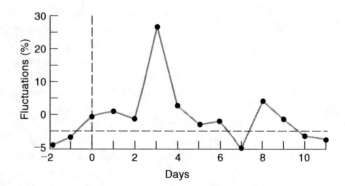

FIGURE 6.4 Daily fluctuations in motor vehicle accident fatalities for a 2-week period before, during (Day 0), and after publication of suicide stories. (From Phillips, 1977.)

that "suicide stories stimulate a wave of imitative suicides, some of which are disguised as motor vehicle accidents."

Table 6.2 contains a list of selected sources of archival information and the nature of the data that might be obtained from them. The types of archival data shown in Table 6.2 are rather arbitrarily classified as running records, those pertaining to the media, and "other records," including records of businesses, schools, and other private institutions. Table 6.2 introduces you to the variety of archival data that can be obtained from archival sources. We will now discuss a critical type of analysis that is used in archival research—content analysis.

Content Analysis

- Content analysis refers to the process of making inferences based on objective coding of archival records.
- Steps for content analysis include identifying a relevant source of archival data, sampling data from the records, and then coding the contents of the records.
- Coding in content analysis involves classifying events and behaviors from archival records into clearly defined categories and recording the amount of time or words devoted to events and behaviors.
- Trained coders use rating scales to make qualitative judgments about the contents of archival records.

Identifying the many sources of archival data is important, but the usefulness of these sources depends ultimately on how their content is analyzed. In the simplest cases, only minimal analysis may be necessary. Recording the votes of state legislators may be as simple as transcribing vote tallies found in legislative documents or on government websites. In many cases, however, gleaning relevant data from an archival source can require careful procedures and relatively complex analysis of the source's content. Furthermore, problems of sampling, reliability, and validity are just as critical when analyzing archival sources as when analyzing data obtained from direct observation.

Content analysis can be generally defined as any technique that allows researchers to make inferences based on specific characteristics they objectively identify in messages (Holsti, 1969). Although content analysis is associated primarily with written communications, it may be used with any form of message, including television and radio programs, speeches, films, interviews, and e-mail messages. For instance, Weigel, Loomis, and Soja (1980) used content analysis to study race relations as depicted on prime-time television. They analyzed the frequency of appearances of Blacks and Whites on evening television shows carried by three major networks. In addition, they rated the quality of Black-White and White-White interactions.

In many content-analysis studies, the communication is written. The units of classification for *quantitative* analysis generally include single words, characters, sentences or paragraphs, themes, or particular items (Holsti, 1969). In a study of bereavement, for example, researchers performed a content analysis of interview transcripts of men who had lost a partner to AIDS (Pennebaker, Mayne, & Francis, 1997). Use of insight and causal words predicted emotional well-being a year later. When newspaper content is analyzed, a frequently used measure is space— for instance, number of column inches devoted to a particular topic. Phillips (1977) used this measure in his study of the relationship between publicized suicides and frequency of motor vehicle fatalities. When television or radio broadcasts are studied, time is often used as a unit of measurement. Weigel et al. (1980) measured both Black appearances and Black-White appearances in terms of the percentage of total human appearance time.

Qualitative measures are also used as part of content analysis. For example, Satterfield and Seligman (1994) used a qualitative measure to investigate the

TABLE 6.2   SELECTED SOURCES OF ARCHIVAL INFORMATION AND ILLUSTRATIVE DATA FOR THREE TYPES OF ARCHIVES*

Source	Illustrative data
Running Records	
Congressional Record	Statements of position on particular issues
Telephone directories	Community ethnic group membership
Salaries of teachers or government employees	Community support
Government agency records (labor, commerce, agriculture departments)	Living trends
Judicial record	Uniformity in sentencing for antisocial behavior
Moody's Handbook	Corporate financial structure
Who's Who in America	Nature of cited accomplishments of successful people
Tax records	Regional differences in patterns of living
City budgets	Perceived value or extent of support of various activities
Media	
Society section of metropolitan newspaper	Upper-middle-class and lower-upper-class activities
Children's books on sale	Qualities of models (heroes and heroines)
Movie announcements in newspapers	Changing taboos and enticements
Want ads	Employer inducements
Obituary columns	Charity preferences
Published speeches	Political, social, economic attitudes
Newspaper headlines	Press bias
Other Records†	
Absentee and tardiness records	Work habits or motivation
Military reenlistment and longevity figures	Morale indicator
Production and other output figures	Performance of individuals, departments, and so on
Sales contest records	Selling effectiveness, effectiveness of incentive plans
Peanut sales at ball games	Excitement indicator (greater after than before seventh inning)
Air trip insurance figures	Public concern before and after air crashes
Sales of layettes by color (blue or pink)	Sex preference in different social classes
Actuarial records: birth, baptismal, death records; marriage licenses	Comparative demographic data (occupation, religion, time of day, cause of death, and so on)
Cemetery documents, burial-lot records	Family membership

*Adapted from Brandt (1972).
†Institutions, businesses, hospitals, schools, and so on; may or may not be open to public inspection.

explanatory styles of George H. W. Bush (the 41st President) and Saddam Hussein during several historical periods of conflict, including the Persian Gulf Crisis. The particular measure used by these researchers is called the CAVE technique. The acronym CAVE stands for "content analysis of verbatim explanations." The CAVE guidelines help researchers identify causal statements in written or spoken verbatim messages. The statements can then be rated on dimensions of

BOX 6.2

THREE BASIC STEPS IN CONTENT ANALYSIS

There are three basic steps in carrying out a content analysis: identifying a relevant archival source, sampling selections from the source, and coding units of analysis for quantitative and qualitative analyses.

Identifying a relevant source. The key to identifying a relevant archival source is defining what we mean by a *relevant* source. What is relevant, of course, depends on the goals of the study and the questions the researcher is asking. Simply stating the purpose of the study is sometimes sufficient to pinpoint an appropriate archival source. A researcher who sets out to study humor in tombstone messages or race relations on television has already identified the relevant archival source. In other situations the identification of relevant sources depends on the ingenuity of the researcher. Lau and Russell's (1980) choice to use the sports page to test the external validity of laboratory findings related to attribution represents an appropriate and clever identification of a relevant archival source. Similarly, Carroll and Russell (1997) identified relevant archival sources for their analysis of film actors' portrayal of emotions, such as disgust and fear, by selecting Hollywood films, such as *Ordinary People* (1980) and *Dead Poets Society* (1989), "noted for their realistic portrayal of modern life and for their highly emotional content."

Sampling selections from the archival source. The second step in content analysis involves the appropriate sampling of selections from the relevant archival source. As is the case when drawing samples for observational studies or for survey research, the goal of sampling is to obtain a representative sample. The extent to which the results of an archival study can be generalized depends on the representativeness of the sample that is used.

For example, Terman's study of genius that we described earlier in the chapter was based on data collected from high IQ, mainly White, middle-class individuals. The same sample was used in the subsequent archival studies of longevity. The external validity of these longevity studies is necessarily less than it would be had the archival source included a more heterogeneous sample. Moreover, we might question the external validity of the findings of the longevity studies based on Terman's original sample for another reason. The impact of parental divorce on children's lives at the beginning of the 20th century, when divorce was less frequent and less socially acceptable, may well not be the same as it is today.

Coding units of analysis. The third and final step in performing a content analysis is *coding*. Similar to the scoring of narrative records, this step requires that relevant descriptive categories and appropriate units of measure be defined (see Holsti, 1969). As with the choice of the archival source itself, what determines a relevant descriptive category is related to the goals of the study. An analysis done by Weigel et al. (1980) in their study of race relations illustrates how the categories used in coding are tied to the study's goals. They defined four major categories: (1) human appearance time, (2) Black appearance time, (3) cross-racial appearance time, and (4) cross-racial interaction time. Each category was operationally defined. For instance, cross-racial interaction was defined as "the time during which black and white characters were engaged in active, on-screen interactions (talking, touching, or clear nonverbal communication). The use of precise operational definitions permitted coders viewing the sample broadcasts to make reliable judgments of events.

explanatory style. The content analysis of verbatim explanations by Bush and Hussein for periods preceding military actions or political conflicts produced an interesting result:

> When the leaders were pessimistic (relative to themselves), their subsequent actions were more cautious and passive. When the leaders were relatively optimistic, their subsequent actions were more aggressive and risky. (Satterfield & Seligman, 1994)

Satterfield and Seligman appropriately acknowledge that the correlational nature of their study means they must "leave open the large class of third-variable accounts before concluding that explanatory style itself causes cautious versus risky actions." For instance, before a definitive conclusion regarding the relationship between explanatory style and political action can be reached, such

FIGURE 6.5 Content analysis of cross-racial interactions between TV actors reveals how race relations are depicted in the American media.

issues as political demands on the leaders or cultural differences in rhetorical style need to be investigated further. Nevertheless, the data suggest that "shifts in explanatory style seem at least to signal corresponding shifts in aggressivity and risk taking." Archival research may help us better understand the psychological nature of political decision making and perhaps even help predict the course of world events.

The use of blind observers is one way to reduce observer bias in studies involving direct observation of behavior. Similarly whenever it is possible to do so, those doing the coding or rating of archival sources should be blind to important aspects of the study, such as the main hypotheses, the source of the messages, and the immediate surrounding context. Judges in the Satterfield and Seligman (1994) study of explanatory style, for example, rated the world leaders' statements only after "all potentially biasing date information was removed" and after source material had been assigned random number codes. Measures of interjudge reliability also should be reported as part of a content analysis.

Problems and Limitations

- Archival data may be biased due to selective deposit and selective survival.
- Selective deposit occurs when biases influence what information is recorded (deposited) in an archival record, or whether a record is made at all; selective survival occurs when archival records are missing or incomplete.
- Archival records are subject to errors and changes in record-keeping procedures.
- Although archival data are considered nonreactive, reactivity can influence the production of archival records; this is particularly true for public records.
- When interpreting the results of correlational analyses of archival data, researchers must be alert to the possibility of spurious relationships.

When discussing the validity of physical traces, we mentioned that biases may result from the way physical traces are established and from the manner in which they survive over time. These biases are referred to as selective deposit and selective survival, respectively, and they are no less a problem for archival records (see Webb et al., 1981). Either of these biases can impose severe limitations on the generality of research findings.

Problems of **selective deposit** arise when biases exist in the production of archival sources. For example, consider the possibility of selective deposit in the context of suicide notes. Osgood and Walker (1959) compared real suicide notes, ordinary letters, and faked suicide notes. A concern with the problem of selective deposit might lead us to ask whether the thoughts and feelings expressed in suicide notes are representative of all suicides. It happens that fewer than a fourth of all individuals who commit suicide leave notes, so it is possible that those who do leave notes are not representative of those who do not leave notes (Webb et al., 1981).

Problems of selective deposit may also arise when individuals associated with archival sources have the opportunity to edit and alter records before they are permanently recorded. Though the *Congressional Record* is ostensibly a spontaneous record of speeches and remarks made before the Congress, legislators actually have the opportunity to edit their remarks before they are published (Webb et al., 1981) and even to enter into the record documents and accounts that were never really read aloud. No doubt remarks that are, in hindsight, viewed as less than politically expedient are changed prior to publication in the *Congressional Record*. Researchers who use archival data must be aware of the biases that may occur when an archive is produced. Consider, for example, what types of biases might cause selective recording of crime statistics, income expense accounts, or sales figures.

Problems associated with **selective survival** arise when records are missing or incomplete (something an investigator may or may not even be aware of). It is important to consider whether there are reasons to suspect systematic biases in the survival of certain records. Are documents missing that are particularly damaging to certain individuals or groups? Following a change of presidential administrations, are some types of archives destroyed or misplaced? Are "letters to the editor" representative of all letters that were received? Schoeneman and Rubanowitz (1985) cautioned that when analyzing the contents of advice columns, they could not avoid the possibility of a preselection bias because advice columnists print only a fraction of the letters they receive. As one prominent group of researchers has commented, when one examines archival data, "the gnawing reality remains that archives have been produced for someone else and by someone else" (Webb et al., 1981).

Beyond the problems of selective deposit and survival, researchers face additional possible problems with archival sources that arise due to errors in record keeping and changes over time in the manner in which the records are kept. Researchers must be able to document that the record keeping was relatively constant and stable over the period of their study. When running records are kept, there is always the possibility that the definitions of categories have been changed midstream. An interesting example of unintended bias appears in the debate over the "home choke" hypothesis. Critics argue that the archival data do not support the hypothesis that sports teams choke in key games when playing at home (Schlenker et al., 1995a, 1995b), When defending the archival analyses supporting the hypothesis, Baumeister (1995) pointed out that during the archival period there had been a rule change for the World Series regarding the use of a designated hitter. The rule change favored the home team, and could have worked against the "home choke" hypothesis.

Archival data represent nonreactive measures of behavior, but their classification as nonreactive applies only to the analysis of archival data. Reactivity can be a problem at the time the archival record was produced. Statements made by public figures and printed in newspapers or reported by other media must be evaluated for possible reactivity. Politicians and others who are constantly exposed to media publicity no doubt learn how to "use" the media, and their public stance may not match their private views. Lau and Russell (1980) had to consider whether the public statements made by players and coaches about a team's performance were really the same as those they made in private. They concluded that differences between public and private statements of attribution no doubt existed but that these differences do not invalidate their generalization of laboratory findings to real-world settings. The only way to control for reactive effects in archival data is to be aware that they may exist and, when possible, to seek other forms of corroborative evidence.

The need to identify possible spurious relationships is yet another problem in the analysis of archival data. A *spurious relationship* exists when evidence falsely indicates that two or more variables are associated. False evidence can arise because of inadequate or improper statistical analysis, A spurious relationship linked to a statistical problem may exist in studies that claim a relationship between frequency of deaths and important occasions. Many people seem to endorse the view that individuals can somehow prolong their life in order to experience certain important events, such as birthdays. Based on their reanalysis of data from several studies, however, Schulz and Bazerman (1980) argue that the supportive evidence may be the result of statistical artifacts—for example, the way in which the period of time before and after a death was measured. Their reanalysis of the data eliminated any evidence for the death-dip hypothesis. But Schulz and Bazerman do not recommend that we abandon the death-dip hypothesis. Instead, they suggest that data supporting the death-dip hypothesis "may well be within reach if we use the proper methodologies and carefully select important events."

Spurious relationships most often occur when variables are accidentally or coincidentally related. This can happen when the correlation between two variables results from changes in another, usually unidentified, *third variable*. For instance, ice cream sales and crime rate are positively correlated. Before we conclude, however, that eating ice cream prompts people to commit crimes, it is important to consider the fact that both variables are likely affected by increases in temperature. Neither eating ice cream nor committing crime directly affects the other; they are correlated because of the third variable they share, temperature.

Several studies (e.g., Baron & Reiss, 1985) have been done to determine whether Phillips' (1983) finding of a relationship between heavyweight prize fights and homicides in the United States reflects a spurious relationship. Critics have questioned whether possible third variables might account for the relationship. Baron and Reiss, for instance, suggested that the third-day peak, which Phillips (1983) admitted he could not readily interpret, was due to the occurrence of holidays or weekends near prize-fight dates or even to fluctuations in the unemployment rate. In spite of questions such as these about possible third variables, extensive reanalysis of Phillips' original data tended to reaffirm a link between violence portrayed in the media and violence acted out in society (see Miller, Heath, Molcan, & Dugoni, 1991).

Researchers tend to be appropriately cautious in reaching final conclusions based solely on the outcome of an archival study (see, for example, Baumeister, 1995). Their cautiousness is due in large part to their recognition of how difficult it can be to identify and rule out possible spurious relationships. Gathering additional evidence from independent sources and subjecting the archival data to more than one kind of analysis is essential in dealing with spurious relationships. Even when these procedures are followed, however, it is hard to draw definitive conclusions from archival data alone. Archival data are most useful when they provide complementary evidence in a multimethod approach to the investigation of a phenomenon.

ETHICAL ISSUES AND UNOBTRUSIVE MEASURES

- Unobtrusive measures such as physical traces and archival data represent an important research method because psychologists can use them to fulfill their ethical obligation to improve individual and societal conditions.

The APA Ethics Code makes clear that "psychologists seek to promote accuracy, honesty, and truthfulness in the science" be "concerned about the ethical compliance of their colleagues' scientific and professional conduct" and commit themselves "to increasing scientific and professional knowledge of behavior and people's understanding of themselves and others and to the use of such knowledge to improve the condition of individuals, organizations, and society" (see Preamble, Principles B and C, of the APA Ethics Code; American Psychological Association, 2002). These are general ethical obligations, of course, that apply when scientists use any methodology. Nevertheless, several studies that we have reviewed in this chapter involving the use of unobtrusive measures provide excellent illustrations of these ethical principles. For instance, we have described research showing how psychologists have contributed meaningfully to our understanding of suicide, race relations, effects of parental divorce, conflict resolution, societal violence, sexual discrimination, and fair scientific practices. This research contributes "knowledge of behavior and people's understanding of themselves and others," and it also has the potential "to improve the condition of individuals, organizations, and society." These contributions arise from only one small sample of psychological research that deals with physical traces or archival data. This impressive list testifies to the ways in which psychologists strive to meet their ethical obligations to create positive change through their research.

It is important to remember that there may be a cost to society of not doing research. A better understanding of such social problems as violence, suicide, and race relations, for example, has the potential to improve many people's lives. Yet, ethical dilemmas arise when there are serious risks to participants that make certain kinds of research difficult to justify when considering a risk/benefit ratio. One potential resolution of this dilemma is to seek alternative methods of data collection that involve lower risk. Research involving the use of physical traces and archival data can be carried out on important psychological problems under conditions where ethical issues are often minimal relative to more intrusive methods. Thus, research using unobtrusive measures may represent an important methodology for investigating important social issues with less risk.

SUMMARY

Unobtrusive measures such as physical traces and archival data are important alternatives to direct observation and surveys. Physical traces are the remnants, fragments, and products of past behavior. Use traces can either result naturally, without any intervention by the investigator, or be planned by the investigator. Physical traces may provide important nonreactive (unobtrusive) measures of behavior and can be used as the sole dependent variable or in combination with other measures of behavior. Multimethod approaches to the study of behavior are particularly recommended because they reduce the chance that results are due to some artifact of the measurement process. In obtaining physical traces, an investigator must be aware of possible biases in the way in which traces accumulate or survive over time.

Archival data are found in records and documents that recount the activities of individuals, institutions, governments, and other groups. These sources of information are valuable because they provide a way of investigating the external validity of laboratory findings, assessing the effect of a "natural treatment" (such as divorce), and analyzing the content of communications. Archival records are nonreactive measures of behavior and, like physical traces, can be used in multimethod approaches to hypothesis testing. The analysis of archival data typically requires some form of content analysis, a process that can involve problems of sampling and coding that are not unlike those that arise in the analysis of narrative records. Problems of selective deposit and selective survival must be investigated when archival data are used, and evidence should be presented showing that observed relationships are not spurious.

Unobtrusive measures can be an important alternative to more intrusive methodologies, permitting psychologists to do research on important social issues with minimal risk to the participants.

KEY CONCEPTS

unobtrusive (nonreactive) measures   content analysis
physical traces   selective deposit
archival data   selective survival

REVIEW QUESTIONS

1. Why are physical traces and archival data especially attractive alternatives to the direct-observation and survey method of measuring behavior and attitudes?

2. Explain why researchers choose to use the multimethod approach to investigate a research question.

3. Identify the two kinds of physical-trace measures that are used by psychologists and briefly describe how they differ.

4. Explain how possible sources of bias can arise when physical-use traces are the dependent variable in a study, and how the validity of these measures can be verified.

5. Describe three reasons researchers use archival data in their research and provide a research example illustrating each of these reasons.

6. What two dimensions can be used to distinguish among the types of archival sources used by psychologists?

7. Briefly describe the three steps that are involved in carrying out a content analysis in archival research.

8. Explain the roles of selective deposit, selective survival, and reactivity in interpreting the results obtained using archival sources.

9. Explain two reasons why spurious relationships can arise in the analysis of archival data.

CHALLENGE QUESTIONS

1 Suggest one physical-trace measure and one source of archival data for each of the following variables. Be sure to specify an operational definition of each variable.

  A Public's interest in cultural events

  B Students' political attitudes

  C Community concern about crime

  D Citizens' attitudes toward their schools

  E Current fads in dress

2 For each of the following archival sources, specify two kinds of data that might be useful in a psychological study. Once again, be sure to specify the operational definition that could be used for the variable you have identified.

  A Weekly news magazine

  B Television soap operas

  C Classified section of newspaper

  D Annual city budgets

  E Student yearbooks

  F List of donors to a university

  G Television commercials

3 A bright female graduate student in psychology has been offered a job with both *Newsweek* and *Time*. The salary offers of the two companies are basically the same, and it appears that both the working conditions and the job responsibilities are similar. To help her decide which job to accept, she resolves to determine whether one magazine has a better attitude toward women than the other. She appeals to you to help her with a content analysis of these two news magazines. What specific advice would you give her regarding each of the following steps of her content analysis?

  A Sampling

  B Coding

  C Reliability

  D Quantitative and qualitative measures

4 An educational specialist was convinced that schoolyard fights among young boys were more violent than those among young girls. To gather evidence relevant to her hypothesis, she checked the records at the nurse's office of her school. She found that, of the 100 injuries resulting from fights which were reported to the school nurse, 75% involved boys and only 25% involved girls. The investigator was convinced on the basis of these findings that her hypothesis was correct. Think critically about her conclusion by considering how these very same findings could result if exactly the opposite of the investigator's hypothesis were true—namely, that fights among young girls are more violent. (Be sure to confine your response to the adequacy of the data that the investigator has presented to support her conclusion.)

Answer to Stretching Exercise

1. There could be a bias in the way the physical trace is laid down if students at the two schools have different expectations concerning the likelihood of disciplinary action for writing obscene words. Since the investigator is recording responses only once a week, either the custodial staff or other students and faculty (unaware of the purpose of the study) might try to remove the words from restroom walls and the "Leave me a note" pads. This potential bias in the way the messages survive over time would be especially troublesome if it differed at the two schools.

2. The external validity of this study could be questioned because comparisons between private and public schools are being made on the basis of only one

school of each type from a particular geographical location with particular staff, and so on. The results of this study could be generalized, however, to schools that were similar to the two schools included in the study.

3. The physical-trace measures of this study could be supplemented by direct observations of youth at the two schools and by conducting a survey of the children at the two schools on their attitudes and behaviors. Important ethical concerns would need to be addressed, however, in attempting to do research on this topic in schools.

Answer to Challenge Question 1

An example of a physical-trace measure (PT) and a possible source of archival data (AD) are listed below for each of the variables. These examples represent only illustrations and not definitive answers. Operational definitions are only sketched here; they should be developed more fully through discussion in class,

A. Public's interest in cultural events: (PT) amount of wear on floors at special exhibit in an Art Museum; (AD) attendance figures for theater and concerts in the past calendar year.

B. Students' political attitudes: (PT) amount of refuse collected after political rallies on campus for different political groups; (AD) records of participation by students at local, state, and national conventions.

C. Community concern about crime: (PT) number of dead bolt locks on front doors of houses; (AD) police records of all calls reporting "suspicious" activities in the community.

D. Citizens' attitudes toward their schools: (PT) condition of playground facilities at elementary schools in the neighborhood; (AD) membership lists for parent-teacher organizations with the implication that active participation suggests positive attitudes.

E. Fads in clothing: (PT) clothing donations to community agencies as an indicator of clothes that were previously in fashion; (AD) recent magazine, newspaper, and television advertisements for clothing as an indicator of current fashion.

Chapter 7

Communication in Psychology

CHAPTER OUTLINE

INTRODUCTION

Scientific research is a public activity. A clever hypothesis, an elegant research design, meticulous data collection procedures, reliable results, and an insightful theoretical interpretation of the findings are not useful to the scientific community unless they are made public. As one writer suggests most emphatically, "Until its results have gone through the painful process of publication, preferably in a refereed journal of high standards, scientific research is just play. Publication is an indispensable part of science" (Bartholomew, 1982). Bartholomew (1982) expresses a preference for a "refereed" journal because refereed journals involve the process of *peer review*. Submitted manuscripts are reviewed by other researchers ("peers") who are experts in the specific field of research addressed in the paper under review. These peer reviewers decide whether the research is methodologically sound and whether it makes a substantive contribution to the discipline of psychology. These reviews are then submitted to a senior researcher who serves as editor of the journal. It is the editor's job to decide which papers warrant publication. Peer review is the primary method of quality control for published psychological research.

There are many journals in which psychologists can publish their research. *Psychological Science, Memory & Cognition, Child Development, Journal of Personality and Social Psychology, Psychological Science in the Public Interest* and *Journal of Clinical and Consulting Psychology* are but a few of the many psychology journals. As we mentioned, editors of these journals make the final decisions about which manuscripts will be published. Their decisions are based on (a) the quality of the research and (b) the effectiveness of its presentation in the written manuscript, as assessed by the editor and the peer reviewers. Thus both content and style are important. Editors seek the best research, clearly described. The editors of the 26 primary journals of the American Psychological Association reviewed about 6,000 (5,978) manuscript submissions in 2003. Journal editors set rigorous standards; *only about one of every three (68% rejection rate) submitted manuscripts is accepted for publication* (American Psychological Association, 2003).

Editorial review and the publication process can take a long time. Up to a year (and sometimes longer) may elapse between when a paper is submitted and when it finally appears in the journal. The review of the manuscript can take several months before a decision whether to accept the paper is made. Several months are also required for the publication process between the time the paper is accepted and when it is actually published in the journal. To provide a more timely means of reporting research findings, professional societies such as the American Psychological Association, the American Psychological Society, the Psychonomic Society, the Society for Research in Child Development, and regional societies such as the Eastern, Midwestern, Southeastern, and Western Psychological Associations sponsor conferences at which researchers give brief oral presentations or present posters describing their recent work. Such conferences provide an opportunity for timely discussion and debate among investigators interested in the same research questions. Research that is "in press" (i.e., waiting completion of the publication process) may be discussed, thus giving conference attendees a preview of important, but yet-to-be-published, research findings.

Researchers often must obtain financial support in the form of a grant from a government or private agency in order to carry out their research. Grants are awarded on the basis of a competitive review of research proposals. Research proposals also typically are required of graduate students when preparing a master's thesis or dissertation. A faculty committee then reviews the proposal before the thesis or dissertation research is begun. So, too, undergraduate students often are required to prepare a research proposal as part of a research methods or laboratory class in psychology. Finally, researchers at all levels will find that research proposals are required by IRBs in order to assess the ethical nature of proposed research at an institution. Research propos-als require a slightly different style and format from a journal article that reports results of a completed study. We provide suggestions for preparing a research proposal later in this chapter.

What do journal articles, oral presentations, and research proposals have to do with you? If you attend graduate school in psychology, you will likely have to describe your research using all three of these types of scientific communication. Even if you do not pursue a professional career in psychology, the principles of good written and oral research reports are applicable to a wide variety of employment situations. For example, a memo to your department manager describing the outcome of a recent sale may have much the same content and format as a short journal article. Of more immediate concern, you may have to prepare a research proposal and write or deliver a research report in your research methods course. This chapter will help you do these things well.

The primary source for scientific writing in psychology is the fifth edition of the *Publication Manual* (2001) of the American Psychological Association. Editors and authors use this manual to ensure a consistent style across the many different journals in psychology. The manual is an invaluable resource for almost any question pertaining to the style and format of a research manuscript. It includes chapters on the content and organization of a manuscript; the expression of ideas and reducing bias; APA editorial style; reference list format including referencing electronic media; manuscript preparation for journal articles and other published research; and on manuscript acceptance and production including guidelines for electronic submission of manuscripts. The manual also includes information about APA policies governing journals and their editorial management as well as information about ethical issues in scientific writing. APA acknowledges that neither editorial style nor the technology of publishing is static. The APA website [www.apastyle.org] provides updates to the *Publication Manual* and the latest changes in APA style and in APA policies and procedures.

Throughout this chapter we have drawn heavily on the *Publication Manual* (2001).[1] This chapter is intended primarily to help you complete successfully the writing you will be doing in your research methods course. It is not intended as a substitute for the *Publication Manual* (2001). If you are planning advanced study in psychology, we recommend that you add the *Publication Manual of the American Psychological Association* (2001) to your personal library. APA also provides helpful resources such as *Mastering APA Style: Student's Workbook and Training Guide* (2001) by H. Gelfand and C. J. Walker. (You can order APA books from the APA website [www.apa.org] or from American Psychological Association, Book Order Department, P.O. Box 92984, Washington, DC 20090-2984.)

Formal communication among researchers through journal articles and convention presentations is not sufficient to sustain the collaborative nature of science. Informal communication is vital to doing research. Research ideas are often formulated in research team meetings or in informal conversations with colleagues. Researchers routinely collaborate at a distance using the Internet and discuss their research using e-mail. Researchers also access electronic databases through the Internet. The Internet has given researchers the ability to access and disseminate information related to their research more quickly and more extensively.

THE INTERNET AND RESEARCH

Access to the Internet has already become an indispensable tool for research psychologists, especially for communication via electronic mail (e-mail). The Internet also serves students and professional psychologists in many other important ways, including as a vehicle for conducting original research (see, for example, Azar, 1994a; 1994b; Birnbaum, 2000; Kardas & Milford, 1996; KelleyMilburn & Milburn, 1995). We describe here a few of the more important ways that psychologists use the Internet in research.

For many researchers *e-mail* is their primary means of communication with colleagues, journal editors, research collaborators, directors of granting agencies, and other professionals. Have a question about an article you just read? Ask the author by sending an e-mail message. E-mailing is simple, efficient, and convenient. The first author of your textbook, for example, can be reached by sending an e-mail message to John J. Shaughnessy (Hope College) [shaughnessy @hope.edu]

There is also a home page on the Web dedicated to this textbook, which can be accessed for student resources (e.g., practice tests) and information about the authors, changes in editions, additional resources for doing psychological research, and errors or omissions in the current edition, publisher's address ordering information, etc. Visit our page [www.mhhe.com/shaughnessy7].

Discussion groups, called "Listservs," allow interested individuals to discuss psychological issues in which they share an interest. The group consists of a "list" of "subscribers" who wish to contribute to an ongoing discussion. List members are immediately "served" any message posted by a subscriber. (If you subscribe to a large Listserv you will likely need to access and edit your e-mail frequently or you may find your mailbox stuffed with messages.) There are hundreds of Listservs on the Internet that link researchers around the world discussing a wide variety of topics, including addiction, religion, and women's studies. Some Listservs are open to anyone who wishes to take part in the discussion, including those who only want to participate passively ("lurk"). Other Listservs are open only to individuals with certain credentials (e.g., members of a particular APA division). APA also sponsors discussion groups for students (psycSTUDENTS) that can be accessed through their website [www.apa.org].

Databases on the Internet are just that: electronic data files that are stored on the Internet and that can be accessed electronically. Databases related to medicine, alcoholism, and opinion polls are available, to mention but a few. Databases are particularly useful when doing archival research and time-series analyses. Large databases, in which data for hundreds of variables and large numbers of participants are available, have become important to many researchers who seek to answer research questions in psychology (e.g., in clinical, social, and developmental psychology). Electronic access to databases frees researchers from the expense and time needed to collect data that may already exist in databases, thereby eliminating wasteful duplication of researchers' and participants' efforts.

Electronic access to journals is now common, and electronic submission of manuscripts is now the norm for journals and for conferences. The wide availability of Internet access and e-mail has facilitated the review process, such that the manuscript submission, peer reviews, and editorial feedback to authors can be completed using the Internet. In addition, some journals are offered exclusively as *electronic journals.* Subscribers receive articles in their electronic mailboxes and readers can electronically submit their comments on the articles. *Psycoloquy, Psyche,* and *Prevention and Treatment* are examples of electronic journals. Whether submitted to electronic journals or journals that are printed, authors seeking publication of their manuscript in respected journals should expect peer review of their research.

Original research, as you saw in earlier chapters, can also be done electronically. The Web allows practically any type of psychological research that uses computers as equipment and humans as participants (Krantz & Dalal, 2000; see especially Kraut et al., 2004, for helpful information about doing online research). How useful you will find the Internet in planning and conducting research will depend both on your specific needs and on your ability to use the Internet. If you are just beginning, we again recommend Fraley's guide, *How to Conduct Behavioral Research Over the Internet* (2004; New York: Guilford Press).

GUIDELINES FOR EFFECTIVE WRITING

Learning to write well is like learning to swim, drive a car, or play the piano. Improvement is unlikely to result solely from reading about how the activity is to be done. Heeding expert advice, though, can help a person get off to a good start. Effective writing begins with having something worthwhile to say, and then being willing to work hard to say it in the best way possible. One key to writing well is getting critical feedback from writing "coaches"—teachers, friends, edi-tors, and even yourself. Lee Cronbach (1992), author of several of the most widely cited articles in the *Psychological Bulletin*, summarizes these ideas well.

My advice must be like the legendary recipe for jugged hare, which begins, "First catch your hare." First, have a message worth delivering. Beyond that, it

is care in writing that counts. . . . Rework any sentence that lacks flow or ca-
dence, any sentence in which first-glance reading misplaces the emphasis, and
any sentence in which comprehension comes less than instantly to that most
knowledgeable of readers, the writer of the sentence. At best, technical writing
can aspire to literary virtues—a change of pace from abstract thesis to memorable example, from brisk to easeful, from matter-of-fact to poetic.

Professional writer Jack Ridl provides the first maxim for effective writing:
"Write, not assuming that you will be understood, but trying to avoid being misunderstood." Good writing, like good driving, is best done defensively. Assume
that whatever can be misunderstood will be! To avoid these writing accidents, we
offer the following tips to consider *before* you begin writing.

* **KNOW YOUR AUDIENCE.** If you assume your readers know more than they
actually do, you will leave them confused. If you underestimate your readers,
you risk boring them with unnecessary details. Either risk increases the likelihood that what you have written will not be read. But if you must err, it is better to underestimate your readers. For example, when you prepare a research
report in a psychology class you might reasonably assume that your intended
audience is your instructor. Writing for your instructor might lead you to leave
a lot out of your paper because, after all, you assume your instructor knows all
that anyway. It would probably be better to consider students in another section of your research methods course as your audience. This might result in
your including more detail than necessary, but it will be easier for your instructor to help you learn to "edit out" the nonessential material than to "edit
in" essential material that you have omitted. Whatever audience you choose,
be sure to make the selection before you begin to write, and keep your audience in mind every step of the way.

* **IDENTIFY YOUR PURPOSE.** Journal articles fall with in the general category of expository writing. *Webster's Dictionary* define sex position as "dis-
course designed to convey information or explain what is difficult to
understand." *The principal purposes of a journal article are to describe and to
convince.* You want first to describe what you have done and what you have
found, and second to convince the reader that your interpretation of these
results is an appropriate one.

* **WRITE CLEARLY.** The foundation of good expository writing is clarity of
thought and expression. The *Publication Manual* (2001) clearly outlines the
road to clarity:

  > You can achieve clear communication, which is the prime objective of sci-
  > entific reporting, by presenting ideas in an orderly manner and by expressing
  > yourself smoothly and precisely. By developing ideas clearly and logically and
  > leading readers smoothly from thought to thought, you make the task of
  > reading an agreeable one.

The *Publication Manual* cites three avenues to clarity:

1. economy of expression,
2. precision, and
3. adherence to grammatical rules.

* **BE CONCISE.** If you say only what needs to be said, you will achieve economy of expression. Short words and short sentences are easier for readers to
understand. The best way to eliminate wordiness is by editing your own writing across successive drafts and asking others to edit drafts of your paper.

* **BE PRECISE.** Precision in using language means choosing the right word for
what you want to say. The *Publication Manual* (2001) contains sage advice
regarding precision of expression:

Make certain that every word means exactly what you intend it to mean. Sooner or later most authors discover a discrepancy between the meaning they attribute to a term and its dictionary definition. In informal style, for example, *feel* broadly substitutes for *think* or *believe*, but in scientific style such latitude is not acceptable.

* **FOLLOW GRAMMATICAL RULES.** Adherence to grammatical rules is absolutely necessary for good writing because failure to do so distracts the reader and can introduce ambiguity. It also makes you, the writer, look bad, and, as a consequence, can serve to weaken your credibility (and your argument) with your reader. Economy of expression, precision, and adherence to grammatical rules do not guarantee effective writing. They do, however, greatly increase the likelihood that your writing will be effective.

* **WRITE FAIRLY.** As a writer you should also strive to choose words and use constructions that acknowledge people fairly and without bias. The American Psychological Association has outlined its policy regarding bias in the language authors use (*Publication Manual*, 2001).

    As a publisher, APA accepts authors' word choices unless those choices are in-accurate, unclear, or ungrammatical. As an organization, APA is committed both to science and to the fair treatment of individuals and groups, and this policy requires authors of APA publications to avoid perpetuating demeaning attitudes and biased assumptions about people in their writing. Constructions that might imply bias against persons on the basis of gender, sexual orientation, racial or ethnic group, disability, or age should be avoided. Scientific writing should be free of implied or irrelevant evaluation of the group or groups being studied.

The *Publication Manual* (2001) describes several guidelines to achieve unbiased communication:

1. Describe the person or persons at the appropriate level of specificity. For example, the phrase *men and women* is more accurate than the generic term man when referring to all human adults. "Chinese Americans" or "Mexican Americans" would be a more specific reference for participants in a study than would be Asian Americans or Hispanic Americans.

2. Be sensitive to the labels we use to refer to people, for example, terms we use to refer to people's racial or ethnic identity. One of the best ways to follow this guideline is to avoid labeling people whenever possible. A label that is perceived by the labeled group as pejorative should never be used. In trying to follow this guideline it is important to remember that preferences for labeling groups of individuals change with time and that people within a group disagree about what label is preferred.

3. "Write about the people in your study in a way that acknowledges their participation." One way to accomplish this is to describe the people who participated in your study using more descriptive terms such as *college students* or *children* rather than the more impersonal term, *subjects*. Active voice is better than passive voice in acknowledging participation—"the students completed the survey" is preferred over "the survey was administered to the students." The *Publication Manual* (2001) includes several good applications and illustrations of these guidelines to the labeling of persons based on their gender, sexual orientation, racial and ethnic identity, disabilities, and age.

* **WRITE AN INTERESTING REPORT.** The *Publication Manual* (2001) provides useful advice about the overall tone of scientific writing:

    Although scientific writing differs in form from literary writing, it need not and should not lack style or be dull. In describing your research, present the ideas and findings directly, but aim for an interesting and compelling manner that reflects your involvement with the problem.

One way to try to achieve an appropriate tone in writing your research reports is to strive to tell a good story about your research. Good research makes for good stories; and well-told stories are good for advancing research.

STRUCTURE OF A RESEARCH REPORT

The structure of a research report serves complementary purposes for the author and for the reader. The structure provides an organization that the author can use to present a clear description of the research and a convincing interpretation of the findings. In this sense, the structure of a research report parallels the structure of a Shakespearean play. In a Shakespearean play, both the playwright and the audience share certain expectations about what should occur in each act as the play unfolds. For example "the stage is set" in the first act, and the climax can be expected in the third act. Similarly, in a research report both author and reader share expectations about the content of each section of the report. As in a play, the reader of a research report can expect to find certain information in each section. If you want to know how an experiment was done, you would look in the Method section; if you want information about the analysis of the data in the study, you would refer to the Results section. The structure is not intended to shackle the playwright or the author. It simply provides a vehicle to make it easier for the audience to focus on the particular point being made in the play or the research report.

A research report consists of the following sections:

Title Page
Abstract
Introduction
Method   } Body of
Results   Report
Discussion
References
Appendixes
Author Note
Footnotes

The body of the report is made up of four sections: Introduction, Method, Results, and Discussion (the four acts of the "play"). The title page and the abstract are like the playbill you see before the play itself begins, and the References, Appendixes, and Notes are analogous to the credits. In this chapter we will provide descriptions of the content and format of each of these sections; more complete descriptions are provided in the *Publication Manual* (2001). Neither this chapter nor the *Publication Manual* will suffice for teaching you how to write a research report. The best preparation for that is to read journal articles reporting research in an area of psychology that interests you. Ultimately, however, you will develop the skills for writing research reports only by actually writing them.

Title Page

The first page of a research report is the title page. It indicates what the research is about (i.e., the title), who did the research (i.e., the authors), where the research was done (i.e., authors' affiliation), and a brief heading to indicate to readers what the article is about (the "running head"). An illustration of a correctly typed title page and succeeding pages of a research report are presented in the Sample Research Report at the end of this chapter. The sample paper includes notes to highlight several important aspects of the final typed draft of a research report.

The title is perhaps the most critical aspect of your paper because it is the part that is most likely to be read! The title should clearly indicate what is the central topic of your paper. In the words of the *Publication Manual* (2001):

> A title should summarize the main idea of the paper simply and, if possible, with style. It should be a concise statement of the main topic and should identify the actual variables or theoretical issues under investigation and the relationship between them.

> Titles are commonly indexed and compiled in numerous reference works. Therefore, avoid words that serve no useful purpose; they increase length and can mislead indexers. For example, the words *method* and *results* do not normally appear in a title, nor should such redundancies as "A Study of" or "An Experimental Investigation of" begin a title. Avoid using abbreviations in the title: Spelling out all terms will help ensure accurate, complete indexing of the article. The recommended length for a title is 10 to 12 words.

The byline for a research report includes the name(s) of the author(s) and the institution with which each author is affiliated. We discussed the criteria for authorship only those who meet these criteria should be listed as authors of a research report. Others who contributed to the research are acknowledged in an author note. The preferred form for an author's name is first name, middle initial, and last name.

The *Publication Manual* (2001) provides a succinct statement describing the last component of a title page, the running head: "The running head is an abbreviated title that is printed at the top of the page of a published article to identify the article for readers." The running head should not exceed 50 characters, and it should appear on the title page, left margin, typed in all uppercase letters one double-spaced line below the first line that includes the page 1 and the manuscript page heading (see Sample Research Report). Note that the running head appears only once in your manuscript, on the title page. The running head is *not* the same as the manuscript page heading that appears on every manuscript page. The manuscript heading includes the first few words of the title and appears on the same line as the page number of each page of the manuscript.

Many journals routinely use masked review or offer masked review for authors who request it. Masked review is intended to enhance the fairness of the review process by withholding the identity of the authors from the reviewers thereby not allowing the reputation of the authors to influence the reviews. The title page must include all information that identifies the authors of the manuscript even if a masked review is to be done. The *Publication Manual* (2001) describes the procedures for a masked review.

> Masked review requires that the identity of the author of the manuscript be concealed from reviewers during the review process. Authors are responsible for concealing their identities in manuscripts that are to receive masked review: For example, the author note must be typed on the manuscript's title page, which the editor removes before the manuscript is reviewed.

Tips on Writing a Title   A common format for the title of a research report is "[The Dependent Variable(s)] as a Function of [the Independent Variable(s)]." For example, "Anagram Solution Time as a Function of Problem Difficulty" would be a good title. The title must not only be informative, but it should also be brief (10 to 12 words). Most important of all, be sure your title describes as specifically as possible the content of your research.

Abstract

The abstract is a one-paragraph summary of the content and purpose of the research report. The abstract should be 100 to 120 words long (about 10 double-spaced typewritten lines). The abstract appears on the second page of the report with the word *Abstract* typed as a centered heading (see Sample Research Report). The abstract should identify four elements of your research:

1. the problem under investigation;
2. the method, including tests and apparatus that were used, data-gathring procedures, and pertinent characteristics of participants;
3. the findings; and
4. the conclusions and implications of the findings.

The abstract, in other words, should highlight the critical points made in the Introduction, Method, Results, and Discussion sections of the research report.

A well-written abstract can have a big influence on whether the rest of a journal article will be read. Abstracts are used by information services to index and retrieve articles. The fate of an article based on a reader's reaction to its abstract is well described in the *Publication Manual* (2001):

> Most people will have their first contact with an article by seeing just the abstract, usually on a computer screen with several other abstracts, as they are doing a literature search through an electronic abstract-retrieval system. Readers fre-quently decide on the basis of the abstract whether to read the entire article; this is true whether the reader is at a computer or is thumbing through a journal. The abstract needs to be dense with information but also readable, well organized, brief, and self-contained. Also, embedding many key words in your abstract will enhance the user's ability to find it.

Tips on Writing an Abstract   Writing a good abstract is challenging. The best way to meet this challenge is to write it last. By writing the abstract after you have written the rest of the report you will be able to *abstract*, or paraphrase, your own words more easily.

Introduction

Objectives for the Introduction   The title of your report appears centered at the top of the third page. The introduction is not labeled with a heading as are the other sections of the paper because the introduction is clearly indicated by its position at the beginning of the paper. Thus, the first paragraph of the Introduction section begins immediately below the title (see Sample Research Report). The introduction serves three primary objectives:

1. to introduce the problem being studied and to indicate why the problem is an important one to study;
2. to describe the theoretical implications of the study and to summarize briefly the relevant background literature related to the study; and
3. to describe the purpose, rationale, and design of the present study with a logical development of the predictions or hypotheses guiding the research.

The order in which you address these objectives in your paper may vary, but the order we describe here is a common one. The *Publication Manual* (2001) describes the common purpose shared by all three objectives. "A good introduction, by summarizing the relevant arguments and the data, gives the reader a firm sense of what was done and why"

The second objective of the introduction includes a summary of related research studies. This review is not intended to provide an exhaustive literature review. Instead, you should carefully select those studies that are most directly related to your research. In summarizing these selected studies, you should emphasize whatever details of the earlier work will best help the reader understand what you have done and why. You must acknowledge the contributions of other researchers to your understanding of the problem. Of course, if you quote directly from another person's work, you must use quotation marks.

More commonly, however, reference is made to the work of other researchers in one of two ways. Either you refer to the authors of the article you are citing by their last names, with the year in which the paper was published appearing in parentheses immediately after the names, or you make a general reference to their work and follow it with both the names and the year of publication in parentheses. For example, if you were citing a study by Lorna Hernandez Jarvis and Patricia V. Roehling that was published in 2003 you would write either "Jarvis and Roehling (2003) found. . ."or "Recent research (Jarvis & Roehling, 2003) showed that . . . ." Complete bibliographical information on the Jarvis and Roehling paper, including the journal title, volume number, and specific pages, would appear in the References section. Footnotes are not used to cite references in a research report in psychology.

You should include in your paper only those references that you have actually read. If you read a paper by Barney (2002) in which the research of Ludwig (2000) is described, you should not cite the Ludwig paper unless you have actually read that paper. Instead, you should use some form such as "Ludwig (2000), as reported by Barney (2002), found that . . ." You should use this approach for two reasons. The first and most obvious one is that you should accurately report what you have read. If this appeal to scholarly integrity does not suffice, you should recognize the risk you are taking. If Barney (2002) has misreported the work of Ludwig (2000) and you repeat this misrepresentation, you are equally subject to criticism. The general rule is simple: Cite only what you have read.

Tips on Writing the Introduction   In order to write an effective introduction, be sure you can answer the following four questions *before* beginning to write:

- "Why is this problem important?
- How do the hypothesis and the experimental design relate to the problem?
- What are the theoretical implications of the study, and how does the study relate to previous work in the area?
- What are the theoretical propositions tested, and how were they derived?" (*Publication Manual*, p. 16).

Searching the Psychological Literature   In the long run, the best way to develop ideas for research and to become familiar with ther elevant literature is to read the journals in your area of interest on a regular basis. If you are just beginning to do research in psychology, you may not have had a chance to read the research literature widely or to have settled on a principal area of interest in psychology. Even if you have identified your primary interest area, you may want to explore research from a literature different from the one that you are used to reading. For example, you may have an idea for an experiment and you may wonder whether the experiment has already been done. Or you may have read an article describing an experiment on which you would like to base an experiment, and you may be interested in finding other studies related to this topic. An important source for additional reading on your topic is the References section of the article. Whatever your topic or research question, there undoubtedly will come a time when you need to search the psychological literature. Resources for searching the psychological literature are available to help you answer these types of questions.

The foundation of present-day methods of searching the psychological literature is *Psychological Abstracts*. The American Psychological Association has published *Psychological Abstracts* since 1927. The abstracts, taken from over 1,000 national and international periodicals, are published monthly in the *Psychological Abstracts*. These abstracts are organized under general categories, such as "Physical and Psychological Disorders." Searching the printed *Psychological Abstracts* was a time-consuming and cumbersome task. Electronic databases have made the task of searching the psychological literature much less labor intensive.

The primary online database for searching the psychological literature is PsycINFO. PsycINFO can be accessed through online databases such as *First-*

Search and *InfoTrac*. Check with your local library staff to find out what online services are available to you. An electronic database makes it possible to scan the titles and abstracts of articles in the database and to identify all those that contain particular keywords. The most effective approach to this type of search is to have intersecting keywords, both of which need to be present before the computer will "flag" an article. For example, a student was interested in conducting a survey to determine the incidence of rapes and other sexual assaults on dates (i.e., date rapes). The student used the keyword RAPE and the letter string DAT to guide her search. She chose the letter string DAT in order to catch such variants as DATE, DATES, and DATING. This intersection led to the identification of 75 references, 73 of which were written in English.

The major advantage of searching electronic databases is that they provide quick access to large amounts of information. There are, however, a few potential problems. One possible problem is that the likelihood that you will obtain all the relevant references you are seeking is directly dependent on the quality of the search you do. When it comes to electronic databases, what you search is what you get. After searching such vast databases multiple times with different keywords, we may become unduly confident that we have identified "all that there is on the subject." However, it is possible that *pertinent information can be missed in any given search of an electronic database*. Keyword scan also prove tricky. The string DAT identified all studies using the word DATA, so a number of the student's ref-erences provided data about rape—but not solely in the context of dating. These potential problems are not problems with the *use* of electronic databases; they are problemsforthe *users* of electronic databases. When electronic databases are used properly, the advantages of searching the psychological literature using PsycINFO far outweigh their disadvantages. Joswick (1994) provides recommen-dations for electronic searches for those who want to move beyond the basics.

Method

The second major section of the body of a research report is the Method section. The Method section starts on the same page on which the introduction ends. It is separated from the introduction with a double-spaced centered heading (Method), and the text of the Method section begins one double-spaced line below the heading (see Sample Research Report). The introduction has provided a broad outline of the research you have done; the method fills in the nitty-gritty details. The *Publication Manual* presents a straightforward description of the goals of the Method section:

> The Method section describes in detail how the study was conducted. Such a description enables the reader to evaluate the appropriateness of your methods and the reliability and the validity of your results. It also permits experienced investigators to replicate the study if they so desire.

Writing a good Method section can be difficult. It sounds easy because all you have to do is describe exactly what you have done. But if you want to get a sense of how challenging this can be, just try to write a clear and interesting paragraph describing how to tie your shoelaces.

The three most common subsections of the Method section are participants, materials (apparatus), and procedure. Each of these subsections is introduced by an italicized subheading that usually begins at the left margin (see Sample Research Report). The *Publication Manual* aptly summarizes the purpose and the content of the *participants* subsection.

> Appropriate identification of research participants and clientele is critical to the science and practice of psychology, particularly for assessing the results (making comparisons across groups); generalizing the findings; and making comparisons in replications, literature reviews, or secondary data analyses.

Tips on Writing the Method Section   The key to writing a good Method section is organization. Fortunately, the structure of this section is so consistent across research reports that a few basic subsections provide the pattern of organization you need for most research reports. Before describing the content of these subsections, however, we must address the question that students writing their first research report ask most frequently: "How much detail should I include?" The quality of your paper will be adversely affected if you include either too much or too little detail. The rule stated in the *Publication Manual* seems simple enough: "Include in these subsections only the information essential to comprehend and replicate the study." As we have said before, the best way to learn how to follow this rule is to read the Method sections of journal articles and to write your own research reports. Be sure to get feedback from your instructor concerning the appropriate level of detail for your research reports.

When humans are the subjects of the study, report the procedures for selecting and assigning them and the agreements and payments made. Report major demographic characteristics such as sex, age, and race/ethnicity, and, where possible and appropriate, characteristics such as socioeconomic status, disability status, and sexual orientation. When a particular demographic characteristic is an experimental variable or is important for the interpretation of results, describe the group specifically—for example, in terms of national origin, level of education, health status, and language preference and use.

When animals are the subjects, report the genus, species, and strain number or other specific identification, such as the name and location of the supplier and the stock designation.

Give the total number of subjects and the number assigned to each experimental condition. If any did not complete the experiment, state how many and explain why they did not continue.

The *apparatus* or *materials* subsection is not always included in a research report. If the only equipment you used is paper, pencils, and a computer, it is better to include this information in the procedure subsection than in a separate apparatus section. On the other hand, if the apparatus or materials played a central role in the study, a separate subsection is useful. If complex or custom-made equipment has been used, a diagram or drawing is helpful for both the reader and the writer of an apparatus subsection. In general, the label *apparatus* is used when mechanical equipment is described. The label *materials* is used when less mechanical instruments, such as a paper-and-pencil questionnaire, have been constructed or used. If you use equipment or materials developed by another investigator, you should cite the work of that investigator, but you should also include the general characteristics of the materials in your own report.

The *procedure* subsection is the most critical component of the Method section. In this subsection you describe what happened from the beginning to the end of the sessions in which you tested your participants. As the previous sentence implies, the organization of the procedure subsection is usually chronological. You should begin writing this subsection by outlining the important steps in testing participants in each group of your study. Next you can either describe the procedure for each group in turn or describe the procedures common to all groups and then point out the distinguishing features of each group. Whichever organization you choose (you may not learn which works best until you have tried to write both), it is best to begin writing only after you have prepared a checklist of the important features of your procedure. The instructions given to participants should be presented in paraphrase form unless they define an experimental manipulation, in which case they should be reported verbatim. The *Publication Manual* recommends that the Method section, and especially the procedure subsection, "should tell the reader *what* you did and *how* you did it in sufficient detail so that a reader could reasonably replicate your study."

RESULTS

The centered heading, Results, introduces this third major section of the body of aresearch report. The Results section begins on the same page on which the Method section ends with a double space separating the heading from the end of the Method section and another double space after the heading (see Sample Research Report). Like the third act of a dramatic play, the Results section contains the climax of the research report—the actual findings of the study. For many students, though, the excitement of describing the climax is blunted by concern about the necessity of reporting statistical information in the Results section. The best way to alleviate this concern, of course, is to develop the same command of statistical concepts that you have of other concepts. Another helpful first step is to adopt a simple organizational structure to guide your writing of the Results section.

You should use your Results section to answer the questions you raised in your introduction. However, the guiding principle in the Results section is to "stick to the facts, just the facts." You will have the opportunity to move beyond just the facts when you get to the Discussion section.

Reporting Statistics The *Publication Manual* provides an excellent overview of the objectives of a Results section:

> The Results section summarizes the data collected and the statistical or data analytic treatment used. Report the data in sufficient detail to justify the conclusions. Mention all relevant results, including those that run counter to the hypothesis. Do not include individual scores or raw data, with the exception, for example, of single-case designs or illustrative samples. Discussing the implications of the results is not appropriate here.

One way to meet these objectives is to use an organizational structure that is typical of paragraphs in the Results section. This structure is outlined in Table 7.1, and

---

TABLE 7.1   STRUCTURE OF A TYPICAL PARAGRAPH IN THE RESULTS SECTION

1. State the purpose of the analysis.
2. Identify the descriptive statistic to be used to summarize results.
3. Present a summary of this descriptive statistic across conditions in the text itself, in a table, or in a figure.
4. If a table or figure is used, point out the major findings on which the reader should focus.
5. Present the reasons for, and the results of, confidence intervals, effect sizes, and inferential statistics tests.
6. State the conclusion that follows from each test, but do not discuss implications. These belong in the Discussion section.

Sample paragraph

To examine retention as a function of instructions given at the time of study, the number of words recalled by each participant in each instruction condition was determined. Words were scored as correct only if they matched a word that had appeared on the target list. Misspelled words were accepted if the spelling was similar to a target item. Mean numbers of words recalled (with the corresponding standard deviations) were: 15.6 (1.44); 15.2 (1.15); and 10.1 (1.00) in the bizarre imagery condition, the standard imagery condition, and the control condition, respectively. The 95% confidence intervals were: bizarre imagery, 13.18–18.02; standard imagery, 12.78–17.62; control, 7.68–12.52. Overall, the mean differences were statistically significant, $F(2, 72) = 162.84$, $p \leq .0005$, $MSE = 1.47$, eta squared (η^2) = .82. Comparisons of the confidence intervals revealed that both the imagery conditions differed from the control condition, but that two imagery conditions did not differ. In conclusion, retention by participants instructed to use imagery was higher than that by participants given no specific study instructions, but retention did not differ for the two types of imagery instructions.

Tips on Writing a Good Results Section   We suggest you follow these steps when writing your Results section.

* *Step 1*. A Results section paragraph begins by stating the purpose of the analysis. The reason(s) for doing an analysis should be stated succinctly; often, no more than a phrase is necessary. In the sample paragraph, for example, the purpose of the analysis is, "to examine retention as a function of the instructions given at the time of study." There are two reasons for making the purpose for each analysis explicit. It helps your reader follow the logic of your analysis plan. And, perhaps more importantly, it ensures that you will never try to report an analysis whose purpose you do not understand.

* *Step 2*. The second step in writing a Results section paragraph is to identify the descriptive statistic that will be used to summarize the results for a given dependent variable. For example, you might use the mean numbers of words recalled, as in the sample paragraph. Other possible descriptive statistics that could be used to summarize the results in each condition of your experiment are the median reaction time or the cumulative number of responses per minute.

* *Step 3*. The third step is to present a summary of this descriptive statistic across conditions. Measures of central tendency should be accompanied by corresponding measures of variability such as reporting a standard deviation along with each mean. A measure of effect size is also strongly recommended. If there are only two or three conditions in your experiment, this summary can be presented in the text itself. For instance, you could summarize the results of a two-group study by saying, "The mean number of correct responses for the experimental group was 10.5 ($SD = 2.1$), whereas that for the control group was 8.2 ($SD = 1.8$). The effect size (d) was 1.20." More commonly, however, you will have more data to summarize and you will need to present your findings in either a table or a figure (graph). We will describe the procedures for constructing tables and figures later in this section. The *Publication Manual* gives good advice regarding the use of tables and figures:

  > To report the data, choose the medium that presents them most clearly and economically. Tables provide exact values and, if well prepared, can present complex data and analyses in a format that is familiar to the reader (e.g., ANOVA tables). Figures of professional quality attract the reader's eye, provide a quick visual impression, and best illustrate complex relationships and general comparisons but are not intended to be as precise as tables.
  >
  > Summarizing the results and the analysis in tables or figures instead of text may be helpful; for example, a table may enhance the readability of complex sets of analysis of variance results. Avoid repeating the same data in several places and using tables for data that can be easily presented in a few sentences in the text.

* *Step 4*. We should not expect a table or figure to be self-sufficient. Your reader will need help to gain as much information as possible from a table or figure. You are in the best position to offer this help because you are the person most familiar with your results. You should direct your reader's attention to the highlights of the data in the table or figure, focusing especially on those aspects of the results that are consistent (or discrepant) with the hypotheses you proposed in the introduction. Usually the same data are not reported in both a table and a figure. Whichever you choose, be sure to highlight in the text itself the critical results that the table or figure reveals.

* *Step 5.* The fifth step in writing a paragraph of the Results section is to pre-sent the results of inferential statistical tests. Three pieces of information should always be reported with any inferential statistics test: the name of the test (usually indicated by a symbol such as *t, r,* or *F*); the degrees of freedom for the test (presented in parentheses after the test is identified); and the value of the test statistic that you obtained. The exact probability of the test outcome should be reported whenever possible along with measures of effect size. The *Publication Manual* makes a strong case for why it is very important to report confidence intervals.

> The reporting of confidence intervals (for estimates of parameters, for functions of parameters such as differences in means, and for effect sizes) can be an extremely effective way of reporting results. Because confidence intervals combine information on location and precision and can often be directly used to infer significance levels, they are, in general, the best reporting strategy. The use of confidence intervals is therefore strongly recommended. (p. 22)

For instance, you might see, "The 95% confidence interval for the control condition was 4.5 to 6.4 and that for the experimental condition was 7.2 to 9.1. The effect of the drug variable was statistically significant, $F(1, 64) = 7.15, p \leq .0005$. The effect size (*d*) was .85."

* *Concluding Step.* The final step in writing a paragraph in the Results section is to state a brief conclusion that follows from each test you report. For example, consider a study in which the mean number correct in the experimental group is 10 and that in the control group is 5 and the confidence intervals for these two means do not overlap. An appropriate concluding statement would be: "The control group did worse than the experimental group." In this simple example the conclusion may seem obvious, but appropriate concluding statements are essential, especially for more complex analyses.

Each paragraph of the Results section follows the structure outlined in Table 7.1. The idea is not to overload your reader with statistics. The challenge is to select those findings that are most critical, being sure to report all the data pertinent to the questions raised in your introduction. Before concluding our discussion of the Results section, we will briefly describe the basic procedures for constructing tables and figures, two key tools in reporting results effectively.

an illustration of a paragraph from the Results section of a published article appears after the table.

Presenting Data in Tables Tables are an effective and efficient means for presenting large amounts of data in concise form. The table should supplement and not duplicate information in the text of the paper, but it should be well integrated into the text. The tables in a research report are numbered consecutively. Numbering the tables makes it easy to refer to them in the text by their numbers. Each table should also have a brief explanatory title, and the columns and rows of the table should be labeled clearly. The data entries in the table should all be reported to the same degree of precision (i.e., all values should have the same number of decimal places), and the values should be consistently aligned with the corresponding row and column headings. An appropriately constructed table appears in the Sample Research Report at the end of this chapter.

Presenting Data in Figures Figures, like tables, are a concise way to present large amounts of information. A figure has two principal axes: the horizontal axis, or *x*-axis, and the vertical axis, or *y*-axis. Typically, the levels of the independent variable are plotted on the *x*-axis and those of the dependent variable are plotted on the *y*-axis. When there are two or more independent variables, the levels of the second and succeeding independent variables serve as labels for the data withinthe figure or are indicated in a figure legend. In Figure 7.1 the values of the dependent variable (mean number recalled) are plotted on the y-axis, the levels of the one independent variable (serial position) are indicated on the x-axis. The levels of the second independent variable (cued [C] or noncued [NC]) label the data within the figures, and the levels of the third independent variable (instructions) serve as the headings for each of the two separate panels of the figure.

Two general types of figures are commonly used in psychology: line graphs and bar graphs. The most common type of figure is the line graph like the one shown in Figure 7.1. When the independent variable plotted on the x-axis is a nominal-scale variable, however, a bar graph is often used. For example, if you were plotting the mean GPA (dependent variable) of students enrolled in different academic majors (independent variable), you could use a bar graph. An illustration of a bar graph is presented in Figure 7.2.

There are alternative ways to construct useful graphic presentations. All figures must include certain features, however. The x- and y-axis must be clearly labeled, with each label printed next to the corresponding axis. Selected points (called grid points) on each axis must be identified with labeled grid marks, and the grid labels are always printed horizontally. The grid scale for the x- and y-axes should be chosen such that the plotted data are legible and span the entire illustration. The figures and the captions for the figures appear separately in a manuscript submitted for publication (see Sample Research Report).

FIGURE 7.1 Mean number of words recalled (of a possible ten) as a function of serial position within blocks, cuing (C = Cued; NC = Noncued), and instructional condition.

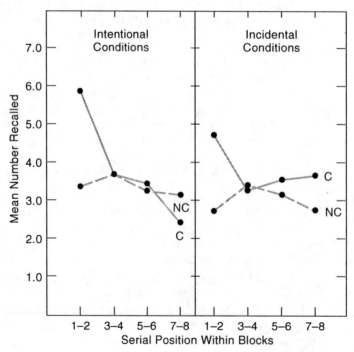

FIGURE 7.2 Proportion recognition errors made by two groups of college students after rating verbal items for either familiarity or meaning. The items were nonwords (NW) and words appearing less than one time, one through ten times and more than forty times per million in the Thorndike-Lorge count.

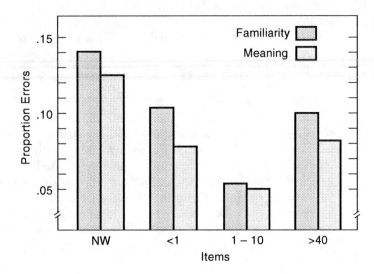

DISCUSSION

The fourth section of the body of your report, the Discussion, begins with a centered heading (see Sample Research Report). The Discussion section (like the Method and Results sections) begins on the same page on which the previous section ended. The Discussion section, unlike the Results section, contains "more than just the facts." In the words of the *Publication Manual:*

> After presenting the results, you are in a position to evaluate and interpret their implications, especially with respect to your original hypothesis. You are free to examine, interpret, and qualify the results, as well as to draw inferences from them.

(*Note:* When the results are relatively brief and discussion is straightforward and also not very lengthy, the two sections can be combined in a Results and Discussion section in some research reports.)

The Discussion begins with a succinct statement of the essential findings. You should give particular attention to how your findings support or refute your original hypotheses. You do not repeat the descriptive statistics in this summary, nor do you necessarily refer to the statistical analyses of the findings. The *Publication Manual* provides good advice about what to do and not to do after the succinct summary of the findings:

> Similarities and differences between your results and the work of others should clarify and confirm your conclusions. Do not, however, simply reformulate and repeat points already made; each new statement should contribute to your position and to the reader's understanding of the problem. Acknowledge limitations, and address alternative explanations of results.

The Discussion is written in a tone and style consistent with the introduction. Becareful, however, to keep the statements you make in the discussion consistent with the data reported in the results. For instance, you should not report that one group did better than another if the difference between the means for these groups was not reliable—at least not without some qualification of what you mean by "better."

As just noted from the *Publication Manual*, the Discussion includes a description of how your findings relate to the relevant literature, most of which you will have cited in the Introduction. If your results are not consistent with your original hypotheses, you should suggest an explanation for these discrepancies. Such post hoc (after-the-fact) explanations should be considered tentative at best. If the reasons for your results are unclear, you should not hesitate to say so. It sometimes is necessary and helpful to include a paragraph describing limitations or problems in the research. One good way to identify limitations or problems is to try to anticipate criticisms of your study that others might make.

If appropriate, conclude the Discussion by proposing additional research that should be done on the problem you are investigating. Strive to be specific about what research should be done and why it needs to be done. That is, be sure to explain what the new research should reveal that we do not already know. The reader will not learn much if you say, "It would be interesting to do this experiment with younger participants." The reader can learn much more if you explain how you would expect the results to differ with younger participants and what you would conclude if the results of the proposed experiment were to turn out as expected. Remember, the watchword in proposing new research is to be specific. Your emphasis when writing your report should definitely be on quality, not quantity.

Tips on Writing the Discussion Section   Again, the *Publication Manual* gives good advice for authors beginning to write their Discussion section: "In this section you might address the following sorts of issues:

* Problem choice: Why is this problem important?
* Level of analysis: How can the findings be linked to phenomena at more complex and less complex levels of analysis?
* Application and synthesis: If the findings are valid and replicable, what real-life psychological phenomena might be explained or modeled by the results? Are applications warranted on the basis of this research?

The responses to these questions are the core of your contribution and justify why readers outside your own specialty should attend to your findings. These readers should receive clear, unambiguous, and direct answers."

REFERENCES

We have already described the procedure for citing references within the body of a research report by using the name(s) of the author(s) and the date of publication. The References section, which appears with a centered heading on a separate page after the discussion (see Sample Research Report), includes the complete citation for each reference. "Just as data in the paper support interpretations and conclusions, so reference citations document statements made about the literature" (*Publication Manual*).

There are four types of references that will cover almost all those needed for most research reports: journal articles, books, chapters in edited books, and Internet sources. The format for each of these reference types is illustrated in Table 7.2. As this table shows, all lines but the first line of each reference are indented (hanging indent). Like the rest of the manuscript, references should be typed double-spaced. The journal article reference includes the authors, the year of publication, the title of the article, the name of the journal, the volume number, and the page numbers. The book citation includes the authors, the copyright date, the title, the city in which the book was published, and the publisher. The reference for a chapter in an edited volume includes the author of thec hapter, the date, the chapter title, the editors of the book, the title of the book, page numbers

TABLE 7.2 ILLUSTRATION OF FORMAT OF REFERENCE CITATIONS

Journal article

Loftus, E. F., & Burns, T. E. (1982). Mental shock can produce retrograde amnesia. *Memory & Cognition, 10,* 318–323.

Book

Posavac, E. J., & Carey, R. G. (2003). *Program evaluation* (6th ed.). Englewood Cliffs, NJ: Prentice Hall.

Chapter in an edited book

Weiss, J. M. (1977). Psychological and behavioral influences on gastrointestinal lesions in animal models. In J. D. Maser & M. E. P. Seligman (Eds.), *Psychopathology: Experimental models* (pp. 232–269). San Francisco: W. H. Freeman.

Article in electronic journal

Kirsch, I., & Sapirstein, G. (1998). Listening to prozac but hearing placebo: A meta-analysis of antidepressant medication. *Prevention and Treatment* [On-line serial], *1.* Available: journals.apa.org/prevention/volume1/pre0010002a.html.

of the chapter, the city of publication, and the publisher. The citation to an electronic journal identifies the specific Internet address.

When citing information from the Internet, especially websites, it is critical that you give the reader the specific information required to locate the source. Be aware, however, that Internet addresses change regularly, as does the information that is found in them. It is recommended (e.g., Harnack & Kleppinger, 1997) that you indicate the date you accessed a website, for example in parentheses following the citation. You can check the APA website [www.apastyle.org] for changes in the format for citing Internet sources and for the latest information in APA style and publication policies and procedures.

You can save your readers much aggravation if you follow the reference formats closely and proofread your reference list carefully. The references are listed in alphabetical order by the last name of the first author of each article. If there are two articles by the same author(s), they are arranged in ascending order by year of publication.

Appendixes

Appendixes are rare in published research articles, but they are a bit more common in students' research reports. When they are intended for a published article, each appendix begins on a separate manuscript page and they appear at the end of the paper following the references. (*Note:* Instructors may require you to submit an appendix including your raw data, the worksheets for a statistical analysis, or the computer printout of the analyses. The appendix can also be used to provide a verbatim copy of the instructions to participants or a list of the specific materials used in an experiment.) Each appendix is identified by letter (A, B, C, and so on), and any reference to the appendix in the body of the text is made using this letter. For instance, you might write, "The complete instructions can be found in Appendix A."

Author Note

The *Publication Manual* provides a concise description of the contents of an author note:

The author note (a) identifies the departmental affiliation of each author, (b) identifies sources of financial support, (c) provides a forum for authors to acknowledge colleagues' professional contributions to the study and personal assistance, and (d) tells whom the interested reader may contact for further information concerning the article.

The author note appears on a separate page under the centered heading "Author Note" immediately after the References section, or after the appendixes, if there are any (see Sample Research Report).

Footnotes

Because they are not used for citing references, footnotes are rare in journal articles and even more rare in students' research reports. When footnotes appear in the text they are of two types: content footnotes and copyright permission footnotes. Content footnotes supplement or expand upon the text material. Copyright permission footnotes acknowledge the source of extensive quotations. Footnotes (of both kinds) are numbered consecutively in the text. In the printed or typed manuscript, footnotes appear on a separate page following the References section under the centered heading "Footnotes" (see Sample Research Report).

Order of Manuscript Pages

The pages of your research report should be numbered consecutively in the following order:

    Title Page
    Abstract
    Text (Introduction, Method, Results, Discussion)
    References (start on a separate page)
    *Appendixes (start each on a separate page)
    Author Note (start on a separate page)
    *Footnotes (list together, starting on a separate page)
    Tables (start each on a separate page)
    Figure Captions (list together, starting on a separate page)
    Figures (place each on a separate page)

    *Appear only infrequently in journal articles.

ORAL PRESENTATIONS

Research psychologists regularly attend professional conventions at which they present brief oral descriptions of their research. Similarly, students may give oral presentations of their research either in class or at a department research symposium involving students from a number of different classes or at undergraduate research conferences. All of these settings share one characteristic—the time allowed for the presentation is usually no more than 10 to 15 minutes. In this length of time it is impossible to provide the detailed description that is included in a journal article. In general, as noted in the *Publication Manual*, "Material delivered verbally should differ from written material in its level of detail, organization, and presentation." To reach your audience the *Publication Manual* recommends that you:

Omit most of the details of scientific procedures, because a listener cannot follow the same level of detail as a reader. The audience wants to know (a) what you studied and why, (b) how you went about the research (give a general orientation), (c) what you discovered, and (d) the implications of your results. A verbal presentation should create awareness about a topic and stimulate interest in it; colleagues can retrieve the details from a written paper, copies of which you may want to have available.

A colleague of ours in the biology department has developed five principles that he distributes to his students to help them prepare the oral presentation required in his class. Like all good maxims these five sound simple enough, but they are all too frequently ignored even by experienced researchers.

Five Principles for Effective Oral Presentations

* AVOID THE TEMPTATION TO TELL EVERYTHING YOU KNOW IN 10 MINUTES. This temptation can best be avoided by limiting your presentation to one or two main points. What are the important "take-home messages"? The brief time available for an oral presentation is barely sufficient to allow you to present the evidence supporting these main points. There simply will not be time to discuss any side issues.

* CULTIVATE A GOOD PLATFORM PRESENCE. This can best be achieved by developing public speaking skills. Most people need a written copy of their presentation in front of them while they are presenting, but your presentation will be more effective if you can appear not to be reading. Many people speak too quickly in front of an audience, particularly if they are reading; it is best to use simple, direct sentences presented at a moderate rate. Most important, speak loudly and clearly.

* USE EFFECTIVE VISUAL AIDS. The use of effective visual aids can help your listeners follow your presentation. Slides, overhead transparencies, and electronic presentations must be distinct enough to be seen clearly at a distance. The successful use of audiovisual aids is a skill and it can be improved with practice. Be sure that whatever visual aids you use are as close to self-explanatory as you can make them.

* LEAVE TIME FOR QUESTIONS. You need to keep in mind the fourth principle, leaving time for questions, because most professional conferences and classroom presentations will require that you reserve time for questions. Although questions from the audience can be somewhat intimidating, the opportunity for questions gives your listeners a chance to become actively involved in your presentation.

* PRACTICE YOUR TALK BEFORE A CRITICAL AUDIENCE BEFORE YOU GIVE IT. This final principle is perhaps the most important. Practicing your talk before an audience is more beneficial than simply rehearsing the talk over and over by yourself. Such private rehearsal is a good way to prepare for your "dress rehearsal," but it is no substitute for practicing before others.

These five principles provide a good coaching manual for oral presentations. The best way to develop this skill, however, is to deliver as many oral presentations as possible under "game conditions." Practice may not make perfect, but it is the best route we know to improvement.

RESEARCH PROPOSALS

In the last section of this chapter we discuss writing again—but this time the writing of research proposals. As we mentioned at the beginning of this chapter, researchers must often seek financial support for their research by submitting grant proposals to private or government agencies. Students in research methods classes are also sometimes required to submit proposals describing research they might do. Even if a written proposal is not required, only a foolhardy researcher would tackle a research project without careful prior consideration of related literature, possible practical problems, workable statistical analyses of the data, and eventual interpretation of the expected results. This careful prior consideration will help you develop a research proposal that is feasible and one that can be analyzed and interpreted appropriately.

The purpose of a research proposal is to ensure a workable experimental design that, when implemented, will result in an interpretable empirical finding of significant scientific merit. No research proposal, no matter how carefully prepared, can guarantee important results. Researchers learn early in their careers about Murphy's Law. In essence, Murphy's Law states, "Anything that can go wrong will go wrong." Nonetheless, it is worthwhile to develop a research proposal, if only to avoid the research problems that are avoidable.

A written research proposal follows the general format of a journal article, but the headings of the various sections are slightly different. The proposal should include the following main sections:

Introduction
Method
Expected Results and Proposed Data Analysis Plan
Conclusions
References
Appendix
Information for Institutional Review Board

An abstract is not included in a research proposal. The introduction of a research proposal is likely to include a more extensive review of the relevant literature than is required for a journal article. The statement of the research problem and the logical development of hypotheses in a research proposal are the same as required in a journal article. Similarly, the Method section in the proposal should be as close as possible to the one that will accompany the finished research. Thus our remarks about the format and content of the Method section of a research report apply equally to the writing of a proposal.

The section of the proposal entitled "Expected Results and Proposed Data Analysis Plan" should include a brief discussion of the anticipated results of the research. In most cases the exact nature of the results will not be known. Nevertheless, you will always have some idea (in the form of a hypothesis or prediction) of the outcome of the research. The Expected Results section may include tables or figures of the results as you expect (hope) that they will come out. The results that are most important to the project should be highlighted. A proposed data analysis plan for the expected results should be in this section. For example, if you are proposing a complex design, you would need to indicate which effects you will be testing and what statistical tests you will use. Reasonable alternatives to the expected results should also be mentioned, as well as possible problems of interpretation that will arise if the results deviate from the research hypothesis. The body of a research proposal ends with a Conclusions section that provides a brief statement of the conclusion sand implications based on the expected results.

The References section should be in exactly the same form as the one you would submit with the final report. An appendix should complete the research proposal and should include a list of all materials that will be used in doing the experiment. In most cases this will mean that a copy of the instructions to participants will be included, as well as the type of apparatus used, a list of the materials or a description of the materials, and so on. For example, if you are doing a study involving students' memory for lists of words, the following must be included in the appendix: actual lists with randomizations made, type of apparatus used for presentation, instructions to participants for all conditions, and randomizations of conditions.

Finally, a research proposal should include material to be submitted to an Institutional Review Board (IRB) or similar committee designed to review the ethics of the proposed research.

A SAMPLE RESEARCH REPORT

First few words of title appear before page number.

5 spaces

False Recall 1

Running head: FALSE MEMORIES

Type flush with left margin.

Type running head all caps.

Number pages consecutively, beginning with title page.

False Recall and Recognition of List Items Following Delay

Jeanne S. Zechmeister and Eugene B. Zechmeister

Loyola University of Chicago

Use upper and lower case for title, name, and affiliation (centered).

Note:
Use one-inch margins at the top, bottom, right, and left of all pages.

No paragraph indentation for abstract.

Center, do not italicize.

Include initials only in Abstract.

False Recall   2

↓

Abstract

Whether false memories persist over a delay was investigated using H. L. Roediger and

K. B. McDermott's (1995) false memory procedure. College students (N = 19) studied

12 15-item lists and either recalled items immediately or following a 90-s delay. A first

recognition test immediately followed recall of lists; a second test occurred 2 days later.

The proportion of correctly recalled list items decreased with the 90-s delay, whereas

the proportion of falsely recalled critical items increased. The overall proportion of items

recognized as "old" was greater for false critical items than for correct list items, but

both false recognition and correct recognition decreased over the 2-day period. These

findings are compared to other studies that examined false memories following delays.

Abstract should be a single paragraph not exceeding 120 words.

Note:
*   Double-space between all lines of the manuscript. There should be no more than 27 lines of text on each page.*
*   When using a word processor, use left justification only (not full). Use italics for statistical symbols and infrequently otherwise, and use one font size throughout the manuscript.*

Leave one space at end of all sentences, and after all commas, colons, and semicolons.

Title appears centered on page 3, with first letter of major words in caps.

False Recall   3

False Recall and Recognition of List Items Following Delay

Roediger and McDermott (1995) captured the attention of memory researchers by reminding us of the importance of examining participants' errors in recall and that these errors can sometimes be quite predictable. Moreover, these "false memories" are relevant to ongoing debates about false memories that may occur in more natural settings (e.g., clinics, courtrooms). Roediger and McDermott, and many others, have demonstrated that false memories are easily created and that participants' phenomenological experience of these memories mimics their memories for actual events (e.g., Mather, Henkel, & Johnson, 1997; Norman & Schacter, 1997; Payne, Elie, Blackwell, & Neuschatz, 1996). The purpose of the present study was to replicate Roediger and McDermott's (1995) findings and to extend their findings by examining the persistence of false memories following delays. If false memories persist following delays, important implications exist regarding courtroom testimony and recovered memories in therapy. For example, memory retrieval in these cases follows varying periods of delay and the accuracy of these memories may thus be questioned.

Identify all authors (surnames only) the first time you cite a source (five or fewer authors).

List multiple sources in alphabetical order, separated by a semicolon.

Indent every paragraph using the tab key (set at five to seven spaces or 1/2 inch).

In this false memory paradigm word lists are constructed such that each word is highly associated with a critical, not-presented word. For example, participants may hear the words *bed, rest, awake, tired, dream*, etc., but never the critical word, *sleep*. False recall and recognition for the word *sleep* is quite high. Underwood (1965) proposed that an implicit associative response (IAR) occurs when participants study an associated word. For example, when participants hear "bed" they may think of "sleep" (the IAR). With the next word, "rest," they again may experience "sleep" as an IAR, and so on. When their memory is tested participants may have difficulty discriminating the

Abbreviated terms are first spelled out, followed by the abbreviation in parentheses.

Use Latin abbreviations (such as e.g. and i.e.) only in parentheses.

Use numbers to express amounts 10 and above, and when numbers are grouped for comparison with numbers 10 and above.

An "s" (with no period) is the abbreviation for second.

Use number for units of time or measure.

Note: Use past tense to describe the study.

Flush with left margin, italicized, only first letter in caps.

Always use words to express numbers that begin a sentence.

IAR from the presented items, resulting in false recall or recognition. An alternative account relies on the extent to which the lists of associated words activate a schema for the words (e.g., a "sleep" schema). According to this account, recall after a delay may be based on memory for the schema rather than the actual list presentation.

In the present study participants listened to 12 lists comprised of 15 words that were associated to a critical, not-presented word. Participants were randomly assigned to recall 4 of the 12 lists in either an immediate-recall condition or following a 90-s delay in a single trial of free recall. When not recalling words (and during the 90-s delays) participants completed distractor tasks consisting of math problems. Additionally, two recognition tests were administered. The first recognition test followed the presentation and recall of the 15 lists; the second was 2 days later.

We hypothesized that the proportions of correct recall and false recall would not differ in the immediate-recall condition because of participants' inability to differentiate their memory for the presented words from the IARs generated for the critical items. In the delayed-recall condition, we expected the proportion of false items recalled to be greater than the proportion of correct items recalled because of participants' activation of a schema for the list to aid recall. This activation was assumed to lead to recall of the highly associated, critical item. Furthermore, we anticipated that correct recall would decrease over time but false recall would increase with the delay. Similar predictions were made for participants' recognition of correct list items and false critical items.

Method

Center, no italics, only the first letter in caps.

Participants

Nineteen students (16 women, 3 men) from a research methods in psychology

Note: Method, Results, and Discussion sections do not begin on new page (unless coincidentally).

Note: "Data" is plural.

Indented, and italicized paragraph heading, followed by a period. Only first letter of first word in caps.

Use words to express numbers less than 10.

False Recall   5

class at Loyola University of Chicago participated as part of a class project. Data for one student were omitted from all analyses because the student attempted recall for the wrong lists; recognition data for two students were omitted from analyses because they missed the second class session in which the experiment was conducted.

Materials

    Word lists. We used 12 15-item word lists from Roediger and McDermott's (1995) study. They constructed 24 lists by selecting 15 words that were highly associated with a critical word that was not presented. Words were ordered such that the strongest associates were presented first, followed by more weakly associated words. For example, the list for the critical word, *needle*, was *thread, pin, eye, sewing, sharp, point, prick, thimble, haystack, thorn, hurt, injection, syringe, cloth,* and *knitting*. Six lists in the present study were identified by Roediger and McDermott as having a high likelihood of creating false memories (identified by the critical item): chair, mountain, needle, rough, sleep, sweet. The other six lists used in the present study for recall were randomly selected from their remaining lists (identified by the critical item): bread, cold, doctor, foot, music, slow.

    Participants recalled words from 4 of the 12 lists in a single trial of free recall. In order to rule out the possibility that proportions of correct and false recall would be determined by the particular lists used for the recall task, the four recall lists were counterbalanced. The 12 lists were randomly divided into three sets of four lists, with the provision that two lists in each set have high likelihoods for creating false memories. Participants were randomly assigned to recall words for four lists. Seven participants recalled the chair, bread, slow, and sleep lists; seven participants recalled the needle, foot, doctor, and rough lists, and four participants recalled the sweet, music, cold, and mountain lists.

Distractor task. Participants completed a distractor task consisting of math problems when not recalling words and during the 90-s delay. We generated 20 pages of math problems. Each page had six complex math problems involving addition, subtraction, multiplication, and division.

Recall packets. We created six different packets to manipulate the recall condition (immediate, delayed) and counterbalance the lists used for recall. Four pages presented recall instructions based on those used by Roediger and McDermott (1995): "Please write down as many words from the list that you remember. A good strategy is to write down the last few items first, then the rest of the words in any order." Twenty pages had math problems. Between each page was a colored sheet of paper, which masked the participants' next task (recall or math problems). The order of the 24 pages depended on whether participants were in the immediate- or delayed-recall condition and which list set participants were assigned to recall. For example, the "music" list was presented first. Following the presentation of the list, participants assigned to recall the music list in the immediate condition opened their packet to a page with recall instructions; all other participants opened their packet to a page of math problems. After 90 s, a tone signaled participants to turn to the next white page (following the colored sheet). If assigned to recall the music list in the delayed-recall condition, participants' next sheet had recall instructions; all other participants received math problems. This sequence was followed for the remaining 11 word lists.

Recognition tests. Participants completed two different recognition tests, the first

Place periods or commas within quotation marks.

followed the presentation and recall of lists (immediate), the second was 2 days later (delayed). Because three list sets were used for recall (to counterbalance recall lists across participants), we created three versions of the first recognition test (session 1) and three versions of the second recognition test (session 2). Following Roediger and McDermott's terminology, recognition-test items that were presented during the recall portion of the study are referred to as "studied," and new distractor items are referred to as "not studied." Each 72-item recognition test consisted of six different types of items: 10 Studied/Recalled items (5 each from two of the four lists participants were asked to recall); 2 corresponding critical items for these lists; 20 Studied/Not Recalled items (5 each from four of the eight lists participants did not recall); 4 corresponding critical items for these lists; 30 Not Studied Distractor items (5 each from six lists that were not presented); and 6 corresponding critical items for the distractor lists (these lists also were from Roediger & McDermott, 1995). The five items selected from the word lists for each recognition test were the first, third, fifth, seventh, and ninth words. The 72 words on each list were randomly ordered. Participants made recognition judgments using a 4-point scale (1 = *sure new*, 2 = *probably new*, 3 = *probably old*, and 4 = *sure old*).

Procedure

A 2 (condition) X 2 (memory type) mixed factorial design was used for the recall portion of the experiment. Students were randomly assigned to either the immediate-recall condition or the delayed-recall condition; thus, the condition variable was manipulated as a random groups design. Memory type was a repeated measures variable with two levels: correct and false memory. The recognition portion of the experiment was a repeated measures independent variable. Participants completed the

A comma separates authors' surnames and year of publication when citation is within parentheses.

Use ampersand to indicate "and" for references within parentheses.

Italicize the anchors of a scale.

Numbers are used to indicate the levels of a design. Include one space to left and right of multiplication sign.

"min" (without a period) is the abbreviation for minute.

first recognition test immediately following the presentation and recall of word lists and completed the delayed recognition test 2 days later. The dependent variables were proportion of correct and false recall and proportion of correct and false recognition.

The experiment was conducted during two scheduled class periods. In the first session, lasting 50 min, the experimenter gave students a consent form and a packet that corresponded to their condition when they entered the class (students were randomly assigned to conditions prior to their arrival). A participant number appeared on top of the packet. Instructions requested students not to open their packet. After students read and signed their consent form, they listened to tape-recorded instructions for the study. Following this, the experimenter stopped the tape recorder and asked if there were any questions. Tape-recorded word lists were then presented. The random order of the lists was as follows (identified by the critical item): music, needle, sleep, doctor, slow, mountain, rough, bread, sweet, cold, chair, and foot. Words were presented at the rate of approximately one word every 1½ s. Following the list presentation, participants heard a tone informing them to turn to the next white page. They then either recalled list items or completed math problems for 90 s. A tone then signaled participants to turn to the next white page. This page instructed them to recall the list items or complete math problems. This procedure was followed for all 12 lists.

After the study and recall phase of the experiment, the experimenter distributed the first recognition test and asked participants to record their participant number on the top of the recognition test. After completing the recognition test, participants were asked to write their participant number in their notebook; they were then dismissed. At the beginning of the next class session (2 days later), participants reported their number

Note: Words are not hyphenated at the end of a line.

Note: Always double-space. Do not insert extra spaces between sections.

Center, no italics.

and they were given the corresponding second recognition test. Each recognition test took approximately 5 min to complete. The instructor then fully debriefed participants regarding the purpose of the experiment.

Results

Results are presented first for participants' recall and then for their recognition of list items. The dependent variables were proportion of correct recall/recognition and proportion of false recall/recognition. Proportion of correct recall was determined by counting the number of words participants correctly recalled and dividing by 60 (the total number of list items they were asked to recall). Proportion of false recall was determined by counting the number of critical items falsely recalled and dividing by 4 (the total number of critical items for the four lists participants recalled).

Similar proportions were computed for recognition data. For ease of comparisons, participants' recognition responses were collapsed such that ratings of 1 or 2 indicated judgments that the word was "new" (i.e., not presented during the recall portion of the study), and ratings of 3 or 4 indicated the word was "old" (i.e., presented during the recall portion). The number of items judged "old" for each type of word (e.g., studied, recalled; not studied distractor) was counted and divided by the total number of words of that type presented on the recognition test.

Recall

Mean proportions for correct and false recall were entered into a 2 (condition) X 2 (memory type) mixed-design analysis of variance (ANOVA). Across the two recall conditions the proportion of falsely recalled critical items (M = .60, SD = .23) tended to be greater than the proportion of correctly recalled list items (M = .48, SD = .12), F(1,

M is the abbreviation for arithmetic mean

SD is the abbreviation for standard deviation.

MSE is the abbreviation for Mean Square Error.

Italicize all statistical terms.

Do not capitalize names of conditions.

Footnotes appear on a separate page near end of manuscript (not at bottom of the page).

Do not abbreviate "Figure." Figure caption and figure appear on separate pages at end of manuscript.

Degrees of freedom for statistical tests are reported in parentheses (with no space after statistical term).

16) = 4.38, p = .053 (MSE = .03, effect size r = .47).[1] The observed power to detect this large effect with the small sample size (n = 9 per condition), at alpha = .05, was estimated to be only .50. The main effect of condition was not significant, F(1, 16) = .10, p > .05 (MSE = .02, r = .10, power = .06). As predicted, however, recall condition and memory type interacted to influence participants' recall, F(1, 16) = 9.50, p < .01 (MSE = .03, r = .61). Comparisons of means revealed that recall differed in the immediate- and delayed-recall conditions in the predicted direction (see Figure 1). Participants in the immediate-recall condition did not differ in their proportions of correct recall and false recall, F(1, 8) = .41, p > .05 (MSE = .036, r = .22, power = .09); however, participants in the delayed-recall condition were more likely to recall a greater proportion of false critical items than correct list items, F(1, 8) = 16.57, p < .005 (MSE = .024, r = .82).[2]

A second set of comparisons of means examined the effect of delay for each type of recall. As expected, the proportion of correctly recalled list items decreased following delay and the proportion of false recall increased following delay (see Figure 1). For correct list items, participants in the delayed-recall condition recalled fewer items than participants who recalled list items immediately, t(16) = 2.08, p = .054 (MSE = .03). The effect size (d) was 1.04, indicating a very large effect of immediate- vs. delayed-recall on participants' correct recall (see Cohen, 1988). In contrast, the proportion of falsely recalled critical items increased following the 90-s delay relative to the immediate-recall condition, t(16) = 2.33, p = .033 (MSE = .03). The effect size (d) was 1.16, indicating a very large effect of recall condition (immediate, delayed) on participants' false recall.

Table appears on separate page near end of manuscript.

Note use of spaces and punctuation when typing statistics.

Variable names in caps when they appear with a multiplication sign.

Recognition

Across two testing sessions separated by 2 days, we examined the proportion of items recognized as "old" as a function of whether items were correct list items or false critical items and whether the items were recalled (vs. not recalled) during the recall portion of the experiment (see Table 1).[3] Distractor items were excluded from the analyses because the proportion of these items judged "old" was generally low across item type and sessions, $M = .18$ ($SD = .12$). Main effects were observed for the time, memory type, and recalled/not recalled variables. As expected, memory for the items decreased over the 2-day period, as the proportion of all items recognized as "old" decreased at Time 2 ($M = .71$, $SD = .14$) relative to Time 1 ($M = .87$, $SD = .11$), $F(1, 14)$ $= 16.40$, $P < .005$ ($MSE = .04$, $r = .73$). Additionally, the main effect of memory type indicated that participants rated a higher proportion of false critical items "old" ($M = .85$, $SD = .11$) than correct list items ($M = .73$, $SD = .13$), $F(1, 14) = 14.72$, $P < .005$ ($MSE = .026$, $r = .71$). Thus, in terms of proportions, false recognition was greater than correct recognition at Time 1 and Time 2. Finally, the proportion of items judged "old" was greater for lists participants were asked to recall ($M = .87$, $SD = .09$) relative to lists they did not recall ($M = .71$, $SD = .14$), $F(1, 14) = 23.57$, $p < .001$ ($MSE = .032$, $r = .79$). This is the "testing effect" identified by Roediger and McDermott (1995), in which rehearsal during the recall portion of the experiment increases subsequent recognition.

There was also a Time X Recalled/Not Recalled interaction effect, $F(1, 14) = 7.49$, $p < .05$ ($MSE = .024$, $r = .59$). This interaction indicated that recognition of words for recalled lists was slightly higher at Time 1 ($M = .90$, $SD = .07$) relative to Time 2 ($M = .83$, $SD = .16$), $F(1, 15) = 3.22$, $p < .10$ ($MSE = .013$, $r = .42$, power = .39). In contrast,

Capitalize nouns that are followed by a number.

False Recall   12

recognition of words from not-recalled lists dropped significantly at Time 2 ($M = .60$, SD = .18) relative to Time 1 ($M = .83$, $SD = .18$), $F(1, 15) = 18.63$, $p < .005$ ($MSE = .023$, $r = .74$). Thus, rehearsal of the lists (through recall) increased the proportion of correct items and false critical items recognized as "old" even after a 2-day period, relative to lists that were not rehearsed.

As noted above, we observed differential effects of delay on the proportion recall of correct list items and false critical items. However, a similar effect was not observed for recognition data, as the Time X Memory Type interaction effect was not statistically significant, $F(1, 14) = .028$, $p > .05$ ($MSE = .014$). The effect size, r, for this interaction was quite small (.04, power = .05). Thus, the 2-day delay between the recognition tests resulted in similar decreases in the proportions of correct list items and false critical items that were recognized as "old."

Discussion

Participants recalled list items in a single trial of free recall immediately after list presentation or following a 90-s filled delay. The proportion of correctly recalled list items decreased as a function of delay, but the proportion of false critical items recalled increased following the 90-s delay. Participants' recognition of correct list items and false critical items was tested following a 2-day delay. In terms of proportions, false recognition of critical items was greater than correct recognition of list items at Time 1 and Time 2, but recognition for both types of items decreased over the 2-day period. A testing effect occurred such that correct and false recognition were greater for lists participants had attempted recall relative to lists not recalled. The effects of rehearsal persisted over the 2-day period. In general, delay produced large effect sizes for both

Note: Make sure you use the "greater than" or "less than" sign correctly.

Center, no italics.

Year of publication
in parentheses after
author's surname.

Do not use
contractions such as
"wasn't."

Year of publication
is not repeated
within a paragraph
if it is clear that
the same study is
being described.

Year of
publication appears
in parentheses
even when
reference has
appeared
previously in
manuscript.

Use "et al."
following surname
of first author for work with three or more authors.
Note: First citation to this work lists all authors (see p. 3).

recall and recognition.

McDermott (1996) used a 30-s filled delay to examine the effects of delay on participants' recall of correct list items and false critical items. Although she observed a decrease in correct recall following delay, her participants' false recall of critical items was not affected by delay. In contrast, we observed an increase in the proportion of false critical items recalled following a 90-s delay. One reason for this discrepancy may be derived from our differing findings for correct list recall. In McDermott's study the proportion of correct list items recalled following a 30-s delay was .50; in our study, the proportion of correct recall following a 90-s delay was .39. To the extent that a longer delay increased participants' forgetting of correct list items in our study, they may have had to rely more on schema-based recall, which we hypothesized to increase the occurrence of false memories. Alternatively, discrimination between IARs and memory for list items may become more difficult with longer delays. As a result, greater proportions of false recall would be expected (as was observed). This explanation is corroborated by McDermott's findings that after a 2-day delay, the proportion of falsely recalled critical items was greater than the proportion of correctly recalled items (similar to our findings for recognition). Thus, in both studies, participants demonstrated high levels of false recall that persisted over time.

Payne et al. (1996) examined participants' recognition memory for correct list items and false critical items in immediate (2 min) and delayed (24 hr) conditions. Similar to our recognition data, Payne et al. observed that false critical items were recognized with higher likelihood at both testing sessions than correct list items. However, they also observed an interaction between item type (correct, false) and "hr" (with no period) is the abbreviation for hour.

retention (immediate, delayed) for their recognition data that we did not. They observed more forgetting for correct list items than false critical items over the 24-hr period, whereas over our 2-day period we observed similar decreases for correct list items and false critical items. Differences in the retention interval (24 vs. 48 hr), the number of word lists (16 vs. 12), or other procedural differences may account for this discrepancy.

The findings of this study and those of other recent studies indicate that false memories are frequent and persist following delays. Moreover, there is accumulating evidence to suggest that false memories for highly associated information may exceed correct memory over time. These data are limited to individuals' recall for highly associated list items. Important areas for future research include false memories for natural categories such as people and events. Also, it is not clear to what extent individuals' emotions may affect correct and false recall. This question is particularly relevant to the issue of false memory in the emotionally charged situations of eyewitness testimony and therapy.

Note: References section begins on a new page immediately after the Discussion section.

Italicize titles of books. Only first letter of first word and word following a colon in caps.

Publisher of book.

Use ampersand before last author's name.

First letter of questionnaire names in caps.

Use initials for first and middle names.

Period after year of publication (in parentheses).

Page numbers.

Use lower case for titles of articles and book chapters (except first word and word after a colon).

Italicize journal name and volume number. Capitalize first letter of major words in journal name. Use comma after journal name and volume number.

Use hanging indents for each reference entry.

Center, no italics.

False Recall   15

References

Cohen, J. (1988). *Statistical power analysis for behavioral sciences* (2nd ed.).
New York: Academic Press.

Keppel, G. (1991). *Design and analysis: A researcher's handbook* (3rd ed.).
Englewood Cliffs, NJ: Prentice-Hall.

Mather, M., Henkel, L. A., & Johnson, M. J. (1997). Evaluating characteristics of
false memories: Remember/know judgments and Memory Characteristics
Questionnaire compared. *Memory & Cognition, 25,* 826-837.

McDermott, K. B. (1996). The persistence of false memories in list recall. *Journal
of Memory and Language, 35,* 212-230.

Norman, K., & Schacter, D. L. (1997). False recognition in younger and older
adults: Exploring the characteristics of illusory memories. *Memory & Cognition,
25,* 838-848.

Separate authors' names with a comma.

Payne, D. G., Elie, C. J., Blackwell, J. M., & Neuschatz, J. S. (1996). Memory
illusions: Recalling, recognizing, and recollecting events that never occurred.
Journal of Memory and Language, 35, 261-285.

Roediger, H. L., & McDermott, K. B. (1995). Creating false memories: Remembering
words not presented in lists. *Journal of Experimental Psychology: Learning,
Memory, and Cognition, 21,* 803-814.

Underwood, B. J. (1965). False recognition produced by implicit verbal
responses. *Journal of Experimental Psychology, 70,* 122-129.

Note: List references in alphabetical order using first author's surname. Double-space references, no extra space between references.

Center, no italics

↓

Author Note

Jeanne S. Zechmeister, Department of Psychology; Eugene B. Zechmeister, Department of Psychology.

Authors' department affiliations in first paragraph.

Acknowledge people who assisted with the research and manuscript preparation.

Last paragraph in Author Note specifies author's address for correspondence. Use this form exactly with your name and address.

Portions of this research were presented at the Annual Meeting of the Psychonomic Society, November 1996. The authors thank the students in the first author's Research Methods in Psychology course at Loyola University of Chicago who participated in and discussed this study, and John J. Shaughnessy for his suggestions for this manuscript.

Send correspondence concerning this manuscript to Jeanne S. Zechmeister, Department of Psychology, Loyola University of Chicago, 6525 N. Sheridan Road, Chicago, IL 60626; e-mail: jzechme@luc.edu.

Footnotes

[1] The effect size, *r*, was derived from ANOVA output that presented η^2 as a measure of effect size. η^2 represents the proportion of variance in the dependent variable that is accounted for by the independent variable. η^2 is analogous to r^2 in analyses involving one *df* for the effect. The square root of η^2 represents *r*, the magnitude of linear relationship between two variables. Cohen (1988) offers the following guidelines for interpreting the size of an effect using *r*: small effect, *r* = .10; medium effect, *r* = .25; large effect, *r* = .40.

[2] Simple main effect analyses were calculated by treating the comparison as a one-way ANOVA, as recommended by Keppel (1991) for mixed designs.

[3] We also examined whether immediate- vs. delayed-recall conditions influenced recognition in the ANOVA. Because this variable did not produce any statistically significant effects in the recognition analyses, it will not be discussed further.

Note: Use footnotes sparingly in manuscript.

Type flush with left margin.

Line separates title from body of table.

Center column headings over appropriate columns.

Line separates headings from table data.

Table title, italicized, with first letters of major words in caps.

False Recall   18

Table 1

Mean Proportions for Recognizing Items as "Old" at Time 1 and Time 2 (48-hr Delay)

	Studied and recalled	Studied and not recalled	Distractor
Correct list items			
Time 1	.84	.79	.19
	(.12)	(.17)	(.12)
Time 2	.76	.56	.18
	(.22)	(.16)	(.16)
False critical items			
Time 1	.97	.88	.28
	(.12)	(.20)	(.13)
Time 2	.91	.64	.17
	(.20)	(.24)	(.10)

Line at end of table data.

Table "notes" are typed flush with left margin.

Note. Standard deviations are in parentheses. "Recalled" and "Not Recalled" refer to whether participants were asked to recall list items at Time 1, not whether these items were produced by participants during recall.

Note: Use double-space in table. Place only one table on a page.

Center, no italics.

↓

False Recall   19

Figure Caption

Flush with left margin. Do not abbreviate "Figure."

→ *Figure 1.* Mean proportions of correct and false recall in the immediate- and delayed-recall conditions.

Note: More than one figure caption may appear on a "Figure Captions" page.

The figure itself appears on a separate page at end of manuscript. If there is more than one figure, each appears on a separate page.

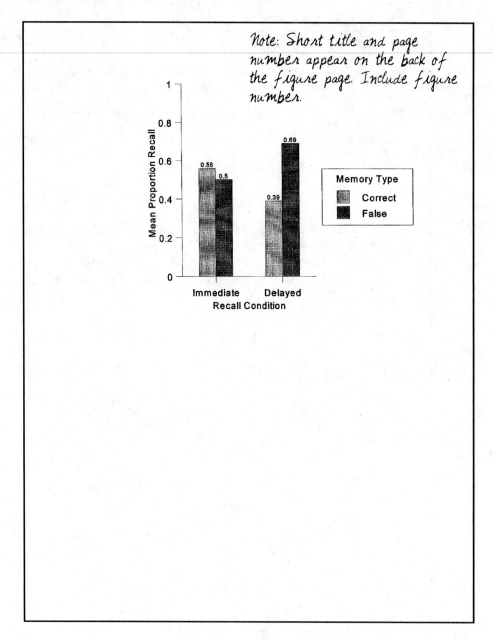

Note: Short title and page number appear on the back of the figure page. Include figure number.

Chapter 8

Ethical Issues in the Conduct of Psychological Research

CHAPTER OUTLINE

INTRODUCTION

Good science requires good scientists. Scientists' professional competence and integrity are essential for ensuring high quality science. Maintaining the integrity of the scientific process is a shared responsibility of individual scientists and the community of scientists (as represented by professional organizations such as APA and APS). Each individual scientist has an ethical responsibility to seek knowledge and to strive to improve the quality of life. Diener and Crandall (1978) identify several specific responsibilities that follow from this general mandate. Scientists should:

—carry out research in a competent manner;
—report results accurately;

—manage research resources honestly;

—fairly acknowledge, in scientific communications, the individuals who have contributed their ideas or their time and effort;

—consider the consequences to society of any research endeavor;

—speak out publicly on societal concerns related to a scientist's knowledge and expertise.

In striving to meet these obligations, individual scientists face challenging and, at times, ambiguous ethical issues and questions. To guide individual psychologists in making ethical decisions, the American Psychological Association (APA) has formulated an Ethics Code that "provides a common set of principles and standards upon which psychologists build their professional and scientific work" (American Psychological Association, 2002). These values are summarized in five General Principles: Beneficence and Non-maleficence; Fidelity and Responsibility; Integrity; Justice; and Respect for People's Rights and Dignity. Based on these five general principles, the APA Ethics Code sets forth standards for ethical behavior for psychologists who do research or therapy or who teach or serve as administrators (see American Psychological Association, 2002). The Ethics Code deals with such diverse issues as sexual harassment, fees for psychological services, providing advice to the public in the media, test construction, and classroom teaching.

As stated in the Preamble to the Ethics Code, psychologists are expected to make "a personal commitment and lifelong effort to act ethically; to encourage ethical behavior by students, supervisees, employees, and colleagues; and to consult with others concerning ethical problems" (American Psychological Association, 2002). It is also important for all students of psychology to make every effort to live up to these stated ideals and standards of behavior. You can familiarize yourself with the Ethics Code by going to the APA website [http://www.apa.org/ethics].

Many of the ethical standards in the APA Ethics Code deal directly with psychological research (see especially Standards 8.01 to 8.15 of the Code), including the treatment of both humans and animals in psychological research. As with most ethical codes, the standards tend to be general in nature and require specific definition in particular contexts. More than one ethical standard can apply to a specific research situation, and at times the standards may even appear to contradict one another. For instance, ethical research requires that human participants be protected from physical injury. Research that involves drugs or other invasive treatments, however, may place participants at risk of physical harm. The welfare of animal subjects should be protected, but certain kinds of research may involve inflicting pain or other suffering on an animal. Solving these ethical dilemmas is not always easy and requires a deliberate, conscientious problem-solving approach to ethical decision making.

The Internet has changed the way many scientists do research, and psychologists are no exception. Researchers from around the world, for example, often collaborate on scientific projects and can now quickly and easily exchange ideas and findings with one another via the Internet. Vast quantities of archival information are accessible though government-sponsored Internet sites (e.g., U.S. Census Bureau). In the last decades of the 20th century, researchers began to collect data from human participants via the World Wide Web. There is the potential to include *millions* of people in one study! Types of psychological research on the Internet include simple observation (e.g., recording "behavior" in chat rooms), surveys (questionnaires, including personality tests), and experiments involving manipulated variables.

Although the Internet offers many opportunities for the behavioral scientist, it also raises many ethical concerns. Major issues arise due to the absence of the researcher in an online research setting, the difficulty of obtaining adequate informed consent and providing debriefing, and concerns about protecting participant confidentiality (see especially Kraut et al., 2004, and Nosek, Banaji, & Greenwald, 2002, for reviews of these problems and some suggested solutions). We discuss some of these ethical issues in the present chapter and also continue this discussion in later chapters when we describe specific research methods.

Ethical decisions are best made after consultation with others, including one's peers but especially those who are more experienced or knowledgeable in a particular area. In fact, review of a research plan by people not involved in the research is legally required in some situations. In the remaining sections of this chapter, we identify those standards from the Ethics Code that deal specifically with psychological research. We also offer a brief commentary on some aspects of these standards and present several hypothetical research scenarios that raise ethical questions. By putting yourself in the position of having to make judgments about the ethical issues raised in these research proposals, you will begin to learn to grapple with the challenges that arise in applying particular ethical standards and with the difficulties of ethical decision making in general. We urge you to discuss these proposals with peers, professors, and others who have had prior experience doing psychological research.

ETHICAL ISSUES TO CONSIDER BEFORE BEGINNING RESEARCH

- Prior to conducting any study, the proposed research must be reviewed to determine if it meets ethical standards.

Researchers must begin to consider ethical issues before they begin a research project. Ethical problems can be avoided only by planning carefully and consulting with appropriate individuals and groups *prior to doing the research*. The failure to conduct research in an ethical manner undermines the entire scientific process, impedes the advancement of knowledge, and erodes the public's respect for scientific and academic communities. It can also lead to significant legal and financial penalties for individuals and institutions. The following ethical standards from the APA Ethics Code (American Psychological Association, 2002, pp. 1069–1071) describe the most important issues that researchers must address as they begin to do psychological research.

APA Ethical Standards

8.01 Institutional Approval When institutional approval is required, psychologists provide accurate information about their research proposals and obtain approval prior to conducting the research. They conduct the research in accordance with the approved research protocol.

Commentary

- Institutional Review Boards (IRBs) review psychological research to protect the rights and welfare of human participants.
- Institutional Animal Care and Use Committees (IACUCs) review research conducted with animals to ensure that animals are treated humanely.

The National Research Act, signed into law in 1974, resulted in the creation of the National Commission for the Protection of Human Subjects of Biomedical and Behavioral Research. This act requires that institutions that seek research funds from specific federal agencies must establish committees to review research sponsored by the institution. Colleges and universities have established these committees that are referred to as *Institutional Review Boards (IRBs)*. You can review the federal regulations for IRBs at the website [http://www.hhs.gov/ohrp]. The IRB review is done so the institution can ensure that researchers protect participants from harm and safeguard participants' rights. Federal regulations impose very specific requirements on the membership and duties of IRBs (*see Federal Register*, June 18,1991). For example, an IRB must be composed of at least five members with varying backgrounds and fields of expertise. Both scientists and nonscientists must be represented, and there must be at least one IRB member who is not affiliated with the institution. Responsible members of the community, such as members of the clergy, lawyers, and nurses, are often asked to serve on these committees.

A psychology student seeking to do research with human participants is likely to submit a research proposal to a department committee charged with reviewing

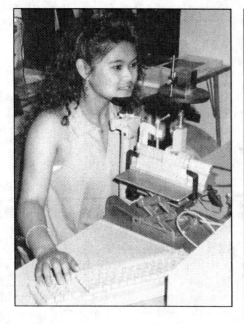
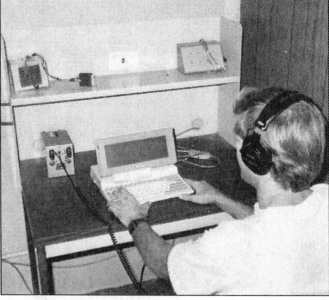

FIGURE 8.1   Many ethical questions are raised when research is performed with humans.

FIGURE 8.2 Following World War II, the Nuremberg War Crimes Court charged German doctors with crimes against humanity, which included performing medical experiments on human beings without their consent. The Court's verdict in these cases led to the development of the Nuremberg Code, which set rules for permissible experimentation with human beings.

research conducted in the psychology department. Depending on the association of this departmental committee with an IRB, research falling into various well-defined categories is either reviewed at the departmental level or referred to the IKB for review. The IRB has the authority to approve, disapprove, or require modifications of the research plan prior to their approval of the research. The IRB also has the ethical responsibility to make sure that their review of the research proposals is fair by considering the perspectives of the institution, the researcher, and the research participants (Chastain & Landrum, 1999).

In 1985, the Department of Agriculture, as well as the Public Health Service, formulated new guidelines for the care of laboratory animals (Holden, 1987). As a result, institutions doing research with animal subjects are now required to have an Institutional Animal Care and Use Committee (IACUC). These committees must include, minimally, a scientist, a veterinarian, and at least one person not affiliated with the institution. Review of animal research by IACUCs extends to more than simply overseeing the research procedures. Federal regulations governing the conduct of animal research extend to specifications of animal living quarters and the proper training of personnel who work directly with the animals (Holden, 1987).

Nearly every college and university require that all research conducted at the institution be reviewed at some stage by an independent committee. Violation of federal regulations regarding the review of research involving humans or animals can bring a halt to research at an institution, spell the loss of federal funds, and result in substantial fines (Holden, 1987). Given the complex nature of federal regulations and the policies of most institutions requiring review of research with humans and animals, *any individual who wants to do research should inquire of the proper authorities, prior to starting research, about the appropriate procedure for institutional review.* Helpful advice is available for students planning to submit a research proposal to an IRB (McCallum, 2001) or to an IACUC (LeBlanc, 2001).

THE RISK/BENEFIT RATIO

- A subjective evaluation of the risks and benefits of a research project is used to determine whether the research should be conducted.

In addition to checking if appropriate ethical principles are being followed, an IRB considers the *risk/benefit ratio* for a study. Society and individuals benefit from research when new knowledge is gained and when treatments are identified that improve people's lives. There are also potential costs when research is not done. We miss the opportunity to gain knowledge and, ultimately, we lose the opportunity to improve the human condition. Research can also be costly to individual participants. For example, research participants risk injury when exposed to potentially harmful circumstances. The principal investigator must, of course, be the first one to consider these potential costs and benefits. An IRB is made up of knowledgeable individuals who do not have a personal interest in the research. As such, an IRB is in a better position to determine the risk/benefit ratio and, ultimately, to decide whether to approve the proposed research.

The **risk/benefit ratio** asks the question, *Is it worth it?* There are no mathematical answers to the risk/benefit ratio. Instead, when deciding whether to approve a research proposal, members of an IRB strive to reach consensus on a subjective evaluation of the risks and benefits both to individual participants and to society When the risks outweigh the potential benefits, then the IRB does not approve the research; when the benefits outweigh the risks, the IRB approves the research. Many factors affect a decision regarding the proper balance of risks and benefits of a research activity. The most basic are the nature of the risk and the magnitude of the probable benefit to the participant as well as the potential scientific and social value of the research (Fisher & Fryberg, 1994). We can tolerate greater risk when we foresee clear and immediate benefits to individuals or when we judge that the research has obvious scientific and social value. For instance, a research project investigating a new treatment for psychotic behavior may entail risk for the participants. If the proposed treatment has a good chance of having a beneficial effect, however, then the possible benefits to both the individuals and society could outweigh the risk involved in the study.

In determining the risk/benefit ratio, researchers also consider whether valid and interpretable results will be produced. Rosenthal (1994b) makes a strong case for considering the quality of the research as a factor in the ethical review of proposed research. "Everything else being equal, research that is of a higher scientific quality is more ethically defensible." More specifically, "If because of the poor quality of the science no good can come of a research study, how are we to justify the use of participants[7] time, attention, and effort and the money, space, supplies, and other resources that have been expended on the research project?" (Rosenthal, 1994b). Thus, *an investigator is obliged to seek to do research that meets the highest standards of scientific excellence.*

When there is potential risk, a researcher must make sure there are no alternative, low-risk procedures that could be substituted. The researcher must also be sure that previous research has not already successfully addressed the research question being asked. Without careful prior review of the psychological literature, a researcher might carry out research that has already been done, thus exposing individuals to needless risk.

Determining Risk

- Potential risks in psychological research include risk of physical injury, social injury, and mental or emotional stress.
- Risks must be evaluated in terms of potential participants' everyday activities, their physical and mental health, and capabilities.

Determining whether research participants are "at risk" illustrates the difficulties involved in ethical decision making. Life itself is a risky affair. Commuting to work or school, crossing streets, and riding on elevators are all activities that have an element of risk. Simply showing up for a psychology experiment has some degree of risk. To say that human participants in psychological research can never face any risks would bring all research to a halt. Decisions about what constitutes risk must take into consideration those risks that are part of everyday life.

We must also consider the characteristics of the participants when we determine risk. Certain activities might pose a serious risk for some individuals but not for others. Running up a flight of stairs may increase the risk of a heart attack for an elderly person, but the same task would probably not be risky for most young adults. Similarly, individuals who are exceptionally depressed or anxious might show more severe reactions to certain psychological tasks than would other people. Thus, when considering risk, researchers must consider the specific populations or individuals who are likely to participate in the study.

We often think of risk in terms of the possibility of physical injury. Frequently, however, participants in social science research risk social or psychological injury. The potential for social risk exists when information gained about individuals through their participation in psychological research is revealed to others. If someone found out that an individual completed a questionnaire inquiring about deviant sexual practices, there is the potential for a social risk for that individual, such as embarrassment. Personal information collected during psychological research may include facts about intelligence, personality traits, and political, social, or religious beliefs. A research participant probably does not want this personal information revealed to teachers, employers, or peers. If researchers do not protect the confidentiality of participants' responses, the social risk for these participants may increase. It has been suggested that the greatest risk to participants in Internet-based research is the possible disclosure of identifiable personal information outside the research situation (Kraut et al., 2004). Other researchers suggest that although the Internet affords a "perception of anonymity" (Nosek, et al., 2002), in some circumstances that perception is false, and investigators must consider ways to protect confidentiality in data transmission, data storage, and post-study interactions with participants.

Some psychological research may pose psychological risk if participants in the study experience serious mental or emotional stress. Imagine the stress a participant may experience when smoke enters the room in which she is waiting. The smoke may be entering the room so the researcher can simulate an emergency. Until the true nature of the smoke is revealed, participants may experience considerable distress. In addition, simply participating in a psychology experiment is anxiety-provoking for some individuals. After learning a list of nonsense syllables, a student participant once said that he was sure the researcher now knew a great deal about him! The student assumed the psychologist was interested in learning about his personality by examining the word associations he used when learning the list. In reality, this person was participating in a simple memory experiment designed to measure forgetting. *A researcher is obligated to protect participants from emotional or mental stress, including, when possible, stress that might arise due to participants' misconceptions about the psychological task.*

Minimal Risk

- A study is described as involving "minimal risk" when the procedures or activities in the study are similar to those experienced by participants in their everyday life.

A distinction is sometimes made between a participant "at risk" and one who is "at minimal risk." **Minimal risk** means that the harm or discomfort participants may experience in the research *is not greater than* what they might experience in their daily lives or during routine physical or psychological tests. As an example of minimal risk, consider the fact that many psychology laboratory studies involve lengthy paper-and-pencil tests intended to assess various mental abilities. Participants may be asked to complete the tests quickly and may receive specific feedback about their performance. Although there is likely to be stress in this situation, the risk of psychological injury is likely no greater than that of being a student. Therefore, such studies would involve only minimal risk for college students. When the possibility of injury is judged to be more than minimal, individuals are considered to be *at risk*. When a study places participants at risk, the researcher has more serious obligations to protect their welfare.

Dealing with Risk

- Whether "at risk" or "at minimal risk," research participants must be protected. More safeguards are needed as risks become greater.
- To protect participants from social risks, information they provide should be anonymous, or if that is not possible, the confidentiality of their information should be maintained.

Even if the potential risk is small, researchers should try to minimize risk and protect participants. For instance, the level of stress that some participants experience can be reduced simply by stating at the beginning of a memory experiment that the tasks are not intended to measure intelligence or personality. In situations where the possibility of harm is judged to be significantly greater than that occurring in daily life, the researcher's obligation to protect participants increases correspondingly. For example, when participants are exposed to the possibility of serious emotional stress in a psychology experiment, an IRB could require that a clinical psychologist be available to counsel individuals about their experience in the study. As you can imagine, online research poses difficult ethical dilemmas in this regard. Participants can experience emotional distress in the context of an Internet study just as they do in a laboratory-based study. Thus, in some research situations, online participants might be at risk, and a risk/benefit evaluation must be made by an IRB. However, because the researcher is absent from the research situation, "the special concern is that researchers may have a diminished ability to monitor subjects in online research and remediate any harm caused by the research" (Kraut et al, 2004). One approach might be to obtain preliminary data with the goal of identifying those who might be at risk and excluding them from the actual study. It may be the case, however, that studies with high risk may not be ethically performed on the Internet (Kraut et al., 2004).

No research activity involving more than minimal risk to participants should be carried out unless alternative methods of data collection with lower risk have been explored. In some cases, descriptive approaches involving observation or questionnaires should be used instead of experimental treatments. Researchers can also take advantage of naturally occurring "treatments" that do not involve experimentally inducing stress. For example, Anderson (1976) interviewed owner-managers of small businesses that had been damaged by hurricane floods. He found that there was an optimum level of stress that led to effective problem-solving and coping behaviors by the participants. Above or below this optimum stress level, problem-solving performance decreased. A similar relationship has been demonstrated in a number of experimental laboratory tasks using experimenter-induced stress.

In order to protect research participants from social injury, data collection should keep participants' responses anonymous by asking participants not to use their names or any identifying information. When this is not possible, researchers should keep participants' responses confidential by removing any identifying information from their records of their responses during the research. When the

STRETCHING EXERCISE

For each of the following research situations, you are to decide whether "minimal risk" is present (i.e., risk not greater than that of everyday life) or if participants are "at risk." If you decide that participants are "at risk," you might think of what recommendations you would make to the researcher to safeguard the participants by reducing the risk. As you do so, you will undoubtedly begin to anticipate some of the ethical issues yet to be discussed in this chapter.

1. College students are asked to complete an adjective checklist describing their current mood. The researcher is seeking to identify students who are depressed so that they can be included in a study examining cognitive deficits associated with depression.

2. Elderly adults in a nursing home are given a battery of achievement tests in the dayroom at their home. A psychologist seeks to determine if there is a decline in mental functioning with advancing age.

3. Students in a psychology research methods class see another student enter their classroom in the middle of the class period, speak loudly and angrily with the instructor, and then leave. As part of a study of eyewitness testimony, the students are then asked to describe the intruder.

4. A researcher recruits students from introductory psychology classes to participate in a study of the effects of alcohol on cognitive functioning. The experiment requires that some students drink 2 ounces of alcohol (mixed with orange juice) before performing a computer game.

researcher must test people on more than one occasion or otherwise track specific individuals, numbers can be randomly assigned to participants at the beginning of a study. Only these numbers need appear on participants' response sheets. If the information supplied by participants is particularly sensitive, a coding scheme may be useful to minimize social risk. One procedure is to assign code numbers to participants. Names are then linked with the code numbers on a master list and access to this list is restricted by keeping it under lock and key. Online researchers need to be particularly sensitive to the possibility of electronic eavesdropping or hacking of stored data and must take appropriate precautions (see Kraut et al., 2004).

Making sure participants' responses are anonymous or confidential can also benefit the researcher if this leads participants to be more honest and open when responding (Blanck, Bellack, Rosnow, Rotheram-Borus, & Schooler, 1992). Participants will be less likely to lie or withhold information if they do not worry about who will have access to their responses.

INFORMED CONSENT

- Researchers and participants enter into a social contract, often using an informed consent procedure.

- Researchers are ethically obligated to describe the research procedures clearly, identify any potential risks that might influence individuals' willingness to participate, and answer any questions participants have about the research.

- Research participants are ethically obligated to behave appropriately during the research by not lying, cheating, or engaging in other fraudulent behavior.

Successful psychological research depends on the willingness of students, patients, clients, and other members of the community to take part in a scientific investigation. In some research, participants are given money or other compensation for their time and effort. Often, people simply volunteer to participate in research with no compensation. In either case, the researcher and the participant

FIGURE 8.3 The U.S. Public Health Service between 1932 and 1972 examined the course of untreated syphilis in poor African American men from Macon County, Alabama, who had not given informed consent. They were unaware they had syphilis and their disease was left untreated.

enter into a social contract. As part of this contract, *a researcher has an ethical responsibility to make clear to the participant what the research entails, including any possible risk to the participant, and to respect the dignity and rights of the individual during the research experience.* Researchers must make every effort to ensure that they obtain the *informed consent* of participants to take part in the research.

The research participants who consent to participate in research also have ethical responsibilities to behave in an appropriate manner. For example, participants should pay attention to instructions and perform tasks in the manner requested by the researcher. Taylor and Shepperd (1996) describe a study that illustrates the possible consequences when participants do not behave responsibly. In the study, participants were briefly left alone by an experimenter who admonished them not to discuss the experiment among themselves. Once they were alone, however, the participants talked about the experiment and obtained information from each other that in effect negated the value of the research. Moreover, when the experimenter later asked the participants about what they knew of the procedures and goals of the study, none revealed that they had gained important knowledge about the study during their illicit conversation. This example illustrates the broader principle that *lying, cheating, or other fraudulent behavior by research participants violates the scientific integrity of the research situation.*

APA Ethical Standards

3.10 Informed Consent

a. When psychologists conduct research or provide assessment therapy, counseling, or consulting services in person or via electronic transmission or other forms of communication, they obtain the informed consent of the individual or individuals using language that is reasonably understandable to that person or persons except when conducting such activities without consent as mandated or prescribed by law or governmental regulation or as otherwise provided in this Ethics Code. The content of informed consent will vary depending on many circumstances; however, informed consent ordinarily requires that the person (1) has the capacity to consent, (2) has been provided information concerning participation in the activity that reasonably might affect his or her willingness to participate including limits of confidentiality and monetary or other costs or reimbursements, (3) is aware of the voluntary nature of participation and has freely and without undue influence expressed consent, and (4) has had the opportunity to ask questions and receive answers regarding the activities. (See also Standards 8.02, Informed Consent to Research; 9.03, Informed Consent in Assessments; and 10.01, Informed Consent to Therapy.)

b. For persons who are legally incapable of giving informed consent, psychologists nevertheless (1) provide an appropriate explanation, (2) seek the individual's assent, (3) consider such persons' preferences and best interests, and (4) obtain appropriate permission from a legally authorized person, if such substitute consent is permitted or required by law. When consent by a legally authorized person is not permitted or required by law, psychologists take reasonable steps to protect the individual's rights and welfare.

c. When psychological services are court ordered or otherwise mandated, psychologists inform the individual of the nature of the anticipated services, including whether the services are court ordered or mandated and any limits of confidentiality, before proceeding.

d. Psychologists appropriately document written or oral consent, permission, and assent. (See also Standards 8.02, Informed Consent to Research; 9.03, Informed Consent in Assessments; and 10.01, Informed Consent to Therapy.)

8.02 Informed Consent to Research

a. When obtaining informed consent as required in Standard 3.10, Informed Consent, psychologists inform participants about (1) the purpose of the research, expected duration, and procedures; (2) their right to decline to participate and to withdraw from the research once participation has begun; (3) the foreseeable consequences of declining or withdrawing; (4) reasonably foreseeable factors that may be expected to influence their willingness to participate such as potential risks, discomfort, or adverse effects; (5) any prospective research benefits; (6) limits of confidentiality; (7) incentives for participation; and (8) whom to contact for questions about the research and research participants' rights. They provide opportunity for the prospective participants to ask questions and receive answers. (See also Standards 8.03, Informed Consent for Recording Voices and Images in Research; 8.05, Dispensing with Informed Consent for Research; and 8.07, Deception in Research.)

b. Psychologists conducting intervention research involving the use of experimental treatments clarify to participants at the outset of the research (1) the experimental nature of the treatment; (2) the services that will or will not be available in the control group(s) if appropriate; (3) the means by which assignment to treatment and control groups will be made; (4) available treatment alternatives if an individual does not wish to participate in the research or wishes to withdraw once a study has begun; and (5) compensation for or monetary costs of participating including, if appropriate, whether reimbursement from the participant or a third-party will be sought. (See also Standard 8.02a, Informed Consent to Research.)

8.03 Informed Consent for Recording Voice and Images in Research

Psychologists obtain informed consent from research participants prior to recording their voice or image for data collection unless (1) the research consists solely of naturalistic observation in public places and it is not anticipated that the recording will be used in a manner that would cause personal identification or harm or (2) the research design includes deception and consent is obtained during debriefing. (See also Standard 8.07, Deception in Research.)

8.04 Client/Patient, Student, and Subordinate Research Participants

a. When psychologists conduct research with clients/patients, students, or subordinates as participants, psychologists take steps to protect the prospective participants from adverse consequences of declining or withdrawing from participation.
b. When research participation is a course requirement or opportunity for extra credit, the prospective participant is given the choice of equitable alternative activities.

8.05 Dispensing with Informed Consent for Research

Psychologists may dispense with informed consent only (1) where research would not reasonably be assumed to create distress or harm and involves (a) the study of normal educational practices, curricula, or classroom management methods conducted in educational settings; (b) only anonymous questionnaires, naturalistic observation, or archival research for which disclosure of responses would not place participants at risk of criminal or civil liability or damage their financial standing, employability, or reputation, and confidentiality is protected; or (c) the study of factors related to job or organization effectiveness conducted in organizational settings for which there is not risk to participants' employability, and confidentiality is protected or (2) where otherwise permitted by law or federal or institutional regulations.

8.06 Offering Inducements for Research Participants

a. Psychologists make reasonable efforts to avoid offering excessive or inappropriate financial or other inducements for research participation, when such inducements are likely to coerce participation.
b. When offering professional services as an inducement for research participation, psychologists clarify the nature of the services, as well as the risks, obligations, and limitations. (See also Standard 6.05, Barter with Clients/Patients.)

4.01 Maintaining Confidentiality

Psychologists have a primary obligation and take reasonable precautions to protect confidential information obtained through or stored in any medium, recognizing that the extent and limits of confidentiality may be regulated by law or established by institutional rules or professional or scientific relationship. (See also Standard 2.05, Delegation of Work to Others.)

Commentary

- Potential research participants must be made aware of all aspects of the study that may influence their willingness to participate.
- Research participants must be allowed to withdraw their consent at any time without penalties.

- Individuals must not be pressured to participate in research.
- Informed consent must be obtained from legal guardians for individuals unable to provide consent (e.g., children, mentally impaired individuals); assent to participate should be obtained from individuals unable to provide informed consent.
- Researchers should consult with knowledgeable others, including an IRB, when deciding whether to dispense with informed consent, such as when research is conducted in public settings. These settings require special attention to protecting individuals' privacy
- Privacy refers to the rights of individuals to decide how information about them is to be communicated to others.

A substantial portion of the Ethics Code dealing with research is devoted to issues related to informed consent. This is appropriate because informed consent is an essential component of the social contract between the researcher and the participant. **Informed consent** is a person's explicitly expressed willingness to participate in a research project based on a clear understanding of the nature of the research, of the consequences of not participating, and of all factors that might be expected to influence that person's willingness to participate. Ethical research practice requires that research participants be fully informed about foreseeable factors that could influence their willingness to participate and they should know what they are consenting to do in the research project. Participants should also know that they are free to withdraw their consent at any time without penalty or prejudice. Researchers must also make reasonable efforts to respond to any questions the participants have about the research. In this way individuals can make an informed decision about their participation. Participants' consent must be given freely, without undue inducement or pressure. Researchers should always obtain informed consent. *Written informed consent is absolutely essential when participants are exposed to more than minimal risk.*

True informed consent cannot be obtained from certain individuals, such as the mentally impaired or emotionally disturbed, young children, and those who

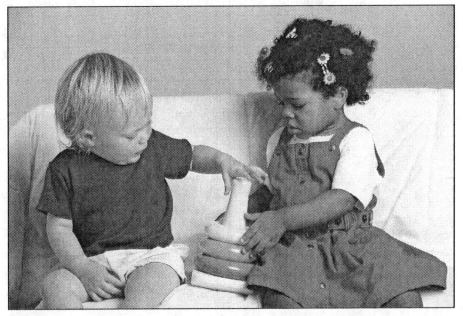

FIGURE 8.4   The issue of informed consent is especially important when children participate in research.

have limited ability to understand the nature of research and the possible risks. Whenever possible, "assent" should always be obtained from the participants themselves. In these cases, however, formal informed consent must be obtained from the participants' parents or legal guardians. Ethical guidelines like those involved with obtaining informed consent also raise methodological issues (see Adair, Dushenko, & Lindsay, 1985). For example, in one study the children of parents who did not provide parental consent for a research project were found to be academically less successful and less popular with their peers than were children of parents who did provide consent (Frame & Strauss, 1987). Studies like this one raise questions about whether findings obtained when studying children whose parents gave consent would also apply to children whose parents did not give parental consent. What is not in question, however, is that doing ethical research takes precedence over these possible methodological concerns.

Once again, online research poses particular ethical problems in this area. Consider that in most cases online participants typically click a button on their computer screen to indicate that they have read and understood the consent statement. But does this constitute a legally binding "signature" of the research participant? How does a researcher know if participants are really of legal age or that they fully understood the informed consent statement? One suggestion for determining whether participants have understood the informed consent statement is to administer short quizzes about its content; procedures to distinguish children from adults might include requiring information that is generally only available to adults (Kraut et al., 2004).

Consider the dilemma faced by a graduate student who was seeking to interview adolescents receiving services from a family planning clinic (Landers, 1988). Parental permission was not required for the teens to attend the clinic. Obtaining permission of parents before conducting research with minors is standard ethical practice and also is mandated by federal laws. Thus, if the investigator asked the parents for permission for their children to participate in the study, she would be revealing to the parents the teens' use of the clinic's services. The graduate student correctly sought advice from members of APA's Committee for the Protection of Human Participants in Research to help her make a decision regarding proper ethical procedures in this difficult case. The student used the expert advice to formulate the procedures that she proposed to use as part of her dissertation research. Whenever ethical dilemmas arise, it is wise to seek advice from knowledgeable professionals, but the *final responsibility for conducting ethical research always rests with the investigator.*

It is not always easy to decide what constitutes undue inducement or pressure to participate. Paying college students $9 an hour to take part in a psychology experiment would not generally be considered improper coercion. Recruiting very poor or disadvantaged persons from the streets with a $9 offer may be more coercive and less acceptable (Kelman, 1972). Prisoners may believe that any refusal on their part to participate in a psychology experiment will be viewed by the authorities as evidence of uncooperativeness and will therefore make it more difficult for them to be paroled. When college students are asked to fulfill a class requirement by serving as participants in psychology experiments (an experience that presumably has some educational value), an alternative method of earning class credit must be made available to those who do not wish to participate in psychological research. The time and effort required for these alternative options should be equivalent to that required for research participation. Alternative assignments that are used frequently include reading and summarizing journal articles describing research, making informal field observations of behavior, attending presentations of research findings by graduate students or faculty, and doing volunteer community service (see Kimmel, 1996).

IRBs require investigators to document that the proper informed consent procedure has been followed for any research involving human participants. In previous editions of this book we provided a sample consent form for use in minimal-risk research when deception is not involved. However, it is important to recognize that, as guidelines from the federal Office for Human Research Protections state, "informed consent is a process, not just a form" One IRB chairperson told us that she tells investigators to imagine they are sitting down with the person and explaining the project. Therefore, in this edition we provide some tips on the process of obtaining proper informed consent (see Box 8.1) and omit a sample form that may imply that "one form fits all." Proper consent procedures and written documentation will vary somewhat across situations and populations. Members of an IRB are a good source for advice on how to obtain and document informed consent in a way that meets ethical guidelines and protects the rights of the participants.

In some situations researchers are not required to obtain informed consent. The clearest example is when researchers are observing individuals' behavior in public places without any intervention. For instance, an investigator might

---

BOX 8.1

TIPS ON OBTAINING INFORMED CONSENT

A proper informed consent should clearly indicate the purpose or research question, the identity and affiliation of the researcher, procedures to be followed, risks/benefits associated with participation, compensation (if any), costs to the participants (if any), alternatives to research participation, procedures for maintaining confidentiality, that participation is voluntary and withdrawal can be made at any time without penalty, information about contacts if there are problems or questions, signatures of researcher(s) and participant, and the date of the research experience. Additional requirements will sometimes be added by the IRB depending on the situation. The federal Office for Human Research Protections (OHRP) has published "tips" to aid researchers in this process. Our adaptation of the OHRP tips follows. The complete text of the OHRP tips, as well as links to important related federal documents, can be obtained from: http://www. hhs.gov/ohrp/ humansubjects/guidance/ictips.htm

- Avoid scientific jargon or technical terms; the informed consent document should be written in language clearly understandable to the participant.
- Avoid use of the first person (e.g., "I understand that . . ." or "I agree to . . ."), as this can be interpreted as suggestive and incorrectly used as a substitute for sufficient factual information. Phrasing such as, "If you agree to participate, you will be asked to do the following," would be preferred. "Think of the document primarily as a teaching tool and not as a legal instrument."
- Describe the overall experience that will be encountered in a way that identifies the nature of the experience (e.g., how it is experimental),

as well as reasonably foreseeable harms, discomfort, inconveniences, and risks.
- Describe the benefits to the participants for their participation. If the benefits simply are helping society or science in general, that should be stated.
- Describe any alternatives to participation. If a college student "participant pool" is being tapped, then alternative ways to learn about psychological research must be explained.
- Participants must be told how personally identifiable information will be held in confidence. In situations where highly sensitive information is collected, an IRB may require additional safeguards such as a Certificate of Confidentiality.
- If research-related injury is possible in research that is more than minimal risk, then an explanation must be given regarding voluntary compensation and treatment.
- Legal rights of participants must not be waived. A "contact person" who is knowledgeable about the research must be identified so that participants who have post-research questions may have them answered. Questions may arise in any of the following three areas, *and these areas must be explicitly stated and addressed in the consent process and documentation*: the research experience, rights of the participants, and research-related injuries. At times this may involve more than one contact person, for example, referring the participant to the IRB or an institutional representative.
- A statement of voluntary participation must be included, which emphasizes the participant's right to withdraw from the research at any time without penalty.

want to gather evidence about race relations on a college campus by observing the frequency of mixed-race versus unmixed-race groups walking across campus. The investigator would not need to obtain students' permission before making the observations. Informed consent would be required, however, if the identity of specific individuals was going to be recorded.

Deciding when behavior is public or private is not always clear-cut. Diener and Crandall (1978) identify three major dimensions that researchers can consider to help them decide what information is private: the sensitivity of the information, the setting, and the method of dissemination of the information. Clearly, some kinds of information are more sensitive than others. Individuals interviewed about their sexual practices, religious beliefs, or criminal activities are likely to be more concerned about how the information will be used than those interviewed about who they believe will win the World Series.

The setting also plays a role in deciding whether behavior is public or private. Some behaviors, such as attending a concert, can reasonably be considered public. In public settings people give up a certain degree of privacy. Some behaviors that occur in public settings, however, are not easily classified as public or private. When you drive in your car, use a public bathroom, or enjoy a family picnic in the park, are these behaviors public or private? Is communication in an Internet "chatroom" public or private? Decisions about ethical practice in these situations depend on the sensitivity of the data being gathered and the ways in which the information, will be used.

When information is disseminated in terms of group averages or proportions, it is unlikely to reflect on specific individuals. In other situations, code systems can be used to protect participants' confidentiality. *Disseminating sensitive information about individuals or groups without their permission is a serious breach of ethics.* When potentially sensitive information about individuals has been collected without their knowledge (e.g., by a concealed observer), researchers can contact the individuals after the observations have been made and ask whether they can use the information. The researcher would not be able to use the information from participants who decline to give their permission. The most difficult decisions regarding privacy involve situations in which there is an obvious ethical problem on one dimension but not on the other two, or situations in which

FIGURE 8.5 Deciding what is public or what is private behavior is not always easy.

STRETCHING EXERCISE

The APA Code of Ethics states that psychologists may dispense with informed consent when research involves naturalistic observation (see Standard 8.05). As we have just seen, however, deciding when naturalistic observation is being done in a "public" setting is not always easy. Consider the following research scenarios and decide whether you think informed consent of participants should be required before the researcher begins the research. It may be that you will want more information from the researcher. If so, what additional information would you want before deciding whether informed consent is needed in the situation? You will see that requiring informed consent can have a dramatic effect on a research situation. Requiring informed consent, for example, can make it difficult for a researcher to record behavior under "natural" conditions. Such are the dilemmas of ethical decision making.

1. In a study of drinking behavior of college students, an undergraduate working for a faculty member attends a fraternity party and records the amount drunk by other students at the party.
2. As part of a study of the gay community, a gay researcher joins a gay baseball team with the goal of recording behaviors of participants in the context of team competition during the season. All the games are played in a city recreation league with the general public as spectators.
3. Public bathroom behavior (e.g., flushing, hand washing, littering, writing graffiti, etc.) of men and women is observed by male and female researchers concealed in the stalls of the respective restrooms.
4. A graduate student wants to investigate cheating behaviors of college students. He conceals himself in a projection booth in an auditorium where exams are administered to students in very large classes. From his vantage point he can see the movements of most students with the aid of binoculars. He records head movements, switching papers, passing notes, and other suspicious exam-taking behaviors.

there is a slight problem on all three dimensions. For instance, the behavior of individuals in the darkened setting of a movie theater would appear to have the potential of yielding sensitive information about the individual, but the setting could be reasonably classified as public.

Privacy refers to the rights of individuals to decide how information about them is to be communicated to others. The APA Ethics Code clearly states that "psychologists have a primary obligation and take reasonable precautions to protect confidential information obtained" from research participants (American Psychological Association, 2002, p. 1066). Whenever possible, the manner in which information about participants will be kept confidential should be explained to participants in psychological research so they may judge for themselves whether the safeguards taken to ensure their confidentiality are reasonable. Implementing the principle of informed consent requires that the investigator seeks to balance the need to investigate human behavior on the one hand with the rights of human participants on the other.

DECEPTION IN PSYCHOLOGICAL RESEARCH

- Deception in psychological research occurs when researchers withhold information or intentionally misinform participants about the research. By its nature, deception violates the ethical principle of informed consent, yet it is considered a necessary research strategy in certain areas of psychology.

The most controversial ethical issue related to research is deception. Some people argue that research participants should *never* be deceived because ethical practice requires that the relationship between experimenter and participant be open and honest. To some, deception is morally repugnant; it is no different from

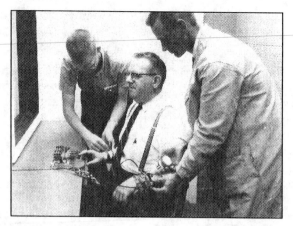

FIGURE 8.6 In the 1960s, participants in Stanley Milgram's experiments were not told that the purpose of the research was to observe people's obedience to authority and many followed instructions of the researcher to give severe electric shock to another human being.

lying. **Deception** can occur either through *omission*, the withholding of information, or *commission*, intentionally misinforming participants about an aspect of the research. Either kind of deception contradicts the principle of informed consent. Despite the increased attention given to deception in research over the last several decades, the use of deception in psychological research has not declined and remains a popular research strategy (Sharpe, Adair, & Roese, 1992). Skitka and Sargis (2005) surveyed social psychologists who used the Internet as a data collection tool and found that 27 percent of the reported studies involved deception of Internet participants.

APA Ethical Standards

8.07 *Deception in Research*

a. Psychologists do not conduct a study involving deception unless they have determined that the use of deceptive techniques is justified by the study's significant prospective scientific educational, or applied value and that effective nondeceptive alternative procedures are not feasible.

b. Psychologists do not deceive prospective participants about research that is reasonably expected to cause physical pain or severe emotional distress.

c. Psychologists explain any deception that is an integral feature of the design and conduct of an experiment to participants as early as is feasible, preferably at the conclusion of their participation, but no later than at the conclusion of the data collection, and permit participants to withdraw their data. (See also Standard 8.08, Debriefing.)

Commentary

- Deception is a necessary research strategy in some psychological research.
- Deceiving individuals in order to get them to participate in the research is always unethical.
- Researchers must carefully weigh the costs of deception against the potential benefits of the research when considering the use of deception.
- Researchers are ethically obligated to explain to participants their use of deception as soon as is feasible.

It is impossible to carry out certain kinds of research without withholding information from participants about some aspects of the research. In other situations, it is necessary to misinform participants in order to have them adopt certain attitudes or behaviors. For example, Kassin and Kiechel (1996) investigated factors affecting whether people will falsely confess to having done something that they did not do. Their goal was to understand what would lead criminal suspects to falsely confess to a crime. In their experiment, the participants' task was to type letters that were being read aloud. They were told not to hit the "Alt" key while typing because this would crash the computer. The computer was rigged to crash after a brief time and the experimenter accused the participant of hitting the "Alt" key. Even though none of the participants had hit the "Alt" key, nearly 70% of the participants signed a written confession that they had done so. If the participants had known in advance that the procedures were trying to elicit their false confessions, they probably would not have confessed. The disclosure required for informed consent would have made it impossible to study the likelihood that people would make a false confession. Although deception is sometimes justified to make it possible to investigate important research questions, deceiving participants for the purpose of getting them to participate in research that involves more than minimal risk is always unethical. As stated in the Ethics Code, *"Psychologists do not deceive prospective participants about research that is reasonably expected to cause physical pain or severe emotional distress"* (Standard 8.70b).

A goal of research is to observe people's normal behavior. A basic assumption underlying the use of deception is that sometimes it is necessary to conceal the true nature of an experiment so that participants will behave as they normally would or so they will act according to the instructions provided by the experimenter. A problem occurs, however, with frequent and casual use of deception (Kelman, 1967). If people believe that researchers often mislead participants, they may expect to be deceived when participating in a psychology experiment. Participants' suspicions about the research may prevent them from behaving as they normally would (see Box 8.2). This is exactly the opposite of what the researchers hope to achieve. Interestingly, Epley and Huff (1998) directly compared reactions of participants who were told or not told in a debriefing following the experiment that they had been deceived. Those who were told of the deception were subsequently more suspicious about future psychological research than were participants who were unaware of the deception. As the frequency of online research increases, it is important that researchers give particular attention to the use of deception, not only because of the potential for increasing the distrust of researchers by society's members, but also because deception has the potential to "poison" a vehicle (i.e., the Internet) that people use for social support and connecting with others (Skitka & Sargis, 2005).

Kelman (1972) suggests that, *before using deception, a researcher must give very serious consideration to (1) the importance of the study to our scientific knowledge, (2) the availability of alternative, deception-free methods, and (3) the "noxiousness" of the deception.* This last consideration refers to the degree of deception involved and to the possibility of injury to the participants. In Kelman's view: "Only if a study is very important and no alternative methods are available can anything more than the mildest form of deception be justified." *When deception is used, the researcher must inform participants in a debriefing after the experiment of the reasons for the deception, discuss any misconceptions they may have, and remove any harmful effects of the deception.* One goal of debriefing is to educate the participant about why the deception was necessary. Participants in the Kassin and Kiechel (1996) experiment on false confessions learned about the reasons for the use of deception in a debriefing. The participants reported that they found the study meaningful and that they thought their own contribution to the research was valuable.

BOX 8.2

TO DECEIVE OR NOT TO DECEIVE: THAT'S A TOUGH QUESTION

Researchers continue to use deceptive practices in psychological research (e.g., Sieber, Iannuzzo, & Rodriguez, 1995). The debate in the scientific community concerning the use of deception also has not abated (see, for example, Broder, 1998; Fisher & Fryberg, 1994; Ortmann & Hertwig, 1997). It is a complex issue, with those taking part in the debate sometimes at odds over the definition of deception (see Ortmann & Hertwig, 1998). Fisher and Fryberg (1994} summarized the debate as follows: "Ethical arguments have focused on whether deceptive research practices are justified on the basis of their potential societal benefit or violate moral principles of beneficence and respect for individuals and the fiduciary obligations of psychologists to research participants" (p. 417). This is quite a mouthful; so let us see if we can break it down,

A moral principle of "beneficence" refers to the idea that research activities should be beneficent (bring benefits) for individuals and society. If deception is shown to harm individuals or society, then the beneficence of the research can be questioned. The moral principle of "respect for individuals" is just that: People should be treated as persons and not "objects" for study, for example. This principle would suggest that people have a right to make their own judgments about the procedures and purpose of the research in which they are participating (Fisher & Fryberg, 1994). "Fiduciary obligations of psychologists" refer to the responsibilities of individuals who are given trust over others, even if only temporarily. In the case of psychological research, the researcher is considered to have responsibility for the welfare of participants during the study and for the consequences of their participation.

These ideas and principles can perhaps be illustrated through the arguments of Baumrind (1985), who argues persuasively that "the use of intentional deception in the research setting is unethical, imprudent, and unwarranted scientifically." Specifically, she argues that the costs to the participants, to the profession, and to society of the use of deception are too great to warrant its continued use. Although these arguments are lengthy and complex, let us attempt a brief summary. First, according to Baumrind, deception exacts a cost to participants because it undermines the participants' trust in their own judgment and in a "fiduciary" (someone who is holding something in trust

for another person). When research participants find they have been duped or tricked, Baumrind believes this may lead the participants to question what they have learned about themselves and to lead them to distrust individuals (e.g., social scientists) whom they might have previously trusted to provide valid information and advice. A cost to the profession is exacted because participants (and society at large) soon come to realize that psychologists are "tricksters" and not to be believed when giving instructions about research participation. If participants tend to suspect psychologists of lying, then one may question whether deception will work as it is intended by the researcher, a point raised earlier by Kelman (1972). Baumrind also argues that the use of deception reveals psychologists are willing to lie, which seemingly contradicts their supposed dedication to seeking truth. Finally, there is harm done to society because deception undermines people's trust in experts and makes them suspicious in general about all contrived events.

Of course, these are not the views of all psychologists (see Christensen, 1988; Kimmel, 1998). Milgram (1977), for instance, suggested that deceptive practices of psychologists are really a kind of "technical illusion" and should be permitted in the interests of scientific inquiry. After all, illusions are sometimes created in real-life situations in order to make people believe something. When listening to a radio program, people are not generally bothered by the fact that the thunder they hear or the sound of a horse galloping are merely technical illusions created by a sound effects specialist. Milgram argues that technical illusions should be permitted in the case of scientific inquiry. We deceive children into believing in Santa Claus. Why cannot scientists create illusions in order to help them understand human behavior?

Just as illusions are often created in real-life situations, in other situations, Milgram points out, there can be a suspension of a general moral principle. If we learn of a crime, we are ethically bound to report it to the authorities. On the other hand, a lawyer who is given information by a client must consider this information privileged even if it reveals that the client is guilty. Physicians perform very personal examinations of our bodies. Although it is morally permissible in a physician's office, the same type of behavior would not be condoned outside the office. Milgram argues that, in the interest of science, psychologists should occasionally be allowed to suspend the moral principle of truthfulness and honesty.

Those who defend deception point to studies showing that participants on the average do not appear to react negatively to being deceived (e.g., Christensen, 1988; Epley & Huff, 1998; Kimmel, 1996). Although people's "suspiciousness" about psychological research may increase, the overall effects seem to be small (see Kimmel, 1998). Nevertheless, the bottom line according to those who argue for the continued use of deception is well summarized by Kimmel (1998): "An absolute rule prohibiting the use of deception in all psychological research would have the egregious consequence of preventing researchers from carrying out a wide range of important studies." No one in the scientific community suggests that deceptive practices be taken lightly; however, for many scientists the use of deception is less noxious (to use Kelman's term) than doing without the knowledge gained by such studies.

What do you think about whether deception should be used in psychological research?

DEBRIEFING

- Researchers are ethically obligated to seek ways to benefit participants even after the research is completed. One of the best ways to accomplish this goal is by providing participants with a thorough debriefing.

Over the years, many researchers have fallen into the trap of viewing human participants in their research chiefly as means to an end. The researchers see participants as if they were "objects" from which researchers can obtain data in order to meet their own research goals. Researchers sometimes have considered that their responsibility to participants ends when the final data are collected. A handshake or "thank you" was frequently all that marked the end of the research session. Participants likely left with unanswered questions about the research situation and with only the vaguest idea of their role in the study. It is important when planning and conducting research to consider how the experience may affect the research participant after the research is completed, and to seek ways in which the participant can benefit from participation. These concerns follow directly from two of the moral principles identified in the Ethics Code, beneficence and respect for people's rights and dignity.

APA Ethical Standards

8.08 *Debriefing*

a. Psychologists provide a prompt opportunity for participants to obtain appropriate information about the nature, results, and conclusions of the -research, and they take reasonable steps to correct any misconceptions that participants may have of which the psychologists are aware.
b. If scientific or humane values justify delaying or withholding this information, psychologists take reasonable measures to reduce the risk of harm.
c. When psychologists become aware that research procedures have harmed a participant, they take reasonable steps to minimize the harm.

Commentary

- Debriefing benefits both participants and researchers.
- Debriefing informs participants about the nature of the research, their role in the study, and educates them about the research process. The overriding goal of debriefing is to have individuals feel good about their participation.

• Debriefing allows researchers to learn how participants viewed the procedures, allows potential insights into the nature of the research findings, and provides ideas for future research.

Earlier we discussed that protecting the confidentiality of participants' responses benefits both the participants (safeguarding them from social injury) and the researcher (e.g., by increasing the likelihood that participants will respond honestly). Similarly, **debriefing** participants at the end of a research session benefits both participants and the researcher (Blanck et al., 1992). When deception has been used in research, *debriefing is necessary to explain to participants the need for deception, to address any misconceptions participants may have about their participation, and to remove any harmful effects resulting from the deception. Debriefing also has the important goals of educating participants about the research (rationale, method, results) and of leaving them with positive feelings about their participation.* Researchers should provide opportunities for participants to learn more about their particular contribution to the research study and to feel more personally involved in the scientific process. For example, researchers can e-mail a report summarizing the study's findings to the participants when the study is completed. Following an online study, a researcher may post debriefing material at a website and even update these materials as new results come in (see Kraut et al., 2004).

Debriefing provides an opportunity for participants to learn more about research in general. For instance, participants can learn that their individual performance in a study is not a direct measure of their abilities. How well they perform on a memory test, for instance, is affected by how good a memory they have, but their performance is also affected by factors such as what the researcher asks them to remember and how they are tested. Because the educational value of participation in psychological research is used to justify the use of large numbers of volunteers from introductory psychology classes, researchers testing college students have an important obligation to ensure that research participation is an educational experience for students. Classroom instructors have sometimes built on the educational foundation of the debriefing and asked their students to reflect on their research experience by writing brief reports describing details about the

FIGURE 8.7   An informative debriefing is critical in ensuring that research participants have a good experience.

study's purpose, the techniques used, and the significance of the research to understanding behavior. An evaluation of one such procedure showed that students who wrote reports were more satisfied with their research experience and they gained a greater overall educational benefit from it than did students who did not write reports (Richardson, Pegalis, & Britton, 1992).

Debriefing helps researchers learn how participants viewed the procedures in the study. A researcher may want to find out whether participants perceived a particular experimental procedure in the way the investigator intended (Blanck et al., 1992). For example, a study of how people respond to failure may include tasks that are impossible to complete. If participants don't judge their performance as a failure, however, the researcher's hypothesis cannot be tested. Debriefing allows the investigator to find out whether participants perceived that they had failed at the tasks or whether they perceived that they had no chance to succeed.

When trying to learn participants' perceptions of the study, researchers shouldn't press them too hard. Research participants generally want to help with the scientific process. The participants may know that in psychological research information may be withheld from them. They may even fear that they will "ruin" the research if they reveal that they really did know important details about the study (e.g., the tasks really were impossible). To avoid this possible problem, debriefing should be informal and indirect. This is often best accomplished by using general questions in an open-ended format (e.g., What do you think this study was about? or What did you think about your experience in this research?). The researcher can then follow up with more specific questions about the research procedures. As much as possible, these specific questions should not cue the participant about what responses are expected (Orne, 1962).

Debriefing also benefits researchers because it can provide "leads for future research and help identify problems in their current protocols" (Blanck et al., 1992). Debriefing, in other words, can provide clues to the reasons for participants' performance, which may help researchers interpret the results of the study. What researchers learn in debriefings can also provide them with ideas for future research. Finally, participants sometimes detect errors in experimental materials—for instance, missing information or ambiguous instructions—and they can report these to the researcher during the debriefing. As we said, debriefing is good for both the participant and the researcher. Because a researcher is absent in an online research setting, an appropriate debriefing process may be difficult, and this aspect of Internet research adds to the list of ethical dilemmas posed by this kind of research (Kraut et al., 2004). The fact that online participants can easily withdraw from the study at any time is particularly troublesome in this regard. One suggestion is to program the experiment in such a way that a debriefing page is presented automatically if a participant prematurely closes the window (Nosek et al., 2002).

Researchers' responsibilities to educate people about their research are not limited to effective debriefing of participants. The goal of science to create change and improve the human condition entails an obligation for scientists to speak out on issues related to their research. Meeting this responsibility presents ethical challenges for scientists. Psychologists do research on important issues of social concern such as discrimination, violent behavior, and childhood sexual abuse. Issues of concern to society are often controversial issues that can be fiercely contested by people with differing political views. Individual researchers who present their research findings in the media risk criticism and even hostile reactions from people who strongly disagree with their conclusions. The American Psychological Society (APS) is making an effort to inform society about how psychological research can contribute constructively to issues of social concern. APS forms study groups made up of experts in an area of research related to an important social issue. The conclusions and recommendations formulated by these study groups are then published in the journal, *Psychological Science in the Public Interest*. Issues addressed in this way include the impact of class size on student achievement and the psychological science of making diagnostic decisions in areas such as predicting violence and diagnosing cancer.

RESEARCH WITH ANIMALS

Each year millions of animals are tested in laboratory investigations aimed at answering a wide range of important questions. New drugs are tested on animals before they are used with humans. Substances introduced into the environment are first given to animals to test their effects. Animals are exposed to diseases in order that investigators may observe symptoms and test various possible cures. New surgical procedures—especially those involving the brain—are often first tried on animals. Many animals are also studied in behavioral research, for example, by ethologists and experimental psychologists. For instance, animal models of the relationship between stress and diabetes have helped researchers to understand psychosomatic factors involved in diabetes (Surwit & Williams, 1996). These investigations yield much information that contributes to human welfare (Miller, 1985). In the process, however, many animals are subjected to pain and discomfort, stress and sickness, and death. Although rodents, particularly rats and mice, are the largest group of laboratory animals, researchers use a wide variety of species in their investigations, including monkeys, fish, dogs, and cats. Specific animals are frequently chosen because they provide good models for human responses. For example, psychologists interested in hearing sometimes use chinchillas as subjects because their auditory processes are very similar to those of humans.

APA Ethical Standards

8.09 Humane Care and Use of Animals in Research

a. Psychologists acquire, care for, use, and dispose of animals in compliance with current federal, state, and local laws and regulations, and with professional standards.

b. Psychologists trained in research methods and experienced in the care of laboratory animals supervise all procedures involving animals and are responsible for ensuring appropriate consideration of their comfort, health, and humane treatment.

c. Psychologists ensure that all individuals under their supervision who are using animals have received instruction in research methods and in the care, maintenance, and handling of the species being used, to the extent appropriate to their role. (See also Standard 2.05, Delegation of Work to Others.)

d. Psychologists make reasonable efforts to minimize the discomfort, infection, illness, and pain of animal subjects.

e. Psychologists use a procedure subjecting animals to pain, stress, or privation only when an alternative procedure is unavailable and the goal is justified by its prospective scientific, educational, or applied value.

f. Psychologists perform surgical procedures under appropriate anesthesia and follow techniques to avoid infection and minimize pain during and after surgery.

g. When it is appropriate that the animal's life be terminated, psychologists proceed rapidly, with an effort to minimize pain, and in accordance with accepted procedures.

Commentary

• Animals are used in research to gain knowledge that will benefit humans, for example, by helping to cure diseases.

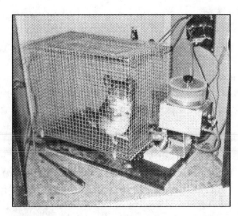 

FIGURE 8.8 Ethical guidelines for the use of animals in research address how animals may be treated before, during, and after they are tested.

- Researchers are ethically obligated to acquire, care for, use, and dispose of animals in compliance with current federal, state, and local laws and regulations, and with professional standards.
- The use of animals in research involves complex issues and is the subject of debate.

The use of animals as laboratory subjects has often been taken for granted. In fact, the biblical reference to humans' "dominion" over all lesser creatures is sometimes invoked to justify the use of animals as laboratory subjects (Johnson, 1990). More often, however, research with animal subjects is justified by the need to gain knowledge without putting humans in jeopardy. Most cures, drugs, vaccines, or therapies have been developed through experimentation on animals (Rosenfeld, 1981). Maestripieri and Carroll (1998) also point out that investigation of naturally occurring infant maltreatment in monkeys can inform scientists about child abuse and neglect.

Many questions, however, have been raised about the role of animal subjects in laboratory research (Novak, 1991; Shapiro, 1998; Ulrich, 1991). These questions include the most basic one, whether animals should be used at all in scientific investigations, as well as important questions about the care and protection of animal subjects. Clearly, according to the APA Ethics Code, *the researcher who uses animal subjects in an investigation has an ethical obligation to acquire, care for, use, and dispose of animals in compliance with federal, state, and local laws and regulations, and with professional standards.* Research with animals is a highly regulated enterprise with the overriding goal of protecting the welfare of research animals. Only individuals qualified to do research and to manage and care for the particular species should be allowed to work with the animals. When researchers expose animals to pain or discomfort, they must justify their procedures with any potential scientific, educational, or applied goals. As we noted earlier, animal review boards (IACUCs) are now in place at research facilities receiving funds from the Public Health Service. These committees determine the adequacy of the procedures for controlling pain, carrying out euthanasia, housing animals, and training personnel. IACUCs also determine whether experimental designs are sufficient to gain important new information and whether the use of an animal model is appropriate or whether nonanimal models could be used (Holden, 1987).

Partly in response to concerns expressed by members of animal rights groups during the 1980s, investigators must satisfy many federal, state, and local requirements, including inspection of animal facilities by veterinarians from the U.S. Department of Agriculture (see National Research Council, 1996). These regulations are often welcomed by members of the scientific community, and many animal researchers belong to groups that seek to protect laboratory animals. The APA has developed a list of specific guidelines to be followed when animal subjects are used in psychological research. These guidelines are at www.apa.org/science/anguide.html.

As with any ethically sensitive issue, however, compromises must be made with regard to the use of animals in research. For example, until alternatives to animal research can be found, the need to conduct research using animal subjects in order to battle human disease and suffering must be balanced against the need to protect the welfare of animals in laboratory research (Goodall, 1987). As APA's former chief executive officer, Raymond Fowler, pointed out, it is also important that the use of animal subjects not be restricted when the application of the research is not immediately apparent (Fowler, 1992). "The charges that animal research is of no value because it cannot always be linked to potential applications is a charge that can be made against all basic research." Such an indictment " "threatens the intellectual and scientific foundation" of all psychology, including both "scientists and practitioners."

Although few scientists disagree that restrictions are necessary to prevent needless suffering in animals, most want to avoid a quagmire of bureaucratic restrictions and high costs that will undermine research. Feeney (1987) suggests that severe restrictions and high costs, as well as the negative publicity (and occasional emotional demonstrations) directed toward individuals and institutions by extremists within the animal activist groups, may deter young scientists from entering the field of animal research. If this were to occur, the (presently) incurably ill or permanently paralyzed could possibly be deprived of the hope that can come through scientific research. Clearly, the issues surrounding the debate over the relevance of animal research to the human condition are many and complex (see Box 8.3). Ulrich (1992) said it well—the discussion of these issues must be approached with "wisdom and balance."

BOX 8.3

MORAL STATUS OF HUMANS AND NONHUMAN ANIMALS?

Ethical decision making often pits opposing philosophical positions against one another. This is clearly seen in the debate over the use of animals in research. At the center of this debate is the question of the "moral status" of humans and non-human animals. As the Australian philosopher Peter Singer (1990) points out, two generally accepted moral principles are:

1. All humans are equal in moral status.
2. All humans are of superior moral status to nonhuman animals.

Thus, Singer continues, "On the basis of these principles, it is commonly held that we should put human welfare ahead of the suffering of nonhuman animals; this assumption is reflected in our treatment of animals in many areas, including farming, hunting, experimentation, and entertainment."

Singer, however, does not agree with these commonly held views. He argues that "there is no rational ethical justification for always putting human suffering ahead of that of nonhuman animals" (p. 9). Unless we appeal to religious viewpoints (which Singer rejects as a basis for making decisions in a pluralistic society), there is, according to Singer, no special moral status to "being human." This position has roots in the philosophical tradition known as utilitarianism, which began with the writings of David Hume (1711–1776) and Jeremy Bentham (1748–1832), as well as John Stuart Mill (1806–1873) (Rachels, 1986). Basically, this viewpoint holds that whenever we have choices between alternative actions we should choose the one that has the best overall consequences (produces the most "happiness") for everyone involved. What matters in this view is whether the individual in question is capable of experiencing happiness/unhappiness, pleasure/pain; whether the individual is human or nonhuman is not relevant (Rachels, 1986).

What do you think about the moral status of humans and animals and its relation to psychological research?

REPORTING OF PSYCHOLOGICAL RESEARCH

- Investigators attempt to communicate their research findings in peer-reviewed scientific journals, and the APA Code of Ethics provides guidelines for this process.

A completed research study begins its journey toward becoming part of the scientific literature when the principal investigator writes a manuscript for submission to one of the dozens of psychology-related scientific journals. The primary goal of publishing research in a psychology journal is to communicate the results of the study to members of the scientific community and to society in general. Publishing research in journals is also a way to enhance the researcher's reputation and even the reputation of the institution that sponsored the research. But getting the results of a scientific investigation published is not always an easy process, especially if the researcher wants to publish in one of the more prestigious scientific journals. Journals sponsored by APA, such as the *Journal of Counseling Psychology, Journal of Educational Psychology, Journal of Experimental Psychology: Learning, Memory, and Cognition,* and *Psychological Review,* have an average rejection rate of 71% with rejection rates as high as 90% (American Psychological Association, 2001).

Manuscripts submitted for publication must be prepared in a style that conforms to the APA *Publication Manual,* must meet rigorous methodological and substantive criteria, and must be appropriate for the particular journal to which the manuscript is submitted. Serious problems in any of these three areas can be sufficient to deny publication, but manuscripts are more likely to be rejected because of problems in the methodology of the study, problems in the statistical treatment of the results, or because the results do not make a significant enough contribution to scientific progress in the field of research related to the particular journal. Decisions about the acceptability of a scientific manuscript are made by the journal's editors, usually on the basis of peer review. *Peer review* involves comments made by several experts in the field who have been asked by the editors for their opinions about the manuscript's scientific value. Researchers need to publish in order to gain professional advancement. In light of these pressures, it is imperative that all scientists adhere strictly to the Code of Ethics governing the reporting of results.

APA Ethical Standards

8.10 Reporting Research Results

a. Psychologists do not fabricate data. (See also Standard 5.Ola, Avoidance of False or Deceptive Statements.)
b. If psychologists discover significant errors in their published data, they take reasonable steps to correct such errors in a correction, retraction, erratum, or other appropriate publication means.

8.11 Plagiarism

Psychologists do not present portions of another's work or data as their own, even if the other work or data source is cited occasionally.

8.12 Publication Credit

a. Psychologists take responsibility and credit, including authorship credit, only for work they have actually performed or to which they have substantially contributed. (See also Standard 8.12b, Publication Credit.)
b. Principal authorship and other publication credits accurately reflect the relative scientific or professional contributions of the individuals involved, regardless of their relative status. Mere possession of an institutional position,

such as department chair, does not justify authorship credit. Minor contributions to the research or to the writing for publications are acknowledged appropriately, such as in footnotes or in an introductory statement.

c. Except under exceptional circumstances, a student is listed as principal author on any multiple-authored article that is substantially based on the student's doctoral dissertation. Faculty advisors discuss publication credit with students as early as feasible and throughout the research and publication process as appropriate. (See also Standard 8.12a, Publication Credit.)

8.13 Duplicate Publication of Data

Psychologists do not publish, as original data, data that have been previously published. This does not preclude repub-lishing data when they are accompanied by proper acknowledgment.

8.14 Sharing Research Data for Verification

a. After research results are published, psychologists do not withhold the data on which their conclusions are based from other competent professionals who seek to verify the substantive claims through reanalysis and who intend to use such data only for that purpose, provided that the confidentiality of the participants can be protected and unless legal rights concerning proprietary data preclude their release. This does not preclude psychologists from requiring that such individuals or groups be responsible for costs associated with the provision of such information.

b. Psychologists who request data from other psychologists to verify the substantive claims through reanalysis may use shared data only for the declared purpose. Requesting psychologists obtain prior written agreement for all other uses of the data.

8.15 Professional Reviewers

Psychologists who review material submitted for presentation, publication, grant, or research proposal review respect the confidentiality of and the proprietary rights in such information of those who submitted it.

Commentary

- Decisions about who should receive publication credit are based on the scholarly importance of the contribution.
- Ethical reporting of research requires recognizing the work of others using proper citations and references; failure to do so may result in plagiarism.
- Proper citation includes using quotation marks when material is taken directly from a source and citing secondary sources when an original source is not consulted.

When a scientific investigation is complete, the investigator usually prepares a manuscript to submit to a professional journal. The ethical standards covering the reporting of the results of a scientific investigation seem more straightforward than in the other areas of the Ethics Code we have discussed. Even here, however, ethical decisions regarding such issues as assigning credit for publication and plagiarism are not always clear-cut. Conducting a research study often involves many people. Colleagues offer suggestions about a study's design, graduate or undergraduate students assist an investigator by testing participants and organizing data, technicians construct specialized equipment, and expert consultants give advice about statistical analyses. When preparing a manuscript for publication, should all these individuals be considered "'authors" of the research? *Publication credit* refers to the process of identifying as authors those individuals who have made significant contributions to the research project. Because authorship of a published scientific study frequently is used to measure an individual's competence and motivation in a scientific field, *it is important to acknowledge fairly those who have contributed to a project.*

It's not always easy to decide whether the contribution an individual has made to a research project warrants being an "author" of a scientific paper or whether that individual's contribution should be acknowledged in a less visible way (such as in a footnote). Also, once authorship is granted, then the order of authors' names must also be decided. "First author" of a multiple-authored article generally indicates a greater contribution than does "second author" (which is greater than third, etc.). Authorship decisions should be based mainly in terms of the scholarly importance of the contribution (e.g., aiding the conceptual aspects of a study), not by the time and energy invested in the study (e.g., Fine & Kurdek, 1993).

Ethical concerns associated with the assigning of authorship can take many forms. For example, not only is it unethical for a faculty member to take credit for a student's work, it is also unethical for students to be given undeserved author credit. This latter situation may arise, for instance, in a misguided attempt by a faculty mentor to give a student an edge when competing for a position in a competitive graduate program. According to Fine and Kurdek (1993), awarding students undeserved author credit may falsely represent the student's expertise, give the student an unfair advantage over peers, and, perhaps, lead others to create impossible expectations for the student. These authors recommend that faculty and students collaborate in the process of determining authorship credit and discuss early on in the project what level of participation warrants author credit. Due to differences in faculty-student power and position, the faculty member should initiate discussions regarding authorship credit for student contributors (see Behnke, 2003).

There is one additional ethical issue related to authorship. As we described earlier, researchers must protect participants' right to privacy by keeping the information they gain from participants confidential. Authors also have a right to privacy when it comes to their ideas. Reviewers of manuscripts that have been submitted for publication or for a research grant must respect the author's right to privacy by maintaining the confidentiality of the information in submitted manuscripts.

A rather troublesome area of concern in the reporting of research, not only for some professionals but frequently for students, is **plagiarism**. Again, the ethical standard seems clear enough: Don't present substantial portions or elements of another's work as your own. But what constitutes "substantial portions or elements," and how does one avoid giving the impression that another's work is one's own? Making these decisions can be like walking a tightrope. On one side is the personal goal of being recognized for making a scholarly contribution; on the other side is the ethical obligation to recognize the previous contributions others have made. The fact that both professionals and students commit acts of plagiarism suggests that many people too often veer from the tightrope by seeking their own recognition instead of giving due credit to the work of others.

Sometimes acts of plagiarism result from sloppiness (failing to double-check a source to verify that an idea that is presented did not originate with someone else, for example). Errors of this kind are still plagiarism; *ignorance is not a legitimate excuse.* Mistakes can be made all too easily. For example, researchers (and students) occasionally ask "how much" of a passage can be used without putting it in quotation marks or otherwise identifying its source. A substantial element can be a single word or short phrase if that element serves to identify a key idea or concept that is the result of another's thinking. Because there is no clear guideline for how much material constitutes a substantial element of a work, students must be particularly careful when referring to the work of others. At times, especially among students, plagiarism can result from failure to use quotation marks around passages taken directly from a source. *Whenever material is taken directly from a source, it must be placed in quotation marks and the source must be properly identified.* It is also important to cite the source of material you include in your paper when you paraphrase the material. *The ethical principle is that you must cite the sources of your ideas when you use the exact words and when you paraphrase.*

Plagiarism also occurs when individuals fail to acknowledge secondary sources. A *secondary source* is one that discusses other (original) work. Secondary sources include textbooks and published reviews of research such as those that appear in scientific journals like the *Psychological Bulletin.* When your only source for an idea or findings comes from a secondary source it is always unethical to report that information in *a way that suggests you consulted the original work.* It is far better to try to locate and read the original source rather than citing a secondary source. If that is not possible, you must inform the reader that you did not read the original source by using a phrase like "as cited in. . ." when referring to the original work. By citing the secondary source, you are telling the reader that you are presenting another person's interpretation of the original material. Again, ignorance concerning the proper form of citation is not an acceptable excuse, and on unfortunate occasions researchers—professors as well as students—have seen their careers ruined by accusations of plagiarism.

STEPS FOR ETHICAL DECISION MAKING

Should research participants be placed at risk of serious injury to gain information about bystander apathy? Should psychologists use deception to learn about the causes of false confessions? Is it acceptable to make animals suffer in order to learn about human drug addiction? These questions require answers; however, you no doubt realize by now that the answers are not easy. It is often unclear what the "right" answer is or even if there is a right answer.

In the face of this uncertainty, researchers and groups such as IRBs and IACUCs can benefit by having an overall plan for approaching ethical decision making. By following a series of steps, researchers can think critically about the ethical issues. Critical thinking about these issues will help protect the rights and welfare of humans and the welfare of animals in research. The following steps are based on reading the ethics literature, and discussions with philosophers involved in ethical decision making.*

1. Find out all the facts of the situation. In other words, determine exactly what is involved in terms of important aspects of the study such as the nature of the participants and the proposed procedure.
2. Identify the relevant ethical issues. An important part of this inquiry will be consulting ethical guidelines that are available, such as the APA Ethics Code we have excerpted in this chapter, as well as policy statements from various professional organizations. Also, make sure you are aware of local, state, and federal regulations or laws that apply to the research area.
3. Decide what is at stake for all parties involved (participants, researchers, institutions). This will mean taking different viewpoints, for example, by asking what is at stake from a scientific point of view, from society's viewpoint, from the view of participants, and from an overall moral viewpoint.
4. Identify alternative methods or procedures, discussing the consequences of each alternative, including their ethical implications. As part of this discussion, consider the consequences of *not* doing the proposed research. Examine the practical constraints of each alternative.

*We wish to acknowledge the contributions in this section of various members of the Loyola University of Chicago Center for Ethics, especially David Ozar, Mark Waymack, and Patricia Werhane.

5. Decide on the action to be taken. Judge the "correctness" of your decision not in terms of whether it makes you feel happy (you may not), but, rather, in terms of the process that was followed. Is it the best that can be done given the circumstances?

SUMMARY

Psychological research raises many ethical questions. Thus, before beginning a research project, you must consider both the specific ethical issues from the APA Ethics Code and the laws and regulations that are relevant to your project. In most cases formal institutional approval—for example, from an IRB or IACUC—must be obtained before beginning to do research. One function of an IRB is to reach a consensus regarding the risk/benefit ratio of the proposed research. Risk can involve physical, psychological, or social injury. Informed consent must be obtained from human participants in most psychological research. Researchers must take special safeguards to protect human participants when more than minimal risk is present and to provide appropriate debriefing following their participation. Serious ethical questions arise when researchers withhold information from participants or misinform them about the nature of the research. When deception is used, debriefing should inform participants about the reasons for having used deception. Debriefing can also help participants feel more fully involved in the research situation as well as help the researcher learn how the participants perceived the treatment or task. Online research presents new ethical dilemmas for a researcher, and consultation with IRB members, as well as researchers experienced with Internet data collection, is urged prior to planning such a study.

Psychologists testing animal subjects must obey a variety of federal and state guidelines and, in general, must protect the welfare of the animals. Animals may be subjected to pain or discomfort only when alternative procedures are not available and when the goals of the research are judged to justify such procedures in terms of the scientific, educational, or applied value of the research. Reporting of psychological findings should be done in a manner that gives appropriate credit to the individuals who contributed to the project. When previously published work contributes to an investigator's thinking about a research study, the investigator must acknowledge this contribution by properly citing the individuals who reported the previous work. Failure to do so represents a serious ethical problem of plagiarism.

KEY CONCEPTS

risk/benefit ratio
minimal risk
informed consent
privacy

deception
debriefing
plagiarism

REVIEW QUESTIONS

1. Explain why researchers submit research proposals to Institutional Review Boards (IRBs) or Institutional Animal Care and Use Committees (lACUCs) before beginning a research project and briefly describe the functions of these committees in the research process.

2. Explain how the risk/benefit ratio is used in making ethical decisions. Briefly describe the characteristics of a research project that are used to assess its potential benefit.

3. Explain why research cannot be risk free and describe the standard that researchers use to determine whether research participants are "at risk." Describe briefly how characteristics of the participants in the research can affect the assessment of risk.

4. Differentiate among the three possible types of risk that can be present in psychological research: physical, psychological, social. How do researchers typically safeguard against the possibility of social risk?

5. What are three important ethical issues raised by online research?

6. What information does the researcher have an ethical obligation to make clear to the participant in order to ensure the participant's informed consent? Under what conditions does the APA Ethics Code indicate that informed consent may not be necessary?

7. What three dimensions do Diener and Crandall (1978) recommend that researchers consider when they attempt to decide whether information is public or private?

8. Explain why deception may sometimes be necessary in psychological research. Describe briefly the questions researchers should ask before using deception and describe the conditions under which it is always unethical to deceive participants.

9. In what ways can debriefing benefit the participant? In what ways can debriefing benefit the researcher?

10. What ethical obligations are specified in the APA Ethics Code for researchers who use animals in their research?

11. What two conditions are required by the APA Ethics Code before animals may be subjected to stress or pain?

12. Explain how researchers decide when an individual can be credited as an author of a published scientific report.

13. Describe the procedures an author must follow to avoid plagiarism when citing information from an original source or from a secondary source.

CHALLENGE QUESTIONS

Note: No answers to the Challenge Questions or Stretching Exercises are provided in this chapter. To resolve ethical dilemmas, you must be able to apply the appropriate ethical standards and to reach an agreement regarding the proposed research after discussion with others whose backgrounds and knowledge differ from your own. You will therefore have to consider points of view different from your own.

We urge you to approach these problems as part of a group discussion of these important issues.

The first two challenge questions for this chapter include a hypothetical research proposal involving a rationale and method similar to that of actual published research. To answer these questions, you will need to be familiar with the APA ethical principles and other material on ethical decision making presented in this chapter, including the

recommended steps for decision making that were outlined at the end of this chapter. As you will see, your task is to decide whether specific ethical standards have been violated and to make recommendations regarding the proposed research, including the most basic recommendation of whether the investigator should be allowed to proceed.

1. IRB Proposal

Instructions Assume you are a member of an Institutional Review Board (IRB). Besides yourself, the committee includes a clinical psychologist, a social psychologist, a social worker, a philosopher, a Protestant minister, a history professor, and a respected business executive in the community. The following is a summary of a research proposal that has been submitted to the IRB for review. You are asked to consider what questions you might want to ask the investigator and whether you would approve carrying out the study at your institution in its present form, whether modification should be made before approval, or whether the proposal should not be approved. (An actual research proposal submitted to an IRB would include more details than we present here.)

Rationale Psychological conformity occurs when people accept the opinions or judgments of others in the absence of significant reasons to do so or in the face of evidence to the contrary. Previous research has investigated the conditions under which conformity is likely to occur and has shown, for example, that conformity increases when people anticipate unpleasant events (e.g., shock) and when the pressure to conform comes from individuals with whom the individuals identify. The proposed research examines psychological conformity in the context of discussions about alcohol consumption among teenage students. The goal of the research is to identify factors that contribute to students' willingness to attend social events where alcohol is served to minors and to allow obviously intoxicated persons to drive an automobile. This research seeks to investigate conformity in a natural setting and in circumstances where unpleasant events (e.g., legal penalties, school suspension, injury, or even death) can be avoided by not conforming to peer pressure.

Method The research will involve 36 high school students between the ages of 16 and 18 who have volunteered to participate in a research project investigating "beliefs and attitudes of today's high school students." Participants will be assigned to four-person discussion groups. Each person in the group will be given the same 20 questions to answer; however, they will be asked to discuss each question with members of the group before writing down their answers. Four of the 20 questions deal with alcohol consumption by teenagers and with possible actions that might be taken to reduce teenage drinking and driving. One member of the group will be appointed discussion leader by the principal investigator. Unknown to the participants, they will be assigned randomly to three different groups. In each group, there will be either 0,1, or 2 students who are actually working for the principal investigator. Each of these "confederates" has received prior

instructions from the investigator regarding what to say during the group discussion of the critical questions about teenage drinking. (The use of confederates in psychological research) Specifically, confederates have been asked to follow a script which presents the argument that the majority of people who reach the legal driving age (16), and all individuals who are old enough (18) to vote in national elections and serve in the armed forces, are old enough to make their own decisions about drinking alcohol; moreover, because it is up to each individual to make this decision, other individuals do not have the right to intervene if someone under the legal age chooses to drink alcohol. Each of the confederates "admits" to drinking alcohol on at least two previous occasions. Thus, the experimental manipulation involves either 0,1, or 2 persons in the four-person groups suggesting they do not believe students have a responsibility to avoid situations where alcohol is served to minors or to intervene when someone chooses to drink and drive. The effect of this argument on the written answers given by the actual participants in this experiment will be evaluated. Moreover, audiotapes of the sessions will be made without participants' knowledge, and the contents of these audiotapes will be analyzed. Following the experiment, the nature of the deception and the reasons for making audiotapes of the discussions will be explained to the participants.

2. IACUC Proposal

Instructions Assume you are a member of an Institutional Animal Care and Use Committee (IACUC). Besides yourself, the committee includes a veterinarian, a biologist, a philosopher, and a respected business executive in the community. The following is a summary of a research proposal that has been submitted to the IACUC for review. You are asked to consider what questions you might want to ask the investigator and whether you would approve carrying out this study at your institution in its present form, whether modification should be made before approval, or whether the proposal should not be approved. (An actual research proposal submitted to an IACUC would include more details than we present here.)

Rationale The investigators seek to investigate the role of subcortical structures in the limbic system in moderating emotion and aggression.

(continued)

This proposal is based on previous research from this laboratory which has shown a significant relationship between damage in various subcortical brain areas of monkey subjects and changes in eating, aggression, and other social behaviors (e.g., courtship). The areas under investigation are those that sometimes have been excised in psychosurgery with humans when attempting to control hyperaggressive and assaultive behaviors. Moreover, the particular subcortical area that is the focus of the present proposal has been hypothesized to be involved in controlling certain sexual activities that are sometimes the subject of psychological treatment (e.g., hypersexuality). Previous studies have been unable to pinpoint the exact areas thought to be involved in controlling certain behaviors; the proposed research seeks to improve on this knowledge.

Method   Two groups of rhesus monkeys will be the subjects. One group ($N = 4$) will be a control group. These animals will undergo a sham operation, which involves anesthetizing the animals and drilling a hole in the skull. These animals then will be tested and evaluated in the same manner as the experimental animals. The experimental group will undergo an operation to lesion a small part of a subcortical structure known as the amygdala. Two of the animals will have lesions in one site; the remaining two will receive lesions in another site of this structure. After recovery, all animals will be tested on a variety of tasks measuring their food preferences, social behaviors with same and opposite-sex monkeys (normals), and emotional responsiveness (e.g., reactions to a novel fear stimulus: an experimenter in a clown face). The animals will be housed in a modern animal laboratory; the operations will be performed and recovery monitored by a licensed veterinarian. After testing, the experimental animals will be sacrificed and the brains prepared for histological examination. (Histology is necessary to confirm the locus and extent of lesions.) The control animals will not be killed; they will be returned to the colony for use in future experiments.

3. Research done by Stanley Milgram on compliance has led to a great deal of discussion about the ethical issues surrounding the use of deception in psychological research (see Box 8.2). Compliance involves the likelihood that a person will follow instructions given by an authority figure. For Part A of this question you are to read a summary describing the basic procedure Milgram used in his experiments. Then you are to treat this summary as if it were a research proposal submitted to an IRB of which you are a member. For the second part of the question you are to consider the additional information in Part B about Milgram's research on compliance using this paradigm. Then you are to explain why you would or would not change the decision you made based on your review in Part A.

A. Two people come to a psychology laboratory supposedly to participate in a learning experiment. They are told that the study was concerned with the effects of punishment on learning. The individuals drew slips of paper to determine who would be the "teacher" and who would be the "learner." One person was actually an accomplice of the principal investigator, and the drawing was rigged so that the real participant in the experiment was always given the role of teacher. The participant watched as the learner was taken to an adjacent room and strapped into a chair and an electrode was attached to the wrist. The participant then heard the experimenter say that the learner would receive an electric shock for every error made while learning a list of word pairs. The teacher was then taken to the laboratory room, which housed an impressive-looking shock generator with 30 lever switches. Each switch was labeled with a voltage designation (ranging from 15 to 450 volts), and next to the switches were verbal labels describing the amount of shock, for example, "Slight Shock," "Strong Shock," "Danger, Severe Shock." Two switches after the last verbal description were simply marked XXX. The teacher was given a sample shock and told to administer the electric shock to the learner whenever the learner made a mistake. The learner's responses were communicated via a set of four switches that lit up a number on the top of the shock generator. The teacher was also told to move one lever higher on the shock generator after each wrong response. As the experiment progressed, the learner offered various protests to the shock. These complaints could be heard through the walls of the room and included shouts to the effect that the shocks were becoming painful, and, later, that the learner wanted the experimenter to end the procedure. When the teacher moved the switch at 180 volts, the learner yelled, "I can't stand it any more" and at the 270 volts gave an agonizing scream. At 300 volts the learner yelled, "I will not give any more answers" but continued to scream. After the switch corresponding to 330 volts was pressed, the learner was not heard from anymore. The learner was not actually shocked, and the major dependent variable was the maximum shock that the participant would give in response to the "orders" of the experimenter. All participants were debriefed after the experiment and, at times, the researcher talked with a participant for some length of time. All participants also received a follow-up questionnaire. Before conducting the experiment Milgram described his planned procedure to 37 psychiatrists; none predicted that participants would administer the most shock.

B. Milgram conducted more than a dozen experiments using this procedure (see Milgram, 1974). In an experiment when the teacher could hear the screams of the learner but not actually see the learner, approximately 60% of the participants gave the learner the maximum shock. The major justification for continuing this line of research after such an unexpected finding was that no participants were apparently seriously injured by the experiment and that an overwhelming majority (84%) said they were glad to have been in the experiment. Many participants (74%) responded to the follow-up questionnaire saying that they had gained something of personal value from the experience. In subsequent experiments Milgram found that the likelihood of participants complying was affected by situational factors. For example, participants were less likely to comply when the learner was in the room with the teacher and participants were least likely to administer the highest shock when the teacher could choose the level of voltage. One interpretation of the original finding is that people will readily comply—they behave like proverbial

sheep. A different view of people's willingness to comply is evidenced by the findings of the entire series of experiments. Milgram demonstrated that people are sensitive to many aspects of the situation in which they are asked to comply. A question remains. Does the benefit of what we have learned about people's tendencies to comply based on Milgrim's findings warrant the risks that his paradigm entails? More generally, how can IRBs best estimate the potential benefits of proposed research when it is impossible for them to use the outcome of the research in their assessment of its potential benefits?

4. Consider the following scenario presented by Fine and Kurdek (1993) as part of their discussion of the issue of determining authorship of a publication.

An undergraduate student asked a psychology faculty member to supervise an honors thesis. The student proposed a topic, the faculty member primarily developed the research methodology, the student collected and entered the data, the faculty member conducted the statistical analyses, and the student used part of the analyses for the thesis. The student wrote the thesis under very close supervision by the faculty member. After the honors thesis was completed, the faculty member decided that data from the entire project were sufficiently interesting to warrant publication as a unit. Because the student did not have the skills necessary to write the entire study for a scientific journal, the faculty member did so. The student's thesis contained approximately one-third of the material presented in the article.

A. Explain what factors of the situation you would consider to determine if the student should be an author of any publication resulting from this work or if the student's work should be acknowledged in a footnote to the article.

B. If you decide that the student should be an author, explain whether you think the student should be first author or the second author of the article.

Chapter 9

A Love Affair with the Brain: A Conversation with Marian Diamond

Janet L. Hopson   *November 1984*

Thirty years of research confirms the lifelong plasticity of the brain.

It's a lucky thing that Marian Cleeves Diamond refused to take her father's advice. British physician Montague Cleeves had settled in the sagebrush foothills north of Los Angeles in the 1920s to practice medicine and rear a family. When his sixth and youngest child reached adolescence, he counseled her to do the "ladylike thing" and become a housewife. But Marian followed her instincts and pursued a career in science in addition to raising four children. With extraordinary energy she worked her way through the cool reception and professional put-downs experienced as a Ph.D. candidate during the 1950s. This same energy helped her become the first female associate dean of the College of Letters and Sciences at the University of California at Berkeley; to produce nearly 100 publications in the field of neuroanatomy; to teach thousands of students, from grade-schoolers to postdoctorates; and to receive more than a dozen awards for scholarship, teaching, and community service. Had her father prevailed, modern science might never have learned some important facts about the brain.

In her best-known research, Diamond and a team of colleagues at Berkeley made a dramatic discovery that contradicted previous notions about the mammalian brain: They found that if a young rat is placed in an environment enriched with toys and playmates, its cortex will begin to thicken after just a few days. More recently, Diamond and her coworkers found that the same principle applies to aged rats—the equivalent of 75-to 90 year-old people. Diamond calls this the "plasticity" of the cortex and draws a straightforward conclusion: Use it or lose it.

Diamond is a vibrant 56-year-old with an implacable dedication to teaching and brain research. Her "love affair with the brain" began nearly four decades ago when, on hospital rounds with her father, she chanced to see a naked brain lying on a table.

Janet L. Hopson

Hopson: Many people would have been shocked at seeing a disembodied brain, and yet it fascinated you. Why?

Diamond: It's because that mass of protoplasm has the capacity to think. We still don't understand what thinking is. But to this day, it fascinates me when I meet people and I imagine the brains inside their skulls. No other organ can store information for 100 years to the degree the brain can. With the intricacies and original creation of ideas that come from the human brain, it is unquestionably the most esoteric functional mass on Earth.

"The human brain . . . is unquestionably the most esoteric functional mass on earth."

Hopson: When you began trying to change an animal's brain by changing its environment, did most biologists believe such changes were possible?

Diamond: No. The general conception in the 1960s, and of course before, was that the brain did not change—that it was a stable structure—and after it developed, it retained its size and eventually decreased. Nutritionists, for example, never included the head in their studies because they felt the brain was so stable.

Hopson: Considering that background, wasn't it a somewhat radical notion to look for environmentally induced changes?

Diamond: There's actually a logical history behind it. Back in the 1920s, Richard Tryon, of the University of California at Berkeley, noticed that some rats ran mazes better than other rats. He bred those rats and developed a "maze-bright" strain of rats. Almost 35 years later, it was David Krech and Melvin Calvin of Berkeley, walking in the hills of Norway one day, who wondered, "If the rats run mazes differently, could their brain chemistry be different?" Krech came back to California and, working with Mark Rosenzweig and Edward Bennett, showed that there was a chemical difference between these strains of rats.

Hopson: How did you get involved in this work?

Diamond: I was at Cornell in the late 1950s and read their paper in *Science*. I thought, that's what I've been waiting for! I came out and joined the team, and this whole enrichment project grew out of that original brain chemistry experiment. Since there was a chemical difference, we wondered whether you could change that chemistry and structure by designing the environment a different way.

Hopson: And you found that you could?

Diamond: Yes. We found that by placing young rats in an enriched environment, we could change the chemistry and structure of the outer layers of the brain, the cortex. After autopsies, we could actually measure an increase in cortical thickness. We later learned we could bring about such changes in only four days.

Hopson: How did you know how to enrich a rat's environment?

Diamond: Donald Hebb in Montreal pioneered the idea of an enriched environment with a bigger cage and playmates. Then you added almost anything—wheels, ladders, blocks—any object the animals can explore. They climb on them, sniff them, crawl under them, explore with their whole sense mechanism.

Hopson: Why does exploring lead to an enlarged cortex?

Diamond: We really don't know what the crucial factors are in inducing the changes. But we know that the cortical thickening is not just the result of a motor response, because if the animals are placed in running wheels alone, they do not experience the cortical change.

Hopson: What does thickening the cortex actually mean?

Diamond: See that picture over there with all the dots? That is one square millimeter of brain tissue that we've blown up to poster size so we can count the cells and find out if a particular area is changing in cortical depth. If it is, we find that the neurons have increased in area but not in number. The glial, or support, cells have divided. The dendrites have grown. There is an increase in dendritic spines. And the post-synaptic thickening has increased in length. So, in other words, every part of the nerve cell has enlarged, and there has been an increase in the number of support cells.

Hopson: Is there proof that rats with cortical thickening are any smarter?

Diamond: They've been exposed to mazes in many laboratories, and they do run a better maze.

Hopson: Are there measures other than maze running?

Diamond: Most researchers measure rat intelligence with maze running—perhaps it's a limitation of us investigators, but maze running does give you a baseline to compare with other rats, and other researchers can know exactly how well the enriched rats have done.

Hopson: What was the impact of your enrichment work?

Diamond: The new idea that the brain is measurably responsive to the environment has been applied with brain-injured people, giving us more hope for the recovery of brain function. And it's helped us to understand the potential of early training. Some teachers and school principals have even told me that it changed their whole view of education.

Hopson: After "enriched rats" grow up and reproduce, do their pups have larger brains?

Diamond: We've been studying this question recently, and we found that rat pups from the enriched parents have increased body weight at birth, but the cortex does not show significant change. Then we wondered if we would see cortical differences when those pups grew up. And we did!

Hopson: Were the pups kept in a standard cage?

Diamond: Yes—no direct enrichment. But their brains were still bigger as adults. We're up to the third generation and the brains are still enlarged, all because the pups coming from enriched parents have greater body weights. We've got the data and now we have to figure out what they mean.

Hopson: And now you are studying brain changes in aging rats?

Diamond: Yes. We are giving the same type of environment to older animals and taking the same type of measurements. We are looking for a normal development and aging curve.

Hopson: And what have you found?

Diamond: We worked with extremely old animals. We kept them in a standard cage until they were 766 days old.

Hopson: What would that be in human years?

Diamond: The rat has the potential to live 1,000 days, and the human being has the potential to live 100 years. So at 766 days, when we moved some rats to enriched environments, we were three quarters of the way through the animal's lives. We added to this experiment the fact that we held the animals as we changed their cages and gave them a little tender loving care. We found that when they were exposed to an enriched environment between 766 and 904 days of age, even these very old rats showed thickening of the cerebral cortex.

Hopson: Is there a connection between longevity and enrichment?

Diamond: Actually, there was a peculiar incident at 900 days. We lost one of the enriched animals, and then in the next three days we lost two more. Yet none of the animals in the control group—the ones we kept in standard cages—had died. We decided to stop the experiment right then and there. And we asked ourselves, "Why did we start losing them in the enriched condition?" My son, who is an architect and interested in housing for the elderly, finds that many of these people find group living stressful. They like some isolation, but they also like the opportunity to come together when they want to. So in our next aging experiment, we'll have a community play-room for the enriched rats but also have radiating side rooms with isolation compartments.

Hopson: You've shown that the cortex can thicken even in old rats, and yet there is a common belief that we lose brain cells as we age.

Diamond: In a nonenriched environment, the normal rat brain does decrease in size with age, but it is not necessarily losing brain cells. It is just the dendrites coming down so the cells get more compact.

Hopson: "Coming down"?

Diamond: When I lecture, I show my hand—my palm is the cell body and my fingers are the dendrites. With use, you can keep those dendrites out there, extended, but without stimulation, they shrink down. It's quite simple: You use it or lose it.

Hopson: What are the implications of this work on the aging brain?

Diamond: For researchers, I think it's terribly important that they pay attention to how they house their animals. So much of aging research is done on isolated animals. Is this normal aging? Until they have stimulating environments, it's not necessarily the normal lifestyle span of the animal. For people's lives, I think we can take a more optimistic view of the aging brain.

Hopson: What would enrichment be for an older person?

Diamond: That depends on the individual, since no two human brains are alike. Some people like to do crossword puzzles. Some go back to school. Some like to visit neighbors. The main factor is stimulation. The nerve cells are designed to receive stimulation. And I think curiosity is a key factor. If one maintains curiosity for a lifetime, that will surely stimulate neural tissue and the cortex may in turn respond.

Hopson: Is there any way to determine the effects of environment on the size and structure of a person's brain?

Diamond: I think some day we will have better records than we do today on the health of the individual—mental health as well as physical health—and when we get the human brains in the laboratory, we'll be able to correlate the structure and function with the environment people had.

Hopson: Would that involve doing some kind of brain anatomy?

Diamond: Very definitely. That's what all these file folders are—bits of data on human brains.

Hopson: Where did those brains come from?

Diamond: People donate their brains—it's a form of immortality, because everything we learn from their brains is embedded in somebody else's brain. So many people are willing to donate their brains. It is amazing. I'll be in a bookstore and somebody will say, "I've heard that you don't have enough female brains. Would you like mine? Let's have tea and discuss it." I was out to dinner just the other night with people who asked if I would like their brains. And there is a musician in Santa Cruz who wants me to have his brain when he dies because he is convinced it is different from those of nonmusicians.

"I found that people who use their brains don't lose them. It was that simple."

Hopson: I understand you did a series of interviews of active elderly people.

Diamond: Yes. I looked for people who were extremely active after 88 years of age. I found that the people who use their brains don't lose them. It was that simple. These people were interested in their professions even after retirement. They kept healthy bodies. They drank milk and ate an egg each day—that was one common denominator that goes against the prevailing thought today. And other denominators were activity, and love of life and love of others and being loved. Love is very basic.

Hopson: Did you learn anything from the interviews that gives you ideas for future directions?

Diamond: I think we need to combat the negative attitude towards the aged, the idea that they can't learn and that we must keep retiring them. I prefer to think of retirement as changing, going in another direction, not removing yourself from life or work altogether.

I was asked to speak at Bell Labs recently. I went hoping that by knowing the potential of the brain to be active at any age, they would treat the older workers with greater dignity. I think it is absolutely essential. And then, to phase them out gradually without losing their potential instead of stopping all these marvelous people at the peak of their careers. To provide dignity at any age is our goal.

Hopson: There's another area of your work with important human implications—the structural differences between male and female brains. Could you summarize those studies?

Diamond: Essentially, we've found that in the male rat, the right hemisphere—that is, the right cerebral cortex—is thicker than the left. We find that it's this way at birth and continues throughout the lifetime of the animals.

Hopson: Do you know why the male shows dominance of the right cortex?

Diamond: We truly wish we knew. We decided to ask the obvious, "How does testosterone, the male hormone, influence the development of one particular side?" So we took the testes out of rats at birth and waited for three months. We found that the anterior two-thirds of the cortex reversed, and developed greater left dominance, but that the posterior one-third remained right-greater-than-left. So it appears that the male's posterior or visual-spatial cortex is what we might call "hard-wired." It's not as easily influenced by the testosterone as is the rest. That surprised us.

Hopson: Why?

Diamond: Because, in the female, we find that the left cortex is significantly thicker than the right. And if we remove the female rat's ovaries at birth, her whole cortex shifts to right dominance over left, especially in the visual-spatial area. In other words, she gets a male pattern. We thought if we took out the testes in males, we'd get a complete reversal to the other picture, but we didn't.

Hopson: Are the right-left differences true for other parts of the brain?

Diamond: If you look at the hippocampus, which we're doing right now, we find that in the male, it is 8 percent greater on the right side than on the left at birth, but it drops to a nonsignificant level of difference later in life. In the female, the left side of the hippocampus is greater than the right, and when she becomes sexually mature, that difference becomes strongly evident. What we're finding is not only that dendrites and thickness change in the cortex, but that brain symmetry patterns change at different stages in the lives of males and females.

Hopson: Would there be an evolutionary advantage to these male-female brain differences?

Diamond: Well, let's consider the female. We autopsied mother rats right after they had given birth, and found that during pregnancy their cortex had grown. And not only mothers raised in enriched environments: Even in females from impoverished environments, the cortex had grown. It would make sense, in evolutionary terms, for the female to be at her optimum behavioral capacity during and after pregnancy. It would help her to prepare for and protect her young.

Hopson: What do these rat brain differences mean for our understanding of human behavior?

Diamond: The results provide baselines for studies on human brains. Several studies show that men are more visually and spatially oriented and women more language oriented. But of course we all know that there are excellent female architects and men who are linguists. There are ranges in basic patterns of behavior as well as changes due to the environment. Men and women will have more tolerance for each other as we learn about our brain similarities and differences.

Hopson: You have also written about a connection between the cortex and the immune system. Aren't female mammals considered to have a more active immune system?

Diamond: Yes, and they have the larger left cortex. A group of French researchers has just found evidence that the left cortex is involved with controlling the immune system.

Hopson: You have suggested that breast cancer may be a model for this.

Diamond: Yes, I think there are reasons to believe that in some individuals breast cancer may develop from six to eight months after severe emotional distress. I was losing my friends and relatives with stress followed by breast cancer, and after five of them in a row, I saw a possible connection.

Hopson: If people know they've had a period of stress, what could they do to prevent a problem later?

Diamond: If the immune system is controlled by the cortex, biofeedback might help. It gets back to Norman Cousins and his theory of laughter and healing. So many people have a common-sense notion that if you have a positive attitude about your body and your life, you're not subject to disease. And the minute you get a negative attitude toward them, disease somehow begins to manifest itself. People have spoken in generalities about this, and we're trying to find a mechanism.

Hopson: What is next in your professional future?

Diamond: I'd like to write up 20 years of research on environmental effects on the brain. We've got file cabinets filled with data that haven't been touched—I'd just take a leave of absence and bring it all together.

Hopson: How about your personal future? What do you hope to be doing by age 88?

Diamond: Eighty-eight is a long way off. And right now, I'm just trying to keep up with my work, be a decent professor. But I'm sure I'll still be learning, teaching and creating somewhere, somehow— perhaps learning more about how the brain can continue to improve our environment, not only how the environment improves the brain.

A SECOND LOOK AT DIAMOND'S LOVE . . .

I had to ask her: Dr. Diamond, are you interested in *anything* besides the brain? From the moment she answered the phone, we had talked about nothing but the brain. There were no little asides about personal achievements or private adventures. Just brain talk. She laughed at herself and then replied, "Well, I have four children. Three have Ph.D.s and one has an M.D. We provided them with a very enriched environment, and . . ."

And we were back into the brain. Clearly this is a woman in love with the brain. Diamond, professor of Anatomy at the University of California at Berkeley, remains actively engaged in research. "Now we're looking at *super*-enriched environments. We not only give the rats objects to explore, but we change the objects every hour, four days a week." The idea is to see whether a super-enriched environment will produce greater improvements in the brain than an enriched environment, or whether it will have detrimental effects. "It could be too much of a good thing. We just don't know."

Another line of research concerns the effects of CAT scans. "Kids are having CAT scans of their heads, and we wondered, 'What is this doing to their brains?' So we decided to see what happens to rat brains. So far it looks like it does no harm, and may even be beneficial, but we're still collecting data."

Diamond is also studying the role of nutrition in brain development. In these experiments, rats are given a protein-deficient diet during pregnancy. When the pups are born, they're given a protein-rich diet and put into an enriched environment. "So many women eat a poor diet during pregnancy. It's important to find out whether the effects on the baby's brain can be overcome."

Will the results of experiments such as these on the role of environment in the brain ever be put to practical use? "They're *already* being used," answers Diamond. "There are enrichment programs for children who are at risk. We're beginning to realize that old people can remain intellectually fit if they live in a stimulating environment."

Diamond is, indeed, in love with the brain. It is a love affair that may benefit us all.

SOMETHING TO THINK ABOUT . . .

1. Diamond's research focuses on what is called brain plasticity. What do you suppose "brain plasticity" means?

2. How do researchers determine if an enriched environment has changed the brain? How could you determine if these changes represent improvements?

3. How do researchers know that increases in brain size are not merely the results of exercise derived from climbing over the "stimulating" objects? Is this control measure adequate?

4. Diamond reports that rat pups from "enriched parents"are heavier and have bigger brains, but she's not sure what this finding means. What do you think it might mean?

5. In what way do the studies with old rats corroborate those with young rats?

6. Most children spend more time in front of the television than they do in school. What effect, if any, do you suppose this is having on brain development? How could you determine the answer?

7. Diamond mentions that pregnancy induces cortical growth in rats. How could you determine if the same thing happens in women?

8. Diamond says that if the immune system is controlled by the cortex, biofeedback might help in fending off disease. How does this follow?

9. Design an enriched environment for a human infant and explain how you could determine whether the enrichment was effective.

10. Could your own environment be considered enriched, when compared to the stimulation most people get? How could you determine whether your environment is improving, or hurting, your brain?

TO LEARN MORE ABOUT IT . . .

The article that got Diamond hooked on brain research was "Cholinesterase Activity." It appeared in *Science* in 1958 (vol. 128, p. 1176). Diamond has written up much of her own research in *Enriching Heredity*, published in 1988 by Free Press.

Chapter 10

The Life Cycle: A Conversation with Erik Erikson

Elizabeth Hall   *June 1983*

The dean of american psychoanalysis reflects on the human life cycle, the perils of the nuclear age, and the power of Gandhi's nonviolence.

Erik Homburger Erikson is the only thinker to have put forth a coherent theory of personality development that covers the entire life span. Trained in Vienna as an orthodox psychoanalyst, he shifted his emphasis from the disturbed individual to the healthy personality, and enlarged his focus from the influence of the family to the influence of society. Because of this broad outlook, his own influence extends far beyond the boundaries of psychoanalysis. In *The Life Cycle Completed*, Erikson looked back on the human life cycle with the wise eyes of a man who had lived for more than 80 years. Recently he talked to *Psychology Today* about the experience of growing old and how it is changing, about his concerns for today's adults, and about the power of Gandhi.

Elizabeth Hall

Hall: Professor Erikson, over the past 30 years your theory of human development has come to dominate our view of the life cycle. Now that you've reached the eighth and final stage of the cycle, has your own experience changed your view of human development?

Erikson: It undoubtedly has. But in *The Life Cycle Completed* I am offering a review of my views, and I emphasize primarily their inner logic. Of course, 30 years ago I lacked the capacity for imagining myself as old, and the general image of old age was different then. Certainly, the theory has not yet taken into account all the recent changes in society. Consider the thousands and thousands of old people alive today who would not have been alive 30 years ago. But I've always emphasized historical relativity in the study of human beings.

Hall: How does the increase in the number of old people affect the experience of old age?

Erikson: Thirty years ago, we spoke of "elders,"the handful of wise old women and men who faced death with dignity. But a society can have only relatively few elders. So our large group of well-preserved old people leads us to speak now of "elderlies." The existence of this group means that we need to rethink the role of old age. Being old is of course a part of life, but—perhaps because we stress youthfulness in our culture—people keep talking about "later adulthood" as if being old were funny or bad.

Hall: Has the large group of elderlies made you consider inserting another stage into the life cycle between middle adulthood and old age?

Erikson: The various life stages are not equal in length, so you can always make one stage longer and describe a transitional stage, although it gets a little odd to talk about a transitional stage at the end of life. I think that the biggest change in the last stage of life would be that old people will be allowed to remain involved in matters that have always been considered too much for them. The stage of middle adulthood, of course, is the stage of generativity, and the question is, how, and how long, can old people remain generative?

Hall: Generativity means a concern with the next generation. How can old people be generative?

Erikson: I've described generativity as including procreativity, productivity, and creativity. Of course, old people can no longer procreate, but they can be productive, and they can be creative; the creative potential of old people has probably been very much underestimated. Only a few elders have been presented as examples of special worth.

Hall: People like Pablo Casals and Picasso and Georgia O'Keeffe.

Erikson: Exactly. But they may be special examples of what more old people can represent. This changing experience of old age doesn't call for a new stage, but perhaps the transition leading to senescence will be longer. People will one day be expected to work longer. And even after they retire, old people can be useful to one another and to the younger generations.

Hall: Are you talking about volunteer work?

Erikson: That depends. Many volunteer projects take on the same quality as the word "elderly." The work is not considered "real" work, and—even if working conditions are adjusted somewhat—it's very important to maintain the quality of real work.

Hall: You mean that if I were doing some volunteer job and I thought that people were just keeping me busy and out of the way, I wouldn't feel good about myself?

Erikson: That's it, exactly. Old people can be generative in another way, too. They can be good grandparents, and not only to their own grandchildren. I'm convinced that old people and children need one another and that there's an affinity between old age and childhood that, in fact, rounds out the life cycle. You know, old people often seem childlike, and it's important that we be permitted to revive some qualities that we had as children.

Hall: Do you mean to look at things afresh with the inexperienced eye of the child, as if you were seeing them for the first time?

Erikson: Yes, something like that. You know, Einstein used the word "wonder" to describe his experience as a child, and he was considered childlike by many people. And I think he claimed that he was able to formulate the theory of relativity because he kept asking the questions that children ask. So when I say old people think like children, I do not mean childishly. But with wonder, joy, playfulness—all those things that adults often have to sacrifice for a while.

Hall: Because they have duties.

Erikson: Things to take care of. The Hindus call it the maintenance of the world. Technology has obviously interfered with this relationship between the old and the young, because it concentrates people in communities for economic reasons. That becomes obvious when old people move into a place that just takes care of old people. But technology has also made it possible for the old and young to get together over long distances—you can fly, drive.

Hall: And you can always phone. So technology both breaks the cycle and makes it possible to mend it. How will this extension of vigorous life change our expectations of the life cycle? What happens when the 25-year-old can expect 60 years of married life?

Erikson: Marriages have changed, too. It may not be coincidence that to be married several times is becoming acceptable.

Hall: Do you think that the culture's recent realization that sexuality may be an important part of old age is changing the experience of aging?

Erikson: I certainly would think so. The old attitude was that sexuality in old age either doesn't exist or ought not to be. The new attitude permits choice. Sexuality in old age is a potential to be enjoyed, not an obligation. In old age, fertility is over, so the question is, "What remains and what is important for life?" I call it generalized sensuality, which has something to do with play and the importance of the moment, getting us back again to the potentially childlike quality in old age.

Hall: If I were writing this up for a human sexuality text, I'd say that you were talking about playful sexuality that may or may not culminate in genital intercourse.

Erikson: That's right, but let's note that the genital engagement can be longer than was once assumed. Of course, sexuality does imply closeness and playfulness. It is recreational by nature when the time for procreation is over.

Hall: The time and the responsibility, and perhaps the fear, are eliminated. But what about the current stress on recreational sex for all ages?

Erikson: We make a distinction between "intimacies" and "Intimacy"—with a capital "I." Sex that is purely recreational involves intimacies. But obviously Intimacy means more for the whole person than intimacies.

Hall: You see the stage of young adulthood as centering on the struggle between Intimacy and isolation. Do you think the culture's fascination with purely recreational sex could affect our capacity for Intimacy?

Erikson: It could. You see, that situation has come about in part because of a misunderstanding of psychoanalysis: the idea that you mustn't repress anything, but must always act it out, so that the most important thing becomes genital recreation. When we speak of the development of Intimacy, we emphasize mature mutuality. Mere intimacies can occupy a period in a person's life—even repeated periods—but they cannot be the final aim of sexuality.

Hall: So purely recreational sex is okay, say, during late adolescence or after divorce. . . .

Erikson: Well, if you bring in "okay," then the question is, "In what environment?" And it depends entirely on what kind of a person somebody is. Some people can cultivate the side issues of the life cycle. The main point is whether they are mature enough to handle the main conflict of each period. For example, some people today may fool themselves in their so-called recreational sexuality and actually feel quite isolated because they lack mutuality—real Intimacy. In extreme cases, you could have a highly active sex life and yet feel a terrible sense of isolation because you're never there as a person; you're never perceiving your partner as a person.

"You could have a highly active sex life and yet feel a terrible sense of isolation."

Hall: And that could lead to an increase in sexual activity in an attempt to get rid of the isolation, because you didn't realize what was causing it.

Erikson: Real Intimacy includes the capacity to commit yourself to relationships that may demand sacrifice and compromise. The basic strength of young adulthood is Love—a mutual, mature devotion.

Hall: In your new book you've moved beyond Freud by proposing a stage of generalized sensuality in old age. His psychosexual stages ended with mature genitality in early adulthood.

Erikson: According to Freud, in the young stage sexuality culminated in genitality, which essentially means mutual genital enjoyment. We've proposed two additional psychosexual stages: procreativity in adulthood and generalized sensuality in old age. But please note that on my chart of thelife cycle I put them both into parentheses, because they haven't been fully discussed in psychoanalytic theory. You see, I believe that there is a procreative drive: There is an instinctual wish to have children, and it's important that we realize that.

Hall: What happens to someone who decides *not* to have children?

Erikson: Since we're in a period of history when the number of births has to be reduced, many people will be making that decision. But it's important that people who decide to remain childless know what they are *not* doing. The danger is that they will repress the sense of frustration and loss that comes with the rejection of procreativity, so that a new kind of unconscious repression develops in place of the sexual repression of the Victorian age.

Hall: By "repression," you mean to push it completely out of mind, so that if someone said, "Don't you sometimes regret having children?" a person could honestly reply, "No." Now what happens when someone who's chosen not to have children wakes up one morning at age 45 or 50 and says, "What have I done?"

Erikson: *Not* done. Well, you don't keep prescriptions ready for such cases; you don't say, "It's easy to handle your problem, you simply have to sublimate." But "sublimate" is the right word; Freud made this very clear many years ago. The procreative urge does need to be directed into socially fruitful channels. Instead of having clear prescriptions, it's better to work out the social structure so that people who never have children of their own will, in the normal course of events, help to take care of all the world's children. You must have noticed how the changes in marriage patterns have led many people to care for children who are not theirs—and do it very well. This is a new trend. Only a few decades ago a child was considered more of a personal possession, and it was very important whose child it was.

Hall: And now we have "his," "hers," and "ours" in many families, as well as the adoption of war orphans from places like Vietnam. The procreative urge is, of course, closely related to generativity, which you regard as a basic tendency of adulthood. Does the urge have to be satisfied by working directly with children?

Erikson: That's why I call it generativity— in order to go beyond procreativity, once we've fully accepted *that*. It can be sublimated into creativity or productivity.

Hall: It's easy for me to see how a childless artist or a writer or a teacher can sublimate generativity in their work. Now how does a plumber do it?

Erikson: Don't underestimate the generative contributions of a good plumber. Also, he or she may be a church member who can do something for all the children in his community. And he or she is still a voter.

Hall: Then the urge to care for future generations can be satisfied by helping to maintain a generative social system?

Erikson: Exactly. That's again why I like so much that Hindu term "the maintenance of the world."

Hall: When you discuss generativity, you contrast it with self-absorption or stagnation as opposing trends during adulthood. If generativity triumphs, a person develops the basic strength of "Care." Generativity also has a regular "dystonic" counterpart: It is "rejectivity."

Erikson: I want to emphasize that those two things belong together. Generativity shouldn't be treated as an achievement that permanently overcomes stagnation. You have both, mostly. If you study the lives of very creative people, you'll find that at times they have a terrible sense of stagnation. And the interaction of such opposites is characteristic of every stage of the life cycle.

Hall: If the crisis of a stage is successfully resolved, the defeated quality doesn't disappear; instead, the balance changes so that there is a preponderance of the positive quality?

Erikson: It's exactly a matter of balance, but we avoid the terms "positive" and "negative." Sometimes what we call the "dystonic tendency" can have positive aspects. For example, during old age the life crisis involves the conflict between integrity and despair. How could anybody have integrity and not also despair about certain things in his own life, about the human condition? Even if your own life was absolutely beautiful and wonderful, the fact that so many people were exploited or ignored must make you feel some despair.

Hall: So people shouldn't expect that if their lives are lived according to Eriksonian theory, they'll go through eight rosy stages. Can a person develop what you call the "syntonic" quality of each life stage without the accompanying dystonic quality? Can you develop generativity without stagnation? Or trust without distrust?

Erikson: Let's take the last one, which describes the psychosocial crisis of infancy. A basic sense of trust means both that the child has learned to rely on his (or her) caregivers to be there when they are needed, and to consider himself trustworthy. But just imagine what somebody would be like who had no mistrust at all.

Hall: Gullible, to say the least. We'd probably think such a person wasn't very bright.

Erikson: Out of the conflict between trust and mistrust, the infant develops hope, which is the earliest form of what gradually becomes faith in adults. If you say that an adult has hope, I'd say, "Well, I hope so," but if you said that a baby has faith, I'd say, "That's quite a baby." Real faith is a very mature attitude.

Hall: So the various strengths take different forms in old age, because they're all tempered by the strength of old age, which is "wisdom."

Erikson: Yes, old age is when a certain wisdom is possible and even necessary, as long as you don't make it too darn wizard-like.

"Old age is when a certain wisdom is possible . . . as long as you don't make it too darn wizard-like."

Hall: Perhaps the prayer of St. Francis of Assisi describes what you mean: changing what you can change and not changing what you can't hope to change, but wise enough to know the difference.

Erikson: Absolutely, although one hesitates to make it all too simple.

Hall: If you consider life as a tapestry, as Mrs. Erikson has done, woven with a different color for each strength, the final pattern would be different for each person. But can one successfully handle the crisis of old age—the struggle between integrity and despair—without having resolved the previous stages favorably?

Erikson: You couldn't possibly imagine a person who has resolved all seven previous crises equally well—in fact, I never hope to meet such a person. At the end of life you attempt to consolidate an existential identity. That sounds stilted, but the existential identity has to emerge from the psychosocial identity.

Hall: I'd think that for people like you, who can carry on your profession as long as you like, there'd not be the same questioning of identity as there is in someone who works until 65 and then retires and loses part of his identity. You're no longer a plumber. Or you're no longer a brain surgeon because you lack the coordination.

Erikson: You notice that you're referring to men exclusively.

Hall: A woman can be a brain surgeon—or a plumber.

Erikson: Yes, and that's certainly going to become more common. The reason that men die earlier than women may be purely biological, or it may have much to do with the fact that so far, man's psychosocial existence has depended so much on his occupation.

Hall: But let's look at the traditional woman. When such a woman is widowed, she loses the identity of "wife," yet she continues to outlive the men around her.

Erikson: In many cultures, "widow" is also an identity. And the surviving wife also has a grand-maternal role, depending on the culture. In China, for example, the role of grandmother has been deeply embedded in tradition.

Hall: And the role of grandmother has traditionally been stronger than the role of grandfather, so it would provide a basis for identity. I guess we solved that problem.

Erikson: Even with this extended life, it's still relatively rare for a couple to grow old together. You know how many more widows than widowers we have.

Hall: Husbands are still generally older than their wives. So if a woman expects to become a widow at 70 instead of at 60, it would mean that we're postponing that experience of old age by expanding the earlier period.

Erikson: That's right, which shows that you don't just prove or disprove a life-cycle theme, but learn to observe the changes and then decide whether the terms you first chose to name the strengths or weaknesses are the right words. Incidentally, we once called the strengths of each stage "virtues"; then we realized that virtue comes from the Latin word *virtus*, which implies manliness. The linguistic implication could be that virtues are male qualities, so I had to change it to "strengths."

Hall: Speaking of women, how does the task of forming an identity differ for adolescent boys and adolescent girls?

Erikson: The task itself doesn't differ; the main stages, strengths, and risks do not differ for men and for women. Rather, they help sexual differences to complement one another. Children do have to learn to become boys and girls, but unless there is very strong sex-typing going on, both sexes have a certain freedom. A little boy can behave a little like a girl, and it's considered charming, or a girl like a boy. It all depends on what the culture makes of it. But essentially, whatever strength has to develop in a certain stage must appear in both boys and girls. Like willpower, for example, or industry. Or identity.

Hall: So the specific tasks of each age are the same for boys and girls, but the content of what they deal with would be somewhat different in different societies, different at different times in the same society, different depending upon both biology and the way the culture brings out the tasks.

Erikson: You sound as if you're ready to teach a course.

Hall: Not yet. Let's go on. A culture can also change the length of time it allows for a stage of life. Take adolescence, when identity is being formed. There is supposed to be a moratorium, when the young person doesn't have the responsibility of adulthood, but in a lot of cultures the official recognition of that period may be only a few weeks, or just puberty rites. When society pays so little attention to a stage, does it affect the way the stage is met?

Erikson: Compressing adolescence into such a short span of time doesn't mean that society cares less. You said in a rather offhand way, "just puberty rites." But take the drama of puberty rites and the enormous existential experience a kid goes through. The transition may take a shorter time, but it may be terribly intense.

Hall: And if society gives you few choices as to what you're going to do afterward, there's no need for all that time to select a future. But let's go back to technological societies. You've pointed out that during identity formation, the adolescent can fall into "totalism," a rigid self-concept that can leave a person susceptible to totalitarian movements. How does the totalism of the 40-year-old member of the Ku Klux Klan differ from the totalism of the adolescent?

Erikson: I don't believe I ever regarded totalism as only an aspect of adolescent thinking. It's an aspect of ideology, which finds easy access to young thinking, but that doesn't mean that there is no totalism after adolescence.

Hall: Would the totalism of a middle-aged Nazi or terrorist be likely to reflect an unsuccessfully resolved adolescent identity crisis?

Erikson: If you study a case history, you may find that the person didn't resolve something earlier. But it can happen to a whole group, as it did to the young Germans after World War I. Because of historical and economic conditions, they could never settle down to adulthood, and so ideological totalism began to dominate them.

Hall: Let's discuss another aspect of identity: its relation to society. You've always stressed the importance of the historical moment when discussing the life cycle.

Erikson: The way a national or communal identity develops depends a lot on the extent to which the national or political or religious ideology strengthens the sense of "I."

Hall: So that in George Orwell's *1984*, there would have been a very limited sense of "I." What about Hitler's Germany?

Erikson: In such a society, the Führer is the one who stands under a thousand banners and says "I" and everybody identifies with that; it gives them a sense of "I." Marching in unison becomes the act of being oneself.

Hall: Joseph Adelson's research showed that German children—not American or English youngsters—said that everybody needs a strong leader.

Erikson: "Everybody needs it" means that everybody needs it for his or her sense of "I." But a historical period can also be host to a most genuine voice of faith. At the time of Jesus, Jewish history was particularly catastrophic for a national sense of "I." In spite of Jehovah's ("I AM") overlordship, the homeland had been in continuous danger of invasion, occupation, and exile. This, I think, helped to open some ears to Jesus' great existential message.

Here I cannot help thinking of how nuclear weapons have done away with the boundaries of whole continents, and how, with their threat of global destruction, they call for the recognition of man's indivisible "specieshood."

"Nuclear weapons have done away with the boundaries of whole continents."

Hall: Both in *Young Man Luther* and in *Gandhi's Truth,* you showed how the attempts of an exceptional man to solve his personal difficulties benefited the whole group. If Luther and Gandhi had each resolved the previous five stages of life in the best possible way, would they have been so content that they would have lacked the urge to make such great changes?

Erikson: I couldn't say. What I tried to show in each book was not only that an exceptional man had the right conflicts, but that he lived in a period that needed just that man, while the historical period needed to resolve collectively what couldn't be resolved personally. As I said in one of the books, he solved for his period in history and for his own people what he could not resolve in his private life. And that makes a leader.

Hall: So it requires the right personal conflict in the right kind of person at the right moment among people who are ready for this conflict. Four elements, all of which are necessary.

Erikson: Yes, it so happened that in each historical situation, the man and his time complemented each other.

Hall: Since the film *Gandhi* was released, there's been renewed interest both in the man and in your book about him. Speaking of generativity, it seemed to me that Gandhi was more concerned with other people than with his own family.

Erikson: He turned into the father of his nation, and he extended his paternal feelings to mankind. Obviously, he acted for the species. Incidentally, Gandhi had a strange and unique mixture of maternal and paternal traits.

"Gandhi had a strange and unique mixture of maternal and paternal traits."

Hall: But isn't that characteristic of most creative people?

Erikson: Yes, because the emphasis is not on your personal procreativity, but on your creativity. People are always asking me how I liked the movie. The film is very different from my book, because I was writing a psychoanalytic book, in which I tried to show the relationship of the hero's personal conflicts to his historical deeds. My aim was to show how Gandhi fitted into that period—the historical moment—and what nonviolence—his truth—meant to him. I couldn't possibly expect to find in the movie a reflection of my developmental point of view.

Hall: Do you feel that anything important was left out?

Erikson: Only one thing—the impression that these nonviolent people made on some of the armed troops. I understood that in several places British soldiers found that they could not resist their nonviolent attackers, and so they threw their weapons away. Perhaps these are just stories, but I'd have liked to see some such reaction in some of the soldiers. For I don't think that all the British were as unfeeling and unresponsive as they were portrayed.

Hall: When Gandhi's followers were lined up five abreast and kept marching toward the clubs, I looked at the soldiers, and they were Indians. And I thought, "What must they be feeling?" How long can you hit somebody without feeling revulsion at what you're doing?

Erikson: In order for nonviolent behavior to be effective it must be shocking—it has to shake up the violent opponent peacefully. In that situation, what is more important? That you are an Indian? That you are a soldier? That you are an officer? That you are a human being? It has to come to the point where suddenly these other people become human to you. Then you can no longer keep hitting them. Incidentally, it's amazing how American audiences are taking to the movie. Aren't you a little surprised?

Hall: If you consider that everybody is terribly concerned right now with the possibility of nuclear war, it's not so surprising. And people are impressed. During the intermission, instead of noise, talking, and a great rush to the snack bar, there's quiet. People are thinking about what they've seen.

Erikson: And these are not intellectuals. The movie about a great man's use of nonviolent resistance reaches people who do not belong to special peace organizations, and it makes them thoughtful. That's why it's such an important film. I honestly believe that it focuses on something our Judeo-Christian culture has not yet quite understood and has not used, and will probably have to face: the invention of nonviolent tactics to get out of the nuclear dilemma.

Hall: That dilemma gets us into rejectivity—the trend that opposes generativity in adulthood. How can it be dangerous?

Erikson: In our scheme, rejectivity is an unwillingness to include certain persons or groups within your generative concern. Human beings spend an awful lot of their imagination on defining just which others they don't care for—in the generative sense. The danger in rejectivity, that is, the rejecting of other people, other groups, or other nations, is that it leads to what I have called "pseudospeciation." People lose the sense of being one species and try to make other kinds of people into a different and mortally dangerous species, one that doesn't count, one that isn't human.

Hall: To the Greeks, everybody else was a barbarian, and the Navajos call themselves "the people"— not "a" people.

Erikson: Many other tribes do the same thing. Other groups are considered to be a different species, and for the sake of decent humanity, you may have to subdue them or get rid of them. You can kill them without feeling that you have killed your own kind.

Hall: If "pseudo" has the connotation of "almost a lie," it indicates that you know what you're doing. But when people do this, they're not really conscious of it, are they?

Erikson: That's exactly the point, and that's why it's so dangerous. The paradox is that pseudospecieshood as a sense of representing the best in mankind binds a group together and inspires loyalty, heroism, and discipline.

Hall: So without pseudospeciation we wouldn't have loyalty and devotion and self-sacrifice. The problem is to keep the positive aspects while getting rid of the negative ones.

Erikson: The very existence of humanity depends on the solution of that paradox.

Hall: If I read you right, this has to be done in a way that enables you to keep your own identity as a group so that there's a culture to hand down.

Erikson: Yes, but what's important is a conviction that one's culture and "system" can go on living in a world that includes one's former enemies.

Hall: Would you like to make odds on our chances of developing an identity that encompasses the whole species? Do you think the odds are better than they were 15 years ago?

Erikson: Absolutely. After all, we are one species.

A SECOND LOOK AT ERIKSON'S LIFE CYCLE . . .

One of Sigmund Freud's most important contributions was the notion that children progress toward adulthood through regular stages. But although Freud focused on sex and concluded that development ended with childhood, Erik Erikson suggested that development meant more than sexual changes and concluded that people continue to develop in predictable ways throughout the life span.

Erikson identified eight stages of development, with each stage involving a crisis to be resolved. In the first year of life, the baby faces a crisis of *trust*. Babies can survive only if others meet their basic needs, if, in other words, they learn to trust. Toddlers face a crisis of *independence*. They must learn to stand on their own two feet, both literally and figuratively. In the third stage, the youngster must learn to take the *initiative* while keeping impulses under control. In the early grades of school, the child faces a crisis of *competence*. Children must master the basic skills that will enable them to meet the demands of adult life. The *identity* crisis is the chief challenge of adolescence. Teens must figure out who they are and where they are going. Young adults must make a commitment to another person to resolve the conflict of *intimacy*. Once adults have learned how to form intimate bonds with others, they face the crisis of *generativity*. They must learn to be productive, creative, and nurturant, especially to the next generation. In the final stage, the crisis is that of *ego integrity*. To resolve it, the elderly must learn to accept the limitations of life and impending death.

Erikson's theory made him one of the giants of developmental psychology. Though he never earned a college degree, he taught at Yale, Harvard, and the University of California. Some of his ideas, particularly the notion that adolescence represents a period of groping for identity, have worked their way into the web of Western society. In fact, Erikson feared that some young people use the identity crisis idea to avoid the difficult task of forming an identity. "Having an identity crisis," he warned, "is neither a boast nor an excuse for late papers."

In this conversation with Elizabeth Hall, Erikson talked about his views of development while he himself was in the eighth stage of development. One gets the impression that he had resolved the crisis of ego integrity quite well.

SOMETHING TO THINK ABOUT . . .

1. Erikson says that he has "always emphasized historical relativity in the study of human beings." What does he mean? Give an example of Erikson's behavior that is historically relative.
2. Erikson says there has been a shift from a handful of *elders* to many *elderly*. How has this changed the relative value society places on old people? How do you think the status of old people will change in the next 30 years?
3. Erikson says that technology has both separated the generations and brought them together. Give examples.
4. Some psychologists say that Western society *invented* adolescence, that it is a by-product of industrialization rather than a natural stage. What do you think? If this view is correct, what are the implications for Erikson's idea of an identity crisis?

5. Erikson suggests that recreational sex can interfere with the capacity for intimacy. What evidence can you muster for or against this view from your own personal observations?

6. According to Erikson," there is an instinctual wish to have children. "Design a study to determine the accuracy of this statement.

7. Hall and Erikson talk about the fact that in different societies developmental stages can vary in length. Adolescence may last no longer than the time it takes to perform a rite, or it may take several years. What are the relative merits of each approach?

8. A common debate in our society concerns when children should be given certain rights: the right to drive an automobile, to hold a job, sign a contract, get married, consume alcoholic beverages, have sex. How could you determine the optimum age for such rights?

9. What does *pseudospeciation* mean? What is its role in war? How might the concept apply to the problem of wife abuse?

10. Erikson suggests that solving the nuclear dilemma will require the invention of nonviolent tactics. Invent such a tactic.

TO LEARN MORE ABOUT IT . . .

For more on Erikson's ideas about development, see his *Childhood and Society*. His final book on development was *The Life Cycle Completed*. Several other theories of development compete with Erikson's and will be of interest to some readers. The notion of developmental stages is of wide interest. *Passages: The Predictable Crises of Adult Life,* by journalist Gail Sheehy, made the bestseller list.